TAKE FINANCIAL CONTROL

BANKRUPTCY UNLOCKED

A Consumer Guide to Financial Fresh Starts in New York & California

NGOZI E. BOLIN, ESQ.

Cover by Jim Olen

Legal Disclaimer

Important Notice to Readers

THIS BOOK IS PROVIDED FOR INFORMATIONAL AND EDUCATIONAL PURPOSES ONLY AND IS NOT INTENDED TO CONSTITUTE LEGAL ADVICE.

No Attorney-Client Relationship

The information contained in this book does not create an attorney-client relationship between the author, publisher, and any reader or user of this material. Reading this book, accessing its content, or using any information contained herein does not establish any professional relationship or create any duties or obligations on the part of the author or publisher to any reader.

Not a Substitute for Professional Legal Counsel

The content of this book is general in nature and may not apply to your specific situation. Legal matters are highly fact-specific and jurisdiction-dependent. Laws, regulations, court decisions, and legal interpretations change frequently and vary significantly between jurisdictions. Nothing in this book should be used as a substitute for competent legal advice from a licensed attorney in your jurisdiction who is familiar with the specific facts of your case.

YOU SHOULD ALWAYS CONSULT WITH A QUALIFIED ATTORNEY BEFORE MAKING ANY LEGAL DECISIONS OR TAKING ANY ACTION BASED ON INFORMATION CONTAINED IN THIS BOOK.

Accuracy and Currency of Information

While every effort has been made to ensure the accuracy of the information contained in this book at the time of publication, the author and publisher make no representations or warranties regarding the completeness, accuracy, reliability, or currency of the information provided. Laws and legal precedents change constantly, and what may have been accurate at the time of writing may no longer be current or applicable.

The information in this book reflects the law as understood by the author as of the publication date. Legal developments occurring after the publication date are not reflected in this material.

Jurisdictional Limitations

Laws vary significantly among different countries, states, provinces, and localities. The information in this book may be based primarily on the laws of specific jurisdictions and may not be applicable in your location. Local laws should always be consulted, and local legal counsel should be retained for matters involving specific jurisdictions.

Limitation of Liability

TO THE FULLEST EXTENT PERMITTED BY LAW, THE AUTHOR, PUBLISHER, EDITORS, CONTRIBUTORS, AND DISTRIBUTORS OF THIS BOOK DISCLAIM ALL LIABILITY FOR ANY LOSS, DAMAGE, OR INJURY ARISING FROM THE USE OF OR RELIANCE ON THE INFORMATION CONTAINED HEREIN, WHETHER SUCH LIABILITY ARISES IN CONTRACT, TORT, STRICT LIABILITY, OR OTHERWISE.

This limitation applies to all damages or injuries, including but not limited to:

- Direct, indirect, incidental, and consequential damages
- Lost profits or business opportunities
- Legal fees and costs

- Punitive or exemplary damages
- Any other economic or non-economic losses

No Warranties

THIS BOOK IS PROVIDED "AS IS" WITHOUT WARRANTY OF ANY KIND, EXPRESS OR IMPLIED, INCLUDING BUT NOT LIMITED TO WARRANTIES OF MERCHANTABILITY, FITNESS FOR A PARTICULAR PURPOSE, OR NON-INFRINGEMENT.

Individual Circumstances

Every legal situation is unique. The examples, case studies, and scenarios presented in this book are for illustrative purposes only and may not reflect the full complexity of actual legal situations. The outcomes described may not be achievable in your circumstances, and past results do not guarantee future outcomes.

Updates and Revisions

The author and publisher are under no obligation to update or revise the content of this book to reflect changes in the law or legal practice. Readers are encouraged to verify all information with current legal sources and qualified legal professionals.

Third-Party Content and References

Any references to third-party materials, websites, organizations, or publications are provided for informational purposes only and do not constitute an endorsement of such materials or entities. The author and publisher are not responsible for the content, accuracy, or availability of third-party materials.

Compliance with Professional Rules

Readers who are legal professionals should ensure that their use of any information in this book complies with applicable professional conduct rules, ethical requirements, and licensing obligations in their jurisdiction.

Intellectual Property Notice

This book is protected by copyright and other intellectual property laws. The information provided is for personal, educational, and non-commercial use only. Any commercial use, reproduction, or distribution requires express written permission from the copyright holder.

Severability

If any portion of this disclaimer is held to be invalid or unenforceable, the remaining portions shall remain in full force and effect.

BY READING AND USING THIS BOOK, YOU ACKNOWLEDGE THAT YOU HAVE READ, UNDERSTOOD, AND AGREE TO BE BOUND BY THE TERMS OF THIS DISCLAIMER.

IF YOU DO NOT AGREE WITH THESE TERMS, DO NOT USE THIS BOOK.

Contents

Introduction

The Phone Call That Changes Everything

The collection call comes at 6:47 AM on a Tuesday. Your heart pounds as you recognize the pattern - the automated voice, the account number you've memorized from countless notices, the demand for "immediate payment to avoid further action." You're not even fully awake, but the familiar knot of anxiety tightens in your stomach as reality crashes back: you're drowning in debt, and nothing you've tried is working.

If this scenario sounds familiar, you're not alone. You're not irresponsible. You're not a failure. You're simply human, facing one of life's most common yet devastating challenges: overwhelming debt that has spiraled beyond your ability to manage.

This book exists because that phone call - and the sleepless nights, the avoided bills, the growing sense of desperation - doesn't have to define your future. There is a way out. There is hope. And there is a legal tool specifically designed to help people exactly like you get back on their feet: bankruptcy.

Breaking Through the Myths and Fear

The word "bankruptcy" carries enormous stigma in our society. It conjures images of failure, shame, and financial ruin. We're told that bankruptcy will destroy our credit forever, that we'll lose everything we own, that it's something only irresponsible people do when they've given up trying to pay their debts.

These beliefs aren't just wrong - they're dangerous. They keep millions of Americans trapped in cycles of debt they can never escape, making minimum payments on obligations they'll never pay off, sacrificing their families' security and their own peace of mind to avoid a legal process that could actually save them.

Here's the truth that creditors don't want you to know: **bankruptcy is not punishment - it's protection.** It's a right created by Congress as authorized by the Constitution, designed specifically to help honest people facing overwhelming debt get a genuine fresh start. Every year, hundreds of thousands of Americans - teachers, nurses, small business owners, veterans, retirees - use bankruptcy successfully to eliminate unmanageable debt and rebuild stable financial lives.

They're not cheating the system. They're using the system exactly as it was designed to be used.

Why This Book, Why Now

Despite bankruptcy's power to transform lives, most people know almost nothing about how it actually works. The information that's available is often confusing, incomplete, or downright misleading. Much of it is written by lawyers for lawyers, using technical language that makes the process seem more complicated than it needs to be.

This book cuts through the confusion and gives you something that's been missing: a complete, honest, practical guide to bankruptcy that speaks in plain English about real-world situations. Written by an attorney with over three decades of experience helping people navigate financial crises in New York and California - America's two most populous states - this guide provides the knowledge you need to make informed decisions about your financial future.

But this isn't just a legal manual. It's a roadmap to recovery that recognizes the human side of financial distress. Behind every bankruptcy case is a person or family facing one of life's most stressful experiences. This book acknowledges that reality while providing the practical tools you need to navigate the process successfully.

What Makes This Guide Different

Complete Coverage of Both Major Types: Unlike many resources that focus on only one type of bankruptcy, this book provides comprehensive coverage of both Chapter 7 ("liquidation") and Chapter 13 ("reorganization") bankruptcy, helping you understand which option - if any - makes sense for your specific situation.

State-Specific Guidance: Bankruptcy is federal law, but the details that determine what property you can keep depend heavily on state law. This guide provides specific, detailed information for residents of New York and California, where nearly one in five Americans live. The principles and processes we cover apply everywhere, but the specific protections and procedures we detail are tailored to these crucial states.

Real-World Focus: Every chapter includes real examples, case studies, and practical scenarios drawn from actual bankruptcy practice. You'll see how bankruptcy works for people facing situations similar to yours - from medical debt and job loss to business failure and divorce.

Beyond Just Filing: Most bankruptcy resources focus only on the filing process itself. This guide takes you further, showing you how to rebuild your credit, protect yourself from future financial problems, and create the stable, secure life that bankruptcy was designed to make possible.

Honest Assessment of Alternatives: Bankruptcy isn't right for everyone, and we don't pretend it is. This book includes comprehensive coverage of alternatives to bankruptcy, helping you understand all your options before making this important decision.

Who This Book Is For

You're considering bankruptcy and want to understand what it really involves, what you can expect, and whether it's the right choice for your situation.

You're facing foreclosure, repossession, or aggressive collection actions and need to understand your immediate options for protection.

You've been told you "make too much money" for bankruptcy and want to understand Chapter 13 and other options for people with higher incomes.

You have complex debts like student loans, tax obligations, or business guarantees and need to understand how bankruptcy treats different types of debt.

You're worried about losing your home, car, or other essential property and want to understand how bankruptcy's property protections actually work.

You're drowning in medical debt from illness or injury and need relief that allows you to focus on recovery rather than creditor calls.

You're going through divorce or other major life changes that have created unmanageable financial obligations.

You're a legal professional seeking practical guidance on consumer bankruptcy issues in New York and California.

You want to help a family member or friend who's struggling with debt and need reliable information about their options.

This book is also for skeptics - people who think bankruptcy sounds too good to be true, or who've been told horror stories about the process. We'll give you the straight facts, including the limitations and drawbacks of bankruptcy, so you can make decisions based on reality rather than myths or fear.

What You'll Learn

The fundamentals of how bankruptcy actually works, stripped of legal jargon and explained in terms that make sense for your daily life.

Whether you qualify for bankruptcy relief and which type of bankruptcy best fits your income, debt, and property situation.

Exactly what property you can keep through bankruptcy, including detailed information about New York and California exemption laws that protect your essential assets.

How to stop foreclosure, repossession, and other collection actions immediately through bankruptcy's powerful automatic stay protection.

The real impact on your credit and how to rebuild your financial life after bankruptcy - including timelines for qualifying for car loans, mortgages, and other credit.

How bankruptcy treats different types of debt, from credit cards and medical bills to student loans, taxes, and domestic support obligations.

Step-by-step guidance through the bankruptcy process, from initial decision-making through final discharge and beyond.

How to avoid bankruptcy fraud and other serious mistakes that could derail your case.

Comprehensive alternatives to bankruptcy that might work better for your specific situation.

Where to find help, including detailed information about free and low-cost legal services, court resources, and other support systems available in New York and California.

How to Use This Book

This book is designed to work for readers with different needs and circumstances:

If you're facing an immediate crisis (foreclosure sale next week, wages being garnished), start with Chapter 16 on stopping foreclosures and repossessions, then circle back to the earlier chapters for comprehensive understanding.

If you're exploring your options but not in immediate danger, start with Chapter 1 (What Is Bankruptcy?) and work through the book systematically.

If you know you need bankruptcy but aren't sure which type, focus on Chapters 2-3 (Should You File? and Types of Bankruptcy) to understand your options.

If you're specifically interested in Chapter 7, read Chapters 6-9 for complete coverage of the liquidation process.

If you're considering Chapter 13, Chapters 10-15 provide comprehensive guidance on reorganization bankruptcy.

If you have special circumstances (divorce, student loans, tax debt, business issues), use the index to find relevant sections throughout the book, then focus on the specialized chapters that address your situation.

Each chapter is written to stand alone while building on information from previous chapters. You can read straight through for complete understanding, or focus on the sections most relevant to your immediate needs.

A Word About Legal Advice

This book provides comprehensive education about bankruptcy law and process, but it cannot provide legal advice for your specific situation. Bankruptcy law is complex and changes frequently. Every person's financial situation is unique, and what works for one person may not work for another.

We strongly encourage you to consult with a qualified bankruptcy attorney who can analyze your specific circumstances and provide personalized guidance. Many attorneys offer free consultations, and legal aid organizations provide low-cost or free help for people who qualify. This book will help you understand your options and ask better questions, but it's not a substitute for professional legal counsel.

Your Journey Starts Here

If you're reading this book, you've already taken the most important step: you've decided to seek information and explore your options rather than continue suffering in silence. That takes courage, especially when you're feeling overwhelmed by your financial situation.

Financial crisis can feel isolating, but you're not alone. Millions of Americans have faced similar challenges and found their way to stability and peace of mind. Some used bankruptcy to get there. Others found different solutions that worked better for their circumstances. All of them had to start where you are now: acknowledging the problem and seeking real solutions.

The path forward may not be easy, but it is possible. You have options. You have rights. And you have the tools you need to build a better financial future.

As we move through this book together, remember that financial difficulties don't define you. A debt problem is just that - a problem. And problems can be solved. Your fresh start is waiting. Let's figure out how to claim it.

The information in this book reflects the law as understood at the time of publication and is based on the author's extensive experience practicing bankruptcy law in New York and California. Laws change, court interpretations evolve, and individual circumstances vary. Always consult with qualified legal professionals before making important decisions about your financial future.

1

What Is Bankruptcy?

Understanding Your Legal Right to Financial Freedom

A Legal Tool, Not a Moral Judgment

Take a deep breath. If you're reading this book, you're likely facing one of the most stressful periods of your life. Perhaps you're lying awake at night, wondering how you'll pay next month's rent. Maybe you're screening calls because you can't face another conversation with a debt collector. Or perhaps you're simply tired - exhausted from the constant worry about money that seems to follow you everywhere.

Here's the first thing you need to know: **bankruptcy is not a moral failure.** It's a legal tool, created by Congress and guaranteed by the U.S. Constitution, designed to help people exactly like you get back on their feet.

Every year, hundreds of thousands of Americans - teachers, nurses, small business owners, veterans, retirees - file for bankruptcy. They do it not because they're irresponsible, but because life happened: a medical emergency, job loss, divorce, or simply the gradual accumulation of debt that became impossible to manage.

What Bankruptcy Actually Is

Bankruptcy is a federal legal process that helps individuals and businesses who are overwhelmed by debt get a **fresh financial start**. It operates through the U.S. Bankruptcy Courts and is governed by federal law, which means the basic process is the same whether you live in Manhattan or Bakersfield.

Think of bankruptcy as a **legal reset button**. It can:

- **Eliminate** most of your unsecured debts (like credit cards and medical bills)
- **Stop** creditor harassment and collection calls
- **Prevent** wage garnishment and lawsuits
- **Halt** foreclosure proceedings on your home
- **Give you breathing room** to reorganize your finances

But bankruptcy isn't magic. It won't solve every financial problem, and it comes with trade-offs you need to understand. What it will do is give you **legal protection** and a **clear path forward** - often the first glimpse of hope you've had in months or years.

The Two Paths: Chapter 7 vs. Chapter 13

For individual consumers, bankruptcy typically comes in two forms, named after the chapters of the federal Bankruptcy Code that govern them:

Chapter 7: The Clean Slate

Also called: "Straight bankruptcy" or "liquidation bankruptcy"

Chapter 7 is designed for people with **limited income** who need to **wipe out debt quickly**. In most cases, it eliminates your unsecured debts - credit cards, medical bills, personal loans - in about three to four months.

How it works:

- You file paperwork listing all your debts, income, and property
- A court-appointed trustee reviews your case

- Most of your debts are "discharged" (legally eliminated)
- You keep most or all of your property thanks to "exemption" laws

Best for: People who can't afford to repay their debts and want a fast fresh start.

Chapter 13: The Repayment Plan

Also called: "Reorganization bankruptcy" or the "wage earner's plan"

Chapter 13 is for people with **steady income** who can afford to repay some of their debt over time, but need help organizing it and stopping creditor pressure.

How it works:

- You propose a 3-to-5-year repayment plan
- You make monthly payments to a court trustee
- The trustee distributes money to your creditors
- At the end, remaining eligible debts are discharged

Best for: People who want to save their home from foreclosure, have valuable property to protect, or earn too much to qualify for Chapter 7.

Your Immediate Protection: The Automatic Stay

The moment you file for bankruptcy - whether Chapter 7 or 13 - a powerful legal protection called the **automatic stay** goes into effect. This court order immediately stops:

- **Collection calls** and letters
- **Lawsuits** by creditors
- **Wage garnishment**
- **Bank account seizures**
- **Foreclosure proceedings**
- **Utility shutoffs** (in most cases)

- **Repossession** of your car

Creditors who violate the automatic stay can face serious penalties. For many people, this immediate relief is worth the price of filing alone - it gives you space to breathe and think clearly for the first time in months.

What Debts Can Be Eliminated?

Bankruptcy is powerful, but it can't erase every type of debt. Here's what typically can and cannot be discharged:

Usually Discharged (Eliminated):

- Credit card balances
- Medical bills
- Personal loans
- Past-due utility bills
- Deficiency balances after car repossession
- Old income taxes (if they meet specific age requirements)
- Collection accounts
- Some court judgments

Usually NOT Discharged:

- Recent income taxes
- Student loans (except in rare hardship cases)
- Child support and alimony
- Court-ordered fines and restitution
- Debts from fraud or intentional wrongdoing
- Some secured debts (unless you surrender the property)

Understanding which of your debts can be eliminated is crucial to determining whether bankruptcy will actually help your situation.

Protecting Your Property: Exemptions

One of the biggest myths about bankruptcy is that you'll lose everything you own. **This is false.** Both federal law and state laws provide "exemptions" - protections for your essential property.

In most consumer bankruptcy cases, people keep:

- Their home (if equity is within exemption limits)
- Their car (if not too valuable)
- Household furniture and clothing
- Work tools and equipment
- Retirement accounts (401k, IRA, pensions)
- Basic personal belongings

The specific amounts you can protect depend on whether you live in New York or California, and which exemption system you choose. We'll cover this in detail in later chapters, but know this: **most people who file bankruptcy keep everything they own.**

The Costs: What You Should Expect

Court Filing Fees

- **Chapter 7:** $338 (may be waived for very low-income filers)
- **Chapter 13:** $313 (payment plans available)

Attorney Fees (Typical Ranges)

- **Chapter 7:** $1,200 - $2,500 in NY/CA
- **Chapter 13:** $3,000 - $5,500 (often paid through your repayment plan)

Required Courses

- **Credit counseling:** Before filing (~$25-50)
- **Financial management course:** After filing (~$25-50)

While bankruptcy isn't free, it's often far less expensive than continuing to struggle with unmanageable debt. Many attorneys offer payment plans or reduced fees for people who qualify.

Common Fears and Misconceptions

"Everyone will know I filed bankruptcy"

Bankruptcy filings are public records, but they're not published in newspapers or announced to your neighbors. In practice, very few people will know unless you tell them.

"I'll never get credit again"

While bankruptcy does impact your credit, many people begin receiving credit offers within months of their discharge. With responsible use, you can rebuild your credit score within 2-3 years.

"I'm taking advantage of the system"

Bankruptcy law exists specifically to help people in financial distress. Using it when appropriate isn't taking advantage - it's using a legal right that Congress created for exactly your situation.

"I should be able to handle this myself"

Financial problems often result from circumstances beyond your control: medical emergencies, job loss, economic downturns, or family crises. Needing help doesn't reflect poorly on your character or abilities.

Signs That Bankruptcy Might Help You

Consider bankruptcy if you're experiencing several of these warning signs:

- You're using credit cards to pay for basic necessities like food or utilities

- You're only making minimum payments on credit cards (or can't even do that)
- You've tried debt consolidation or credit counseling without success
- You're facing foreclosure, eviction, or repossession
- Your wages are being garnished
- You can't realistically pay off your debt within 5 years, even with a strict budget
- You're losing sleep or experiencing health problems due to financial stress
- You're avoiding friends and family because of money issues

The Emotional Side of Financial Crisis

Before we dive into the legal details, let's acknowledge something important: **financial crisis is emotionally devastating.** You might be feeling:

- **Shame** about your situation
- **Fear** about the future
- **Anxiety** about making the wrong decision
- **Isolation** because you think you're the only one going through this
- **Anger** at yourself or your circumstances

These feelings are normal and valid. Bankruptcy isn't just a legal process - it's an emotional journey toward rebuilding your life. Give yourself permission to feel these emotions while also taking concrete steps to improve your situation.

Why This Book Focuses on New York and California

While bankruptcy is federal law and works similarly everywhere, important details - especially what property you can keep - depend heavily on your state's laws. New York and California are home to nearly 60 million Americans and have some of the most consumer-friendly exemption laws in the country and the author is admitted in both jurisdictions.

If you live in one of these states, this book will give you specific, actionable guidance. If you live elsewhere, the general principles still apply, but you'll need to research your state's specific exemption laws.

Federal Law, Local Implementation

Bankruptcy may be federal law, but it's implemented locally. New York has four federal bankruptcy districts (Southern, Eastern, Northern, and Western), while California also has four (Northern, Central, Eastern, and Southern). Each district has its own local rules, procedures, and court culture.

This local variation means that while the big picture is the same everywhere, the details - filing procedures, trustee expectations, local deadlines - can vary. It's one reason why working with a local bankruptcy attorney familiar with your specific court can be valuable.

What Happens Next in This Book

The chapters ahead will take you step-by-step through everything you need to know:

- **Chapters 2-3:** Should you file bankruptcy, and if so, which type?
- **Chapters 4-5:** How bankruptcy affects your credit, property, and future
- **Chapters 6-10:** Complete guide to Chapter 7 bankruptcy
- **Chapters 11-15:** Complete guide to Chapter 13 bankruptcy
- **Chapters 16-20:** Special situations (divorce, student loans, taxes, fraud prevention)
- **Chapters 21-24:** Finding help, alternatives to bankruptcy, and rebuilding your life

Each chapter builds on the previous ones, but they're also designed to stand alone if you need to focus on a specific topic.

A Word About Legal Advice

This book provides **educational information** about bankruptcy law, not legal advice for your specific situation. Bankruptcy law is complex and changes frequently. Every person's financial situation is unique, and what works for one person may not work for another.

Always consult with a qualified bankruptcy attorney before making important decisions about your case. Many attorneys offer free consultations, and legal aid organizations provide low-cost or free help for people who qualify.

This book will help you understand your options and ask better questions, but it's not a substitute for personalized legal guidance.

Your Journey Starts Here

Financial crisis can feel like you're drowning in an ocean of debt with no land in sight. Bankruptcy - when it's the right choice - is like a life raft that can carry you to shore. It's not a luxury cruise, and the journey isn't always smooth, but it can get you to safety.

You've already taken the most important step by seeking information and exploring your options. That takes courage, especially when you're feeling overwhelmed or ashamed about your situation.

As we move through this book together, remember: **you are not alone, you are not out of options, and this crisis does not define you.** Thousands of people have walked this path before you and found their way to financial stability and peace of mind.

Your fresh start is waiting. Let's figure out how to claim it.

In the next chapter, we'll help you determine whether bankruptcy is actually the right choice for your situation - because while it can be a powerful solution, it's not right for everyone.

2

Should You File?

Making the Most Important Financial Decision of Your Life

The Question That Keeps You Up at Night

You know bankruptcy exists. You may have even visited a bankruptcy attorney's website or called a legal aid hotline. But you're still asking yourself the same question that brought you to this book: **Should I actually file for bankruptcy?**

This isn't a decision to make lightly, and it's not one you should make in desperation at 3 AM when the bills are spread across your kitchen table and you can't see any other way out. Bankruptcy can be a powerful tool for financial recovery, but it's not right for everyone - and it's definitely not a decision to rush into.

In this chapter, we'll walk through a systematic way to evaluate whether bankruptcy makes sense for your specific situation. We'll help you distinguish between temporary financial stress and true financial crisis, analyze what types of debt you're carrying, and explore alternatives that might work better for your circumstances.

Understanding the Difference: Behind vs. Drowning

Everyone falls behind on bills sometimes. A car repair comes at the wrong time, you get sick and miss work, or an unexpected expense throws off your budget for a month or two. **Being behind on bills is not the same as needing bankruptcy.**

Bankruptcy is designed for people who are **financially insolvent** - meaning your debts have grown so large compared to your income that you cannot realistically repay them in the foreseeable future, even with significant lifestyle changes.

Signs You're Temporarily Behind (May Not Need Bankruptcy):

- You've missed 1-2 months of payments due to a specific event
- You can see a clear path to catching up within 6-12 months
- Your total debt is less than your annual income
- You have assets you could sell to address the problem
- The issue is primarily one or two large debts, not overwhelming overall debt
- You have family or other resources that could help in an emergency

Signs You May Be Drowning (Bankruptcy Might Help):

- You've been struggling for 6+ months with no improvement
- You're borrowing money or using credit cards just to buy food or pay rent
- Your minimum monthly payments exceed 40% of your take-home income
- You've stopped opening bills because it's too overwhelming
- You're considering payday loans or title loans to pay other debts
- You can't imagine being debt-free even in 5-10 years
- You're experiencing physical symptoms of stress (insomnia,

headaches, anxiety)

The Debt Analysis: What You Owe Matters

Not all debt is created equal in bankruptcy.

Understanding what types of debt you're carrying is crucial to determining whether filing will actually help your situation.

Dischargeable Debts (Can Usually Be Eliminated):

Credit Card Debt

- Regular credit card balances
- Store credit cards
- Gas cards
- *Why it matters*: This is the debt bankruptcy handles best

Medical Debt

- Hospital bills
- Doctor bills
- Ambulance charges
- Medical equipment costs
- *Why it matters*: Medical debt is a leading cause of bankruptcy and is almost always dischargeable

Personal Loans

- Bank personal loans
- Credit union loans
- Loans from friends or family (though this can get complicated)
- *Why it matters*: These unsecured debts are typically eliminated completely

Deficiency Balances

- Amount still owed after car repossession
- Shortfall after foreclosure (in some states)
- *Why it matters*: You can eliminate these "phantom debts" even though you no longer have the property

Old Utility Bills

- Past-due electric, gas, water bills from previous addresses
- *Why it matters*: These collection accounts can be eliminated

Non-Dischargeable Debts (Usually Survive Bankruptcy):

Student Loans

- Federal student loans
- Most private student loans
- *The reality*: Very difficult to discharge, though new rules make it somewhat easier

Recent Taxes

- Income taxes less than 3 years old
- Payroll taxes
- Fraud-related tax debt
- *The strategy*: Chapter 13 can help you pay these over time

Domestic Support Obligations

- Child support
- Alimony/spousal support
- *Why it matters*: These obligations always survive bankruptcy

Criminal Fines and Restitution

- Court-ordered fines
- Criminal restitution

- *The bottom line*: These debts are considered non-dischargeable

Secured Debts (Tied to Property):

Mortgage

- *In Chapter 7*: You can keep the house if you stay current on payments
- *In Chapter 13*: You can catch up on missed payments over time

Car Loans

- *In Chapter 7*: Keep the car if current on payments, or surrender it and eliminate any deficiency
- *In Chapter 13*: Catch up on missed payments, or sometimes reduce the loan balance

The Financial Reality Check

Before considering bankruptcy, you need to honestly assess your financial situation. This can be painful, but it's essential for making the right decision.

Step 1: Calculate Your Total Debt

Make a list of every debt you owe:

- Credit cards (include the interest rates)
- Medical bills
- Personal loans
- Back taxes
- Student loans
- Any other debts

Total Unsecured Debt: $__________

Step 2: Calculate Your Monthly Take-Home Income

Include all sources:

- Job income (after taxes)
- Social Security
- Disability payments
- Unemployment benefits
- Side gig income
- Any other regular income

Monthly Take-Home Income: $__________

Step 3: Calculate Essential Monthly Expenses

Be realistic about what you actually need:

- Housing (rent/mortgage, utilities)
- Food
- Transportation
- Insurance
- Minimum debt payments
- Basic clothing and personal care

Essential Monthly Expenses: $__________

Step 4: The Math Test

Available for Debt Payment = Income - Essential Expenses

If this number is:

- **Negative:** You're spending more than you earn on basics - bankruptcy likely makes sense
- **Less than minimum payments:** You can't even service your debts - bankruptcy probably helps
- **Enough for minimums but no principal:** You'll never get out of debt - bankruptcy might help

- **Enough to make real progress:** You might not need bankruptcy

The 5-Year Test

Here's a crucial question: **Even if you paid every available dollar toward debt, could you realistically be debt-free in 5 years?**

Take your total unsecured debt and divide by 60 months. If that monthly payment is more than you can afford (from Step 4 above), bankruptcy starts to make sense.

Example:

- Total debt: $45,000
- ÷ 60 months = $750/month needed
- Available for debt payment: $200/month
- **Result:** You'd need 19 years to pay off the debt, and that's assuming no interest and no new emergencies

Asset Protection: What You Stand to Lose (Or Keep)

Many people avoid bankruptcy because they're afraid of losing everything they own. In reality, **most people keep all their property** thanks to exemption laws.

Property You'll Almost Certainly Keep:

- Basic household furnishings
- Clothing and personal items
- One vehicle (if not too valuable)
- Work tools and equipment
- Retirement accounts (401k, IRA, pensions)
- Life insurance (if not too valuable)

Property That Might Be at Risk:

- Second homes or rental property
- Expensive cars with significant equity
- Valuable collections (art, coins, etc.)
- Business equipment (beyond basic tools)
- Large amounts of cash or investments

The Homestead Exemption

Both New York and California protect home equity, but the amounts vary:

- **New York:** Up to approximately $179,950 in most counties
- **California:** Up to $678,000+ (System 1) or about $32,000 (System 2)

If your home equity exceeds these amounts, Chapter 13 might be better than Chapter 7, as it allows you to keep all property while repaying debts over time.

Have You Tried Alternatives?

Bankruptcy should generally not be your first attempt at debt relief. Courts and trustees look favorably on people who have made good-faith efforts to resolve their debts before filing.

Credit Counseling

What it is: Working with a nonprofit agency to create a debt management plan

How it works: You make one payment to the agency, which distributes funds to creditors at reduced interest rates

Pros:

- Can significantly reduce interest rates
- Simplifies payments
- Doesn't appear as negatively on credit reports

Cons:

- You still pay the full balance owed
- Not all creditors participate
- Takes 3-5 years
- If you miss payments, you're back where you started

Best for: People with steady income and moderate debt who want to avoid bankruptcy

Debt Settlement

What it is: Negotiating with creditors to accept less than the full balance owed

How it works: You (or a company) negotiate lump-sum settlements for less than you owe

Pros:

- Can reduce total debt owed
- Faster than debt management plans

Cons:

- Severely damages credit
- No guarantee creditors will negotiate
- May owe taxes on forgiven debt
- Debt settlement companies often charge high fees

Best for: People with access to lump-sum cash who can't qualify for bankruptcy

Informal Negotiation

What it is: Calling creditors yourself to arrange payment plans or hardship programs

How it works: You explain your situation and ask for reduced payments, interest rate reductions, or settlement options

Pros:

- Free to attempt
- Some creditors have generous hardship programs
- Can buy you time to improve your situation

Cons:

- No guarantee of success
- Temporary solutions may not address underlying problems
- Can be time-consuming and stressful

Best for: People with temporary hardships who need short-term relief

Special Circumstances That Favor Bankruptcy

Certain situations make bankruptcy particularly attractive:

Medical Debt

If medical bills are a significant portion of your debt, bankruptcy is often the best solution. Medical debt is completely dischargeable, and courts are very sympathetic to people overwhelmed by healthcare costs.

Job Loss or Income Reduction

If your income has permanently decreased (due to job loss, disability, or retirement), bankruptcy can eliminate debts based on your old income level and give you a fresh start with your new financial reality.

Divorce

Divorce often leaves people with debt they can't handle on a single income. Chapter 7 can eliminate joint debts, while Chapter 13 can discharge certain divorce-related property settlement debts.

Business Failure

If a failed business left you with personal guarantees or business debt, bankruptcy can provide relief that business closure alone cannot.

Garnishment or Lawsuits

If creditors are already garnishing your wages or have sued you, bankruptcy's automatic stay provides immediate relief that other debt relief options cannot match.

Red Flags: When Bankruptcy Might Not Be Right

You Just Want to Avoid Paying Debts You Can Afford

Bankruptcy is for people who genuinely cannot pay their debts, not for those who simply don't want to. Filing when you can afford to pay is considered abuse of the bankruptcy system.

You Recently Ran Up Large Debts

If you've recently charged large amounts on credit cards or taken cash advances knowing you planned to file bankruptcy, those debts may not be dischargeable, and you could face fraud allegations.

You've Filed Bankruptcy Recently

You can only receive a Chapter 7 discharge once every 8 years. If you've filed recently, you may not be eligible for relief.

Your Debt Is Mostly Non-Dischargeable

If most of your debt consists of student loans, recent taxes, and child support, bankruptcy may not provide significant relief.

You're About to Receive Money

If you're expecting a large tax refund, inheritance, or legal settlement that could resolve your debts, it might make sense to wait rather than file bankruptcy.

The Emotional Readiness Factor

Beyond the financial calculations, bankruptcy requires emotional readiness. Ask yourself:

Are you ready to:

- Face the reality of your financial situation honestly?
- Complete detailed paperwork about your finances?
- Attend court proceedings and answer questions under oath?
- Change your financial habits to avoid future problems?
- Accept that your credit will be impacted for several years?
- Live within a strict budget during the process?

Are you filing for the right reasons:

- To get genuine relief from overwhelming debt?
- To stop creditor harassment and regain peace of mind?
- To protect essential property like your home or car?
- To get a fresh start and rebuild your financial life?

Or the wrong reasons:

- To spite creditors or avoid paying debts you can afford?
- Because someone told you it would "fix everything" quickly?
- To hide assets or avoid legitimate obligations?
- As a quick fix without addressing underlying financial problems?

Making the Decision: A Practical Framework

Here's a step-by-step approach to making this crucial decision:

1. Complete the Financial Analysis

Use the calculations earlier in this chapter to understand your true financial position.

2. Identify Your Goals

What are you trying to achieve?

- Stop creditor harassment?
- Save your home from foreclosure?
- Eliminate overwhelming debt?
- Get a fresh start?

3. Consider Your Timeline

- How urgent is your situation?
- Are creditors actively pursuing you?
- Do you have time to try alternatives?

4. Evaluate Alternatives

Based on your analysis, would credit counseling, debt settlement, or negotiation realistically work?

5. Consider the Consequences

- How will bankruptcy affect your specific goals?
- Can you live with the credit impact?
- Will it actually solve your problems?

6. Seek Professional Input

A bankruptcy attorney can provide case-specific guidance that no book can offer.

When to Act Quickly

Sometimes you need to file bankruptcy immediately:

Foreclosure: If your home is scheduled for foreclosure sale, bankruptcy's automatic stay can stop it, but only if you file before the sale occurs.

Wage Garnishment: Bankruptcy can stop garnishment immediately, but every day you wait means more money taken from your paycheck.

Lawsuit: If creditors have sued you and obtained judgments, they may be able to seize bank accounts or other assets.

Utility Shutoffs: While bankruptcy can prevent utility disconnections, it's easier to restore service if you file before it's disconnected.

The Bottom Line: Three Questions

Before moving forward with bankruptcy, honestly answer these three questions:

1. **Can I realistically pay off my debts within 5 years, even with a strict budget and no new emergencies?**
2. **Have I tried reasonable alternatives, or are my circumstances so severe that alternatives won't work?**
3. **Will bankruptcy actually solve my problems, or do I have issues (like insufficient income) that bankruptcy can't fix?**

If you answered "no" to question 1 and "yes" to questions 2 and 3, bankruptcy likely makes sense for your situation.

Moving Forward with Confidence

Deciding whether to file bankruptcy is one of the most difficult financial decisions you'll ever make. It requires brutal honesty about your situation, careful analysis of your options, and the courage to take action when necessary.

Remember: **bankruptcy is not a sign of personal failure.** It's a legal tool created specifically for people facing the kind of financial crisis you're experiencing. Millions of honest, hardworking people have used bankruptcy to get their lives back on track.

If your analysis suggests that bankruptcy is the right choice, don't let shame or fear prevent you from taking action. The longer you wait while your situation deteriorates, the harder it becomes to recover.

On the other hand, if you determine that bankruptcy isn't right for your situation, that's valuable information too. You can focus your energy on alternatives that better fit your circumstances.

In the next chapter, we'll explore the different types of bankruptcy available to consumers and help you understand which option might work best for your specific situation.

3

Types of Bankruptcy

Finding the Right Path to Your Fresh Start

Choosing Your Route to Financial Freedom

If you've decided that bankruptcy might be right for your situation, the next crucial question is: **Which type of bankruptcy should you file?**

This isn't a one-size-fits-all decision. The type of bankruptcy that works for your neighbor might be completely wrong for you. Your choice depends on your income, the types of debt you have, what property you own, and what you're trying to accomplish.

Think of bankruptcy chapters like different routes to the same destination. Chapter 7 is like taking the highway - it's fast and direct, but not everyone qualifies for the on-ramp. Chapter 13 is more like taking the scenic route - it takes longer, but it allows you to see more of the landscape and may get you to places the highway can't reach.

In this chapter, we'll explore each type of consumer bankruptcy in detail, help you understand who qualifies for what, and give you the tools to determine which path is right for your specific situation.

Chapter 7: The Express Route to Debt Relief

What Chapter 7 Really Means

Chapter 7 bankruptcy, officially called "liquidation bankruptcy," is designed to give people with limited income a fast, clean slate. The term "liquidation" scares many people, but here's the reality: **most Chapter 7 filers keep everything they own.**

The Basic Process:

1. File your petition and supporting documents
2. A trustee is assigned to review your case
3. Attend a short "Meeting of Creditors" (usually by phone/video)
4. Most unsecured debts are discharged (eliminated) 3-4 months after filing
5. Case closed - you're debt-free

Who Chapter 7 Is Designed For

Ideal Chapter 7 Candidates:

- People with **low to moderate income** (below state median or who pass the "means test")
- Those with primarily **unsecured debt** (credit cards, medical bills, personal loans)
- Individuals who want a **quick resolution** (3-4 months vs. 3-5 years)
- People with **limited assets** or assets that are fully protected by exemptions
- Those who are **current on house and car payments** (if they want to keep them)

What Chapter 7 Can Do for You

Debts Typically Eliminated:

- Credit card balances
- Medical bills
- Personal loans
- Collection accounts
- Old utility bills
- Payday loans
- Deficiency balances after repossession
- Some older tax debts (if they meet specific criteria)
- Most court judgments

Immediate Benefits:

- **Automatic stay** stops all collection activity immediately
- **No more creditor calls** or letters
- **Wage garnishment stops** immediately
- **Lawsuits are halted**
- **Bank account freezes are lifted**

What Chapter 7 Cannot Do

Debts That Survive:

- Student loans (except in rare hardship cases)
- Recent income taxes (less than 3 years old)
- Child support and alimony
- Criminal fines and restitution
- Debts from fraud or willful injury to others

Property Limitations:

- If you have **non-exempt property** worth significant money, the trustee may sell it

- You can't use Chapter 7 to **catch up on missed mortgage or car payments**
- **Secured debts** continue (you must stay current or surrender the property)

The Income Test: Do You Qualify?

Not everyone can file Chapter 7. You must pass the **"means test,"** which compares your income to your state's median income for a household of your size.

2025 Approximate Median Incomes *(these change annually)*:

Household Size New York California1 person $65,000 $68,0002 people $83,000 $87,0003 people $96,000 $97,0004 people $112,000 $114,000

If your income is below the median: You automatically qualify for Chapter 7 (subject to other requirements).

If your income is above the median: You must complete a more complex calculation that considers your actual expenses. Many people still qualify even with higher incomes.

Real-Life Chapter 7 Example

Maria's Story - Los Angeles, CA:

- Single mother, works as a school aide
- Annual income: $42,000 (below CA median)
- Debts: $35,000 in credit cards, $8,000 in medical bills
- Assets: 2010 Honda Civic, basic household items, small savings account
- **Result:** All unsecured debt eliminated in 4 months, kept all property

Chapter 13: The Reorganization Route

What Chapter 13 Really Means

Chapter 13 bankruptcy, called "reorganization bankruptcy" or the "wage earner's plan," allows people with regular income to keep their property while repaying all or part of their debts over 3-5 years.

Think of Chapter 13 as a **court-supervised payment plan** that gives you powerful legal protections while you get back on your feet.

The Basic Process:

1. Propose a repayment plan based on your income and expenses
2. Make monthly payments to a court trustee for 3-5 years
3. The trustee distributes money to creditors according to your plan
4. Remaining eligible debts are discharged at the end
5. You keep all your property

Who Chapter 13 Is Designed For

Ideal Chapter 13 Candidates:

- People with **steady, regular income** (job, pension, Social Security, etc.)
- Those who are **behind on mortgage or car payments** and want to catch up
- Individuals with **valuable property** they want to protect
- People who **don't qualify for Chapter 7** due to higher income
- Those who owe **non-dischargeable debts** they need time to pay
- Homeowners facing **foreclosure**

What Chapter 13 Can Do for You

Powerful Protections:

- **Stop foreclosure** immediately and allow you to catch up over time
- **Prevent car repossession** and let you catch up on payments
- **Reduce car loan balances** in some cases (if the car is worth less than

you owe)

- **Strip off second mortgages** if your home is underwater
- **Stop all collection activity** for the entire 3-5 year period
- **Discharge remaining debt** at the end of the plan

Debt Management:

- **Catch up on missed mortgage payments** over the life of the plan
- **Pay priority debts** (like taxes and child support) over time without penalties
- **Reduce payments** on unsecured debt (sometimes to $0)
- **Stop interest** on most unsecured debts

How Chapter 13 Payments Work

Your monthly payment is based on what you can afford after essential living expenses, not what you owe.

Example Payment Calculation:

- Monthly take-home income: $4,500
- Essential expenses (housing, food, transportation, etc.): $3,800
- Available for debt payment: $700
- **Chapter 13 payment: $700/month**

Where the Money Goes:

1. **Priority debts** (taxes, child support) - must be paid in full
2. **Secured debt arrears** (missed mortgage/car payments) - paid over time
3. **Unsecured debts** (credit cards, medical bills) - often paid very little or nothing

Chapter 13 Plan Length

3-Year Plans:

- If your income is **below** the state median
- **Minimum:** You must pay at least what unsecured creditors would receive in Chapter 7

5-Year Plans:

- If your income is **above** the state median
- **Maximum:** Plans cannot exceed 60 months

Real-Life Chapter 13 Example

David's Story - Buffalo, NY:

- Married couple, combined income $85,000
- $15,000 behind on mortgage, facing foreclosure
- $25,000 in credit cards, $8,000 in medical bills
- **Plan:** $450/month for 60 months
  - Caught up on mortgage over 5 years
  - Paid taxes and child support in full
  - Paid 20% to unsecured creditors
- **Result:** Kept home, eliminated most unsecured debt

Chapter 11: Business Reorganization (Rarely for Consumers)

What Chapter 11 Is

Chapter 11 is primarily designed for businesses, but it's sometimes used by individuals with **very high debt levels** or **complex financial situations.**

Typical Chapter 11 Individual Cases:

- Debt exceeding Chapter 13 limits ($2.75 million in total debt)
- Complex business and personal finances

- High-income individuals with substantial assets

Why Most Consumers Avoid Chapter 11:

- **Expensive:** Legal fees often exceed $50,000-$100,000
- **Complex:** Requires detailed business-style planning and reporting
- **Time-consuming:** Cases often take 2+ years
- **Public:** More scrutiny and publicity than other chapters

Bottom Line: Unless you have extraordinarily high debt or complex business interests, Chapter 11 is probably not for you.

Other Bankruptcy Chapters (Not for Most Consumers)

Chapter 12: Family Farmers and Fishermen

Specialized reorganization for family farmers and commercial fishermen with regular annual income.

Chapter 9: Municipalities

For cities, towns, and other governmental entities.

Chapter 15: Cross-Border Cases

For cases involving assets in multiple countries.

Note: These chapters are included for completeness but don't apply to typical consumer situations.

Chapter 7 vs. Chapter 13: The Direct Comparison

- **Time to Complete:** Chapter 7: 3-4 months; Chapter 13: 3-5 years
- **Income Requirements:** Chapter 7: Below median or pass means test; Chapter 13: Regular income required
- **Monthly Payments:** Chapter 7: None (after filing); Chapter 13: Yes, for entire plan period

- **Property at Risk:** Chapter 7: Non-exempt assets may be sold; Chapter 13: Keep all property
- **Foreclosure Relief:** Chapter 7: Temporary delay only; Chapter 13: Can catch up over time
- **Car Loan Relief:** Chapter 7: Limited options; Chapter 13: Can catch up or reduce balance
- **Unsecured Debt:** Chapter 7: Eliminated completely; Chapter 13: Partially paid, remainder discharged
- **Credit Report Impact:** Chapter 7: 10 years; Chapter 13: 7 years
- **Best For:** Chapter 7: Quick clean slate; Chapter 13: Saving home/car, higher income

How to Choose: The Decision Framework

Start with Income

Step 1: Income Qualification

- Calculate your average monthly income over the past 6 months
- Compare to your state's median income for your household size
- If **below median:** Chapter 7 is likely available
- If **above median:** May need Chapter 13 or must pass complex means test

Consider Your Goals

Step 2: What Are You Trying to Accomplish?

Choose Chapter 7 if:

- You want to eliminate debt quickly
- You're current on house/car payments (if keeping them)
- You have mostly unsecured debt
- You don't have significant non-exempt property

- You want to "surrender" property you can't afford

Choose Chapter 13 if:

- You're behind on mortgage and want to save your home
- You're behind on car payments and need the vehicle
- You have valuable property you want to protect
- You have significant non-dischargeable debt (taxes, child support)
- You don't qualify for Chapter 7 due to income

Analyze Your Debts

Step 3: Debt Composition Analysis

Chapter 7 is better for:

- High credit card balances
- Large medical bills
- Personal loans and payday loans
- Collection accounts

Chapter 13 is better for:

- Mortgage arrears (missed payments)
- Car loan arrears
- Recent tax debt
- Priority debts that must be paid in full

Asset Protection Considerations

Step 4: Property Analysis

Chapter 7 works if:

- All your property is exempt (protected)
- You don't mind surrendering non-exempt property

- You don't have significant equity in non-exempt assets

Chapter 13 is necessary if:

- You have valuable non-exempt property
- Your home equity exceeds exemption limits
- You own business assets or investment property

Common Misconceptions About Chapter Choice

"Chapter 13 is better because it shows you're trying to pay"

Reality: Both chapters are legitimate legal options. Chapter 7 isn't "cheating" - it's using the law as Congress intended.

"Chapter 7 will ruin my credit worse than Chapter 13"

Reality: Both significantly impact credit initially. Chapter 7 stays on your report longer (10 vs. 7 years) but allows faster rebuilding since you're debt-free immediately.

"I should file Chapter 13 to keep my house"

Reality: You can often keep your house in Chapter 7 if you're current on payments and your equity is within exemption limits.

"Chapter 13 is only for rich people"

Reality: Chapter 13 is often used by working-class families to save their homes from foreclosure.

Special Situations That Affect Chapter Choice

Recent Bankruptcy Filing

- **Chapter 7 to Chapter 7:** Must wait 8 years

- **Chapter 13 to Chapter 7:** Must wait 6 years (with exceptions)
- **Chapter 7 to Chapter 13:** Must wait 4 years
- **Chapter 13 to Chapter 13:** Must wait 2 years

Domestic Support Obligations

If you owe child support or alimony, you must be **current** to receive a Chapter 7 discharge. Chapter 13 allows you to catch up over time.

Previous Dismissals

If you've had a bankruptcy case dismissed in the past year, the automatic stay may be limited or not apply at all.

Fraud or Abuse

Recent large purchases, cash advances, or attempts to hide assets may make Chapter 7 unavailable and require Chapter 13.

Making Your Decision: A Practical Checklist

Chapter 7 Checklist ✓

- [ ] My income is below the state median OR I pass the means test
- [ ] I want to eliminate debt quickly
- [ ] I'm current on house/car payments (if keeping them)
- [ ] Most of my debt is unsecured (credit cards, medical bills)
- [ ] I don't have significant non-exempt property
- [ ] I haven't filed Chapter 7 in the past 8 years

Chapter 13 Checklist ✓

- [ ] I have regular, steady income
- [ ] I'm behind on mortgage/car payments and want to catch up

- [ ] I have property I want to protect that might not be exempt
- [ ] I don't qualify for Chapter 7 due to income or other factors
- [ ] I owe significant priority debts (taxes, child support)
- [ ] I can commit to 3-5 years of monthly payments

When You're Not Sure: Getting Professional Help

Red Flags That You Need Attorney Guidance

- Your income is close to the median limits
- You have significant assets or complex property ownership
- You're facing immediate foreclosure or repossession
- You have recent large purchases or unusual financial transactions
- You've filed bankruptcy before
- You have business interests or rental property

The Cost of Getting It Wrong

- **Filing the wrong chapter** can cost you property, time, and money
- **Missing deadlines** can result in dismissal and loss of protection
- **Incorrect paperwork** can lead to fraud allegations or denial of discharge

How to Find the Right Attorney

- Look for attorneys who specialize in bankruptcy (not general practice)
- Check state bar associations for referrals
- Ask about experience with your specific type of case
- Inquire about flat fees vs. hourly billing
- Consider legal aid organizations if you qualify

Your Next Steps

Understanding the different types of bankruptcy is just the beginning. Once you've identified which chapter might work for your situation, you'll need to dive deeper into the specifics:

- **Income and expense calculations**
- **Property exemption analysis**
- **Debt classification and treatment**
- **Timeline and procedural requirements**

The good news is that you don't have to figure this all out alone. In the chapters that follow, we'll walk through each type of bankruptcy in detail, giving you the tools and knowledge you need to move forward with confidence.

Remember: **the right choice is the one that best fits your specific situation and goals.** There's no shame in needing help, and there's no "better" or "worse" chapter - only what works for you.

In the next chapter, we'll explore how federal and state laws work together in bankruptcy, and why understanding this relationship is crucial to protecting your property and maximizing your fresh start.

4

Federal vs. State Law

Understanding the Legal Framework That Protects Your Property

Why This Matters to You

When most people think about filing bankruptcy, they assume it's all federal law - the same everywhere in the United States. And they're partially right. The basic structure of bankruptcy **is** federal, which means you'll follow the same general process whether you file in Brooklyn or Bakersfield.

But here's what catches many people off guard: **the most important question - what property you get to keep - depends heavily on your state's laws.**

This interplay between federal and state law can mean the difference between keeping your home and losing it, between protecting your savings and having them seized, between walking away with your tools for work and starting over with nothing.

Understanding this relationship isn't just legal trivia - it's essential to making smart decisions about your bankruptcy case and protecting everything you've worked for.

The Federal Foundation

Constitutional Authority

Bankruptcy law exists because the U.S. Constitution specifically gives Congress the power to create "uniform Laws on the subject of Bankruptcies throughout the United States." This is found in Article I, Section 8, right alongside Congress's power to regulate interstate commerce and coin money.

This constitutional foundation means that:

- **Bankruptcy is a federal right**, not a privilege granted by states
- **The basic process is uniform** across all 50 states
- **Federal courts handle all bankruptcy cases**, not state courts
- **Core protections** (like the automatic stay) apply everywhere

What Federal Law Controls

The U.S. Bankruptcy Code (Title 11 of the United States Code) sets the rules for:

Case Structure and Process:

- Which chapters of bankruptcy are available
- Who can file and when
- How cases are administered
- What forms must be completed
- Timeline requirements and deadlines

Core Legal Protections:

- The automatic stay (stops collections immediately)
- Discharge of debts (legal elimination of obligations)
- Treatment of different types of debts

- Creditor rights and limitations

Eligibility and Qualification:

- Income limits and means testing
- Credit counseling requirements
- Previous bankruptcy restrictions
- Fraud prevention measures

Court Procedures:

- How trustees are appointed
- Meeting of creditors procedures
- Court hearings and requirements
- Appeal processes

Federal Bankruptcy Districts

While bankruptcy law is federal, it's administered through **94 federal judicial districts** across the country. These districts handle the practical, day-to-day operations of the bankruptcy system.

New York's Four Districts:

- **Southern (SDNY):** Covers Manhattan, Bronx, Westchester, Rockland, Orange, Putnam, Sullivan, Dutchess; main courthouses: White Plains, Poughkeepsie
- **Eastern (EDNY):** Covers Brooklyn, Queens, Staten Island, Nassau, Suffolk; main courthouses: Brooklyn, Central Islip
- **Northern (NDNY):** Covers Albany area, Syracuse, Utica, Binghamton; main courthouses: Albany, Syracuse, Utica
- **Western (WDNY):** Covers Buffalo, Rochester, Elmira; main courthouses: Buffalo, Rochester

California's Four Districts:

- **Northern (NDCA):** Covers San Francisco Bay Area, Oakland, San Jose, Sacramento (bankruptcy only); main courthouses: San Francisco,

Oakland, San Jose

- **Central (CDCA):** Covers Los Angeles, Orange County, Riverside, San Bernardino, Ventura, Santa Barbara; main courthouses: Los Angeles, Riverside, Santa Ana, Woodland Hills
- **Eastern (EDCA):** Covers Sacramento, Fresno, Modesto, Bakersfield; main courthouses: Sacramento, Fresno, Modesto
- **Southern (SDCA):** Covers San Diego, Imperial County; main courthouses: San Diego

Why Districts Matter:

- Each has **local rules** that supplement federal law
- **Different trustees** with varying policies and expectations
- **Local court culture** and practices
- **Varying efficiency** and processing times

Where State Law Takes Over

While federal law creates the bankruptcy framework, state law fills in crucial details - particularly when it comes to **what property you can protect.**

The Exemption System: Your Financial Lifeline

Exemptions are laws that protect certain property from being taken to pay creditors. Think of them as your financial lifeline - they ensure you don't lose everything and can maintain a basic standard of living.

Why Exemptions Exist:

- Prevent debtors from becoming destitute
- Allow fresh start with basic necessities
- Protect tools needed to earn a living
- Preserve family stability and dignity

How Exemptions Work:

- If your property is **exempt**, you keep it (even in Chapter 7)

- If property is **non-exempt**, it may be sold to pay creditors
- Exemptions have **dollar limits** (e.g., "up to $5,000 in car equity")
- You must **choose an exemption system** when you file

State vs. Federal Exemptions: The Choice

Here's where it gets interesting (and potentially confusing): **Some states let you choose between state and federal exemptions, while others require you to use only state exemptions.**

States That Allow Choice (including New York):

- You can pick either federal exemptions OR your state's exemptions
- You **cannot mix and match** - it's all or nothing
- Your choice can dramatically affect what you keep

States That Require State Exemptions (including California):

- You **must** use your state's exemption system
- Federal exemptions are not available
- Some states (like California) offer multiple state systems to choose from

The New York Exemption Choice

New York residents get to choose between **two complete exemption systems.**

Federal Exemptions (2025 approximate amounts):

- **Homestead:** $27,900 (individual), $55,800 (joint)
- **Vehicle:** $4,450
- **Household Goods:** $700 per item, $14,875 total
- **Jewelry:** $1,875
- **Tools of Trade:** $2,800

- **Wildcard:** $1,475 + unused homestead (up to $13,950)
- **Retirement Accounts:** Unlimited (401k, IRA, etc.)

New York State Exemptions (2025 approximate amounts):

- **Homestead:** $179,950 (varies by county)
- **Vehicle:** $5,000
- **Household Goods:** Reasonable amounts
- **Tools of Trade:** $3,750
- **Cash/Bank Accounts:** $6,000
- **Wildcard:** $1,175 (if no homestead claimed)
- **Retirement Accounts:** Unlimited

Key Differences:

- **New York's homestead** is much higher (great for homeowners)
- **Federal wildcard** is more flexible for various assets
- **Federal household goods** protection is more generous
- **New York vehicle** exemption is slightly higher

California's Dual System Approach

California doesn't allow federal exemptions but offers **two different state systems:**

System 1 (CCP § 704) - "The Homeowner's System":

- **Homestead:** $678,000+ (adjusted annually)
- **Vehicle:** $3,625
- **Household Goods:** Reasonable amounts
- **Tools of Trade:** $9,525
- **Jewelry:** $1,850

- **Wildcard:** None
- **Retirement Accounts:** Unlimited

System 2 (CCP § 703) - "The Renter's System":

- **Homestead:** $31,950
- **Vehicle:** $7,500
- **Household Goods:** $700 per item, $14,875 total
- **Jewelry:** $2,050
- **Tools of Trade:** $2,800
- **Wildcard:** $1,550 + unused homestead (up to $30,400)
- **Retirement Accounts:** Unlimited

Key Differences:

- **System 1** protects much more home equity
- **System 2** offers more flexibility with the large wildcard
- **System 2** protects more vehicle equity
- **System 2** is better for renters or those with diverse assets

Strategic Exemption Planning

Choosing the Right System: New York

Choose Federal Exemptions if:

- You rent rather than own
- You have valuable personal property (electronics, jewelry, collections)
- You want maximum flexibility with the wildcard exemption
- You have moderate vehicle equity
- You own tools or equipment worth more than $3,750

Choose New York State Exemptions if:

- You own a home with significant equity
- You live in a high-cost county (NYC area, Westchester, etc.)
- You have substantial cash savings
- Your personal property is modest
- You want maximum homestead protection

Real Example - Brooklyn Homeowner: Sarah owns a Brooklyn home worth $600,000 with a $450,000 mortgage (equity = $150,000).

- **Federal exemptions:** Only protect $27,900 - she'd lose the house
- **NY state exemptions:** Protect up to $179,950 - she keeps the house
- **Choice:** New York state exemptions, clearly

Real Example - Albany Renter: Mike rents an apartment but owns a collection worth $15,000, a car worth $8,000, and has $5,000 in savings.

- **Federal exemptions:** Wildcard can protect the collection, car partially protected
- **NY state exemptions:** Collection not well protected, but car and cash better covered
- **Choice:** Depends on priorities - probably federal for the wildcard flexibility

Choosing the Right System: California

Choose System 1 (704) if:

- You own a home with substantial equity
- You're a long-term homeowner in an expensive market
- Your other assets are modest
- You want maximum homestead protection

Choose System 2 (703) if:

- You rent or have limited home equity

- You have diverse assets (cash, investments, collections)
- You own a valuable vehicle
- You want flexibility to protect different types of property

Real Example - San Diego Homeowner: Carlos owns a home worth $850,000 with a $200,000 mortgage (equity = $650,000).

- **System 1:** Protects $678,000+ of equity - he keeps the house
- **System 2:** Only protects $31,950 - he'd lose significant equity
- **Choice:** System 1, without question

Real Example - Sacramento Renter: Maria rents but has $25,000 in savings, a paid-off car worth $15,000, and valuable work equipment.

- **System 1:** No wildcard to protect savings, limited vehicle protection
- **System 2:** Large wildcard can protect savings, better vehicle protection
- **Choice:** System 2 for the flexibility

The Residency Requirement: Anti-Forum Shopping Rules

You can't just move to a state with better exemptions and immediately use them. The **730-day rule** prevents "forum shopping":

The Two-Year Rule

To use a state's exemptions, you must have lived there for **730 days (2 years)** before filing bankruptcy.

The Domicile Test

If you haven't lived in one state for the full 730 days, you use the exemptions of the state where you lived for **the majority of the 180-day period** before the 730-day period.

Example Timeline:

- **Today:** File bankruptcy in California
- **730 days ago:** Must have been living in California
- **If not:** Look at where you lived during the 180 days before that 730-day mark

Special Rules for Homestead Exemptions

If you acquired your home within **1,215 days** (about 3.3 years) before filing, your homestead exemption may be capped at **$189,050**, regardless of what your state allows.

Why These Rules Exist:

- Prevent people from moving just to take advantage of generous exemptions
- Ensure exemptions serve people with genuine ties to the state
- Stop abuse of the bankruptcy system

Local Court Rules and Procedures

While the big picture is federally controlled, each bankruptcy district has **local rules** that affect the practical aspects of your case.

What Local Rules Cover

Filing Procedures:

- Specific formatting requirements for documents
- Electronic filing procedures and requirements
- Local deadlines that supplement federal rules
- Required local forms in addition to federal forms

Trustee Practices:

- How trustees conduct 341 meetings
- What documentation trustees typically request

- Local trustee policies on asset sales and exemptions
- Payment procedures and timing

Court Scheduling:

- How quickly cases are processed
- Availability of court hearings
- Judge assignment procedures
- Local court calendars and scheduling

Attorney Requirements:

- Local bar admission requirements
- Continuing education requirements
- Local ethical rules and expectations

Examples of Local Variations

341 Meetings:

- **Some districts:** Conducted entirely by video/phone
- **Others:** Require in-person attendance
- **Timing:** May be scheduled 20-60 days after filing

Document Requirements:

- **Some courts:** Require additional local forms
- **Others:** Have specific formatting requirements for standard forms
- **Electronic filing:** Procedures vary by district

Trustee Policies:

- **Asset sales:** Some trustees are more aggressive about selling non-exempt property
- **Payment timing:** Varies for Chapter 13 plans
- **Communication:** Some prefer email, others require written

correspondence

Practical Impact on Your Case

Why Understanding This Framework Matters

Property Protection:

- **Wrong exemption choice** can cost you your home, car, or savings
- **Understanding residency rules** prevents unpleasant surprises
- **Local court knowledge** helps set proper expectations

Case Strategy:

- **Chapter choice** may depend on exemption availability
- **Timing of filing** can be affected by residency requirements
- **Local procedures** impact how quickly your case resolves

Cost and Complexity:

- **Different exemption systems** require different levels of planning
- **Local attorney knowledge** becomes more valuable
- **Court requirements** affect preparation time and costs

Common Mistakes to Avoid

Exemption Planning Errors:

- Assuming you can "mix and match" exemption systems
- Not researching which system works better for your assets
- Failing to consider the residency requirements
- Waiting too long to file when facing exemption timing issues

Local Procedure Mistakes:

- Not understanding your specific court's requirements

- Missing local deadlines or formatting requirements
- Choosing an attorney unfamiliar with your local court
- Underestimating local trustee practices

Working with the System

Getting Expert Guidance

When Local Knowledge Matters Most:

- You have significant assets near exemption limits
- You've moved between states recently
- You have complex property ownership issues
- You're facing immediate foreclosure or repossession

Finding the Right Attorney:

- Look for attorneys who practice regularly in your specific district
- Ask about experience with your local trustees
- Inquire about knowledge of local court procedures
- Consider attorneys who handle similar cases to yours

Maximizing Your Protections

Pre-Filing Planning:

- Understand your exemption choices before you need them
- Consider how residency requirements might affect timing
- Plan major asset purchases or sales with exemptions in mind
- Document your residency history if you've moved recently

During Your Case:

- Choose exemptions carefully with professional guidance

- Comply with all local court requirements
- Maintain clear records of exempt property
- Communicate promptly with trustees and court personnel

The Bottom Line: Federal Structure, State Protections

The genius of the American bankruptcy system is that it provides **uniform access** to debt relief while allowing **state-specific protections** that reflect local values and cost of living.

What This Means for You:

- You have the **federal right** to bankruptcy relief regardless of where you live
- Your **state's laws determine** how much property you can protect
- **Local court procedures** affect the practical experience of your case
- **Expert guidance** becomes crucial for navigating both levels of law

Key Takeaways:

1. **Federal law** creates your right to bankruptcy and the basic process
2. **State law** determines what property you can keep
3. **Local rules** affect the practical details of your case
4. **Professional guidance** helps you navigate all three levels effectively

Understanding this framework isn't just academic - it's essential to making informed decisions about your financial future. The interplay between federal and state law can mean the difference between a successful fresh start and a disappointing outcome.

In the next chapter, we'll explore exactly how bankruptcy affects your credit, assets, and financial future - separating the myths from the realities so you can make decisions based on facts, not fears.

5

Credit & Assets

Separating Bankruptcy Myths from Financial Reality

The Fear That Keeps People Trapped

If you're considering bankruptcy, you've probably heard horror stories: "You'll never get credit again." "They'll take everything you own." "Your credit will be ruined forever." "No one will rent to you." "You'll never buy a house."

These myths keep millions of Americans trapped in cycles of debt, struggling with payments they can't afford, avoiding bankruptcy even when it would dramatically improve their lives. The reality is far different - and far more hopeful - than these scare stories suggest.

In this chapter, we'll separate bankruptcy myths from reality. We'll show you what actually happens to your credit score, what property you'll likely keep, and how quickly you can rebuild your financial life. Most importantly, we'll help you understand that bankruptcy isn't the end of your financial story - it's often the beginning of a much better chapter.

The Credit Score Reality Check

What Actually Happens to Your Credit

Let's start with the hard truth: **Yes, bankruptcy will initially lower your credit score.** But here's what the scare stories don't tell you:

For most people filing bankruptcy, their credit is already severely damaged. If you're behind on payments, have accounts in collections, or are facing judgments and garnishments, your credit score has likely already dropped significantly.

The Credit Timeline: What to Expect

Before Bankruptcy:

- Missed payments: -35 to -125 points each
- Collection accounts: -50 to -125 points each
- Charge-offs: -50 to -150 points
- Judgments: -50 to -200 points
- High credit utilization: -10 to -45 points

Immediately After Filing:

- Bankruptcy filing: Additional -100 to -200 points
- **BUT:** All the negative accounts are now showing $0 balances
- Collection activity stops completely
- No more late payments accumulating

The Recovery Timeline: What Typically Happens

- **1-3 months:** Discharged debts show $0 balance on credit report
- **6-12 months:** Score begins steady improvement
- **12-18 months:** May qualify for secured credit cards and credit-builder loans
- **18-24 months:** Often receive unsecured credit offers (high interest initially)
- **2-3 years:** May qualify for auto loans at reasonable rates
- **2-4 years:** May qualify for FHA mortgage

- **4-7 years:** May qualify for conventional mortgage
- **7-10 years:** Bankruptcy notation removed from credit report

How Long Bankruptcy Stays on Your Report

Chapter 7: 10 years from filing date **Chapter 13:** 7 years from filing date

Important Note: The bankruptcy notation staying on your report doesn't mean your credit will be poor for that entire time. Most people see significant improvement long before the bankruptcy disappears from their report.

Credit Score Recovery: Real Examples

Sarah's Story (Brooklyn, NY):

- Pre-bankruptcy score: 485 (due to collections and missed payments)
- 6 months post-discharge: 520
- 12 months: 580
- 24 months: 650
- 36 months: 720 (qualified for conventional mortgage)

Miguel's Story (Los Angeles, CA):

- Pre-bankruptcy score: 520 (multiple charge-offs)
- 6 months post-discharge: 540
- 18 months: 625
- 30 months: 680 (qualified for car loan at 6.5% APR)

Why Credit Often Improves Faster Than Expected

Debt-to-Income Ratio Improvement:

- Bankruptcy eliminates most unsecured debt
- Your debt-to-income ratio drops dramatically
- This is a major factor in credit scoring

Payment History Reset:

- No more late payments on discharged debts
- New accounts (used responsibly) build positive history
- Payment history is 35% of your credit score

Credit Utilization Drops:

- With discharged debts, your utilization drops to zero on those accounts
- New credit (used carefully) can maintain low utilization
- Utilization is 30% of your credit score

Property Protection: What You Actually Keep

The Biggest Bankruptcy Myth

Myth: "Bankruptcy means losing everything you own." **Reality:** Most people keep everything they own, thanks to exemption laws.

What "Exemption" Really Means

An **exemption** is legal protection for specific types of property. If your property is exempt, the bankruptcy trustee cannot take it to pay creditors - period.

Think of exemptions as a protective bubble around your essential possessions, ensuring you don't become destitute and can maintain basic dignity while getting your fresh start.

Property You'll Almost Certainly Keep

Your Home (in most cases):

- **If you're current on payments** and your equity is within exemption limits
- **New York:** Up to $179,950 in equity protected

- **California:** Up to $678,000+ (System 1) or $31,950 (System 2)
- **Even if behind on payments:** Chapter 13 can help you catch up

Your Vehicle:

- **New York:** $5,000 in equity protected
- **California:** $3,625 (System 1) or $7,500 (System 2)
- Most people's cars fall well within these limits
- Even if over the limit, trustees often don't pursue low-value vehicles due to costs

Household Goods and Personal Property:

- Furniture, appliances, clothing
- Basic electronics (TV, computer, phone)
- Jewelry (within reasonable limits)
- Books, photos, personal items
- Children's toys and necessities

Retirement Accounts:

- 401(k) plans: **100% protected**
- Traditional and Roth IRAs: **100% protected**
- Pension plans: **100% protected**
- These are never at risk in bankruptcy

Tools of Your Trade:

- **New York:** Up to $3,750
- **California:** Up to $9,525 (System 1) or $2,800 (System 2)
- Includes professional equipment, tools, licenses
- Computers needed for work

Property That Might Be at Risk

Non-Exempt Assets:

- Expensive jewelry or collectibles
- Second homes or investment property
- Boats, RVs, or luxury vehicles
- Large amounts of cash (beyond exemption limits)
- Business equipment (beyond tools of trade limits)

Important Note: Even if you have non-exempt property, Chapter 13 allows you to keep it while repaying creditors over time.

Real-Life Asset Protection Examples

Example 1: Middle-Class Family (Buffalo, NY)

- Home worth $180,000, mortgage $120,000 (equity: $60,000)
- Two cars worth $8,000 and $12,000, loans $5,000 and $15,000
- Normal household furnishings
- 401(k) worth $85,000
- **Result:** Kept everything - all within exemption limits

Example 2: Renter with Savings (San Diego, CA)

- Rents apartment
- Car worth $18,000, loan $10,000 (equity: $8,000)
- $15,000 in savings account
- Tools worth $5,000
- **Using System 2:** Large wildcard protects savings, car equity partially protected
- **Result:** Kept everything using strategic exemption planning

Example 3: Homeowner with High Equity (San Francisco, CA)

- Home worth $1.2 million, mortgage $400,000 (equity: $800,000)

- **Using System 1**: $678,000+ homestead exemption
- **Result**: Kept home (though had to pay trustee the excess equity over time in Chapter 13)

Secured Debts: Your House and Car

Understanding Secured vs. Unsecured Debt

Secured Debt: Backed by collateral (house, car)

- Lender can repossess/foreclose if you don't pay
- Debt is tied to specific property

Unsecured Debt: Not backed by collateral (credit cards, medical bills)

- Lender cannot automatically take property
- Must sue and get judgment first

What Happens to Your Mortgage

If You're Current on Payments:

- **Chapter 7**: You can keep the house by continuing payments
- **Chapter 13**: Same - continue regular payments
- Bankruptcy doesn't affect your right to keep current secured debts

If You're Behind on Payments:

- **Chapter 7**: Provides temporary relief, but you must catch up quickly or face foreclosure
- **Chapter 13**: Allows you to catch up on missed payments over 3-5 years while stopping foreclosure

If You Can't Afford the House:

- **Either chapter**: You can surrender the house and eliminate any deficiency balance
- This is often called a "strategic foreclosure" within bankruptcy

What Happens to Your Car

If You're Current on Payments:

- Continue paying and keep the car
- Bankruptcy doesn't change this arrangement

If You're Behind on Payments:

- **Chapter 7:** Limited options - may need to surrender if you can't catch up
- **Chapter 13:** Can catch up over time and keep the car

If the Car Is Worth Less Than You Owe:

- **Chapter 13:** May be able to reduce the loan balance to the car's actual value ("cramdown")
- This can save thousands of dollars

If You Can't Afford the Car:

- Surrender it and eliminate any deficiency balance
- Walk away debt-free from an unaffordable payment

Strategic Decisions About Property

Keep or Surrender? Key Questions:

1. Can I afford the monthly payments going forward?
2. Is the property worth keeping (not underwater)?
3. Do I need this property for work or family?
4. Are there better/cheaper alternatives available?

Example Decision Matrix:

- Current on mortgage, affordable payments: Keep in Chapter 7 or 13
- Behind on mortgage, want to keep house: Chapter 13 to catch up
- Mortgage underwater, can't afford payments: Surrender and

eliminate deficiency

- Car current, need for work: Keep and continue payments
- Car behind, need for transportation: Chapter 13 to catch up
- Expensive car, could buy cheaper one: Surrender and buy affordable replacement

Life After Discharge: Rebuilding Your Financial Life

The Immediate Benefits

Day One After Discharge:

- **No legal obligation** to pay discharged debts
- **Creditors cannot contact you** about discharged debts
- **Wage garnishments stop** permanently
- **Lawsuits dismissed** or cannot be filed
- **Fresh start** with significantly reduced debt load

Building New Credit Responsibly

Secured Credit Cards (6-12 months after discharge):

- Put down $200-$500 deposit
- Spend small amounts and pay in full monthly
- Builds positive payment history
- Often converts to unsecured card after 12-18 months

Credit-Builder Loans:

- Small loans where payments go into savings
- You get the money after the loan is paid off
- Creates positive payment history
- Available from credit unions and online lenders

Become an Authorized User:

- Ask family member with good credit to add you to their card
- You benefit from their payment history
- Don't need to use the card - just being listed helps

The Credit Building Timeline

Months 1-6: Foundation

- Monitor credit reports for accuracy
- Open secured credit card
- Use card for small purchases, pay in full
- Set up automatic payments for all bills

Months 6-18: Building

- May qualify for additional secured cards
- Consider credit-builder loan
- Keep credit utilization below 30%
- Continue perfect payment history

Months 18-36: Expanding

- May receive unsecured credit offers
- Could qualify for auto loan (higher rates initially)
- Continue responsible credit use
- Monitor credit score improvement

Years 3-5: Normalizing

- Credit score typically 650-700+ if managed well
- Qualify for conventional credit products
- May qualify for mortgage (FHA after 2 years, conventional after 4)
- Interest rates approaching standard market rates

What Lenders Actually Care About

The 4 Factors Post-Bankruptcy:

1. **Payment history since bankruptcy** (most important)
2. **Current income and employment stability**
3. **Debt-to-income ratio** (should be excellent post-bankruptcy)
4. **Time elapsed since bankruptcy**

Lenders often prefer bankruptcy over:

- Multiple collections and charge-offs
- Debt settlement
- Ongoing payment struggles
- High debt-to-income ratios

Why? Bankruptcy provides a clear "before and after," and many lenders know that people who've filed bankruptcy are often more financially responsible afterward.

Housing and Employment: Practical Considerations

Renting After Bankruptcy

The Reality:

- **Many landlords** will rent to people with discharged bankruptcies
- **Some landlords** prefer bankruptcy over ongoing collections
- **Smaller/private landlords** often more flexible than large companies

Strategies for Renting:

- Be honest about your bankruptcy on applications
- Explain the circumstances that led to filing
- Emphasize current income stability

- Offer larger security deposit if needed
- Get letters of recommendation from current/previous landlords
- Consider having a co-signer initially

Employment Considerations

What Employers Can and Cannot Do:

- **Private employers:** Generally cannot discriminate based on bankruptcy alone
- **Government jobs:** Some restrictions for certain positions
- **Financial industry:** May have restrictions for positions handling money
- **Security clearances:** Bankruptcy may affect clearance applications

Best Practices:

- Be honest if directly asked about bankruptcy
- Focus on lessons learned and improved financial management
- Emphasize that bankruptcy resolved your financial issues
- Most employers care more about reliability and skills than past financial troubles

Insurance and Banking

Auto Insurance:

- Bankruptcy may initially affect rates
- Shop around - companies vary widely in their policies
- Rates typically improve as credit improves

Banking:

- Most banks will open checking/savings accounts
- Some may require secured credit initially

- Credit unions often more friendly to bankruptcy filers

Life Insurance:

- Term life insurance typically not affected
- Whole life policies may be more expensive initially

Protecting Your Fresh Start

Building an Emergency Fund

Why It's Crucial:

- Prevents future debt when unexpected expenses arise
- Builds confidence and reduces financial anxiety
- Creates buffer against income disruptions

How to Start:

- Begin with $25-50 per month if that's all you can afford
- Use automatic transfers to savings
- Keep emergency fund in separate account
- Goal: 3-6 months of essential expenses

Avoiding Financial Traps

High-Risk Products to Avoid:

- **Payday loans:** Extremely high interest, debt trap cycle
- **Title loans:** Risk losing your vehicle
- **Rent-to-own:** Extremely expensive way to buy furniture/electronics
- **Subprime auto dealers:** Often prey on bankruptcy filers with terrible terms

Better Alternatives:

- **Credit union loans:** Often much better terms

- **Secured credit cards:** Build credit without risk
- **Save for purchases:** Avoid debt when possible
- **Shop around:** Don't accept the first offer

Red Flags in Credit Offers

Legitimate vs. Predatory:

Legitimate Offers:

- Reasonable fees and terms
- Clear disclosure of costs
- Gradual credit limit increases
- Reports to credit bureaus

Predatory Offers:

- Excessive fees and penalties
- Hidden costs and terms
- Immediate high limits with poor terms
- Doesn't help build credit

The Emotional Journey of Financial Recovery

Dealing with Shame and Stigma

Common Feelings After Bankruptcy:

- Relief mixed with embarrassment
- Worry about judgment from others
- Anxiety about financial decisions
- Fear of making mistakes again

Healthy Perspective:

- **Bankruptcy is a legal tool**, not a moral failing
- **Millions of successful people** have filed bankruptcy
- **You took action** to solve your problems
- **Focus on the future**, not the past

Building Financial Confidence

Education and Knowledge:

- Learn about personal finance and budgeting
- Understand credit scores and how they work
- Stay informed about your rights as a consumer

Small Wins:

- Celebrate paying bills on time
- Acknowledge credit score improvements
- Recognize successful money management decisions

Long-term Perspective:

- View bankruptcy as one chapter, not the whole story
- Focus on the lessons learned
- Build on the fresh start you've earned

Real Success Stories

Sarah's Journey (3 Years Post-Bankruptcy)

- **Before**: $65,000 in credit card debt, facing foreclosure, credit score 480
- **Filed**: Chapter 7, discharged $52,000 in unsecured debt, kept home
- **18 months later**: Credit score 620, qualified for car loan
- **3 years later**: Credit score 715, refinanced mortgage, has emergency

fund

Key factors: Disciplined spending, automatic savings, responsible credit use

Marcus's Story (5 Years Post-Bankruptcy)

- **Before:** $85,000 in debt from failed business, behind on everything
- **Filed:** Chapter 13, repaid $30,000 over 5 years
- **2 years after completion:** Bought home with FHA loan
- **5 years later:** Owns successful small business, excellent credit

Key factors: Used bankruptcy to restructure, learned from business mistakes, rebuilt systematically

Your Fresh Start Action Plan

Immediate Steps (Months 1-6)

- [ ] Obtain copies of credit reports from all three bureaus
- [ ] Verify discharged debts show $0 balances
- [ ] Dispute any errors on credit reports
- [ ] Open basic checking and savings accounts
- [ ] Create realistic monthly budget
- [ ] Start small emergency fund ($25-50/month)

Short-term Goals (Months 6-18)

- [ ] Apply for secured credit card
- [ ] Use credit card for small purchases only
- [ ] Pay credit card in full every month
- [ ] Continue building emergency fund
- [ ] Monitor credit score monthly

- [ ] Avoid new debt except for rebuilding credit

Medium-term Goals (Years 2-3)

- [ ] Build emergency fund to $1,000-2,500
- [ ] Qualify for unsecured credit card
- [ ] Consider auto loan if needed (shop for best rates)
- [ ] Continue improving credit score
- [ ] Start saving for major goals (house down payment)

Long-term Goals (Years 3-5+)

- [ ] Emergency fund: 3-6 months expenses
- [ ] Credit score 700+
- [ ] Qualify for mortgage if desired
- [ ] Build retirement savings
- [ ] Achieve long-term financial stability

The Bottom Line: Bankruptcy as a Tool, Not a Tragedy

The fear of bankruptcy often does more damage than bankruptcy itself. While filing bankruptcy does have consequences - particularly for your credit in the short term - it also provides powerful benefits:

What Bankruptcy Actually Does:

- Eliminates overwhelming debt
- Stops creditor harassment immediately
- Protects essential property
- Provides legal fresh start
- Allows faster financial recovery than struggling with unpayable debt

What Bankruptcy Doesn't Do:

- Ruin your life permanently
- Make you a financial pariah
- Prevent you from ever getting credit again
- Take away your essential possessions
- Make you a bad person

The Most Important Truth: For most people who file bankruptcy, **their financial situation improves dramatically** within 2-3 years. They have less debt, better cash flow, reduced stress, and often better credit than they had before filing.

The key is viewing bankruptcy not as an ending, but as a beginning - the start of a more sustainable, responsible financial life.

In the next chapter, we'll dive deep into Chapter 7 bankruptcy: how it works, who qualifies, what to expect throughout the process, and how to maximize the benefits of this powerful fresh start tool.

6

Chapter 7 Overview

Liquidation and a Clean Slate

Chapter 7: Your Express Route to Debt Freedom

If Chapter 13 bankruptcy is like taking a scenic route that requires a 3-5 year journey, then Chapter 7 is like taking the express highway. You'll reach your destination - a debt-free life - in just 3-4 months instead of years.

Chapter 7 bankruptcy, officially called "liquidation bankruptcy," is designed for people who genuinely cannot afford to repay their debts and need a complete fresh start. Despite the scary name "liquidation," the reality is that **most people who file Chapter 7 keep everything they own** and walk away completely free of most debts.

In this chapter, we'll walk you through everything you need to know about Chapter 7: who it's designed for, what it can and cannot do, how the process works, and what your life will look like on the other side.

Who Chapter 7 Is Really For

The Ideal Chapter 7 Candidate

Chapter 7 works best for people who fit this profile:

Financial Situation:

- Income at or below state median levels
- Primarily unsecured debt (credit cards, medical bills, personal loans)
- Little to no disposable income after essential expenses
- Unable to pay off debt within 5 years even with strict budgeting
- Already experiencing severe financial stress

Asset Situation:

- Own modest assets that fall within exemption limits
- Don't have significant equity in expensive property
- Current on secured debts they want to keep (house, car)
- Not hiding or recently transferring assets

Goals:

- Want debt relief as quickly as possible
- Prefer clean slate over partial repayment
- Need immediate relief from creditor pressure
- Ready to commit to responsible financial habits

Real-Life Chapter 7 Profiles

Profile 1: The Medical Debt Overwhelm *Maria, 34, Los Angeles*

- Works as school aide, earns $38,000/year
- $45,000 in medical bills from cancer treatment
- $12,000 in credit cards used during illness
- Current on car payment, rents apartment
- **Result:** Perfect candidate - all debt dischargeable, keeps all property

Profile 2: The Job Loss Spiral *David, 52, Albany*

- Lost manufacturing job, now works retail for $28,000/year
- $38,000 in credit cards accumulated during unemployment
- Owns modest home with $15,000 equity, current on mortgage
- $8,000 in collections from when he couldn't pay bills
- **Result:** Excellent candidate - income below median, home equity protected

Profile 3: The Divorce Financial Fallout *Jennifer, 41, Buffalo*

- Divorced, raising two kids alone on $42,000/year
- $29,000 in debt from legal fees and living expenses during divorce
- Rents apartment, owns 2012 Honda Civic
- Current on all bills but can't make progress on debt
- **Result:** Strong candidate - single parent income, manageable assets

What Chapter 7 Can Eliminate

Debts That Disappear Forever

When you receive your Chapter 7 discharge, these debts are legally eliminated - you never have to pay them, and creditors can never try to collect them:

Credit Card Debt:

- Regular credit cards (Visa, MasterCard, etc.)
- Store cards (Target, Macy's, Home Depot)
- Gas station cards
- Business credit cards (if personally guaranteed)

Medical Debt:

- Hospital bills
- Doctor and specialist bills

- Ambulance charges
- Medical equipment costs
- Dental and vision bills
- Mental health treatment costs

Personal Loans:

- Bank personal loans
- Credit union loans
- Payday loans
- Title loans (if you surrender the collateral)
- Loans from friends or family

Collection Accounts:

- Debt buyer collections
- Original creditor collections
- Medical collections
- Utility collections

Deficiency Balances:

- Amount still owed after car repossession
- Shortfall after foreclosure (in most states)
- These "phantom debts" for property you no longer own

Court Judgments:

- Most civil court judgments for money
- Credit card lawsuit judgments
- Collection lawsuit judgments

Utility Bills:

- Past-due electric, gas, water bills

- Cable and internet bills
- Phone bills

Old Tax Debts:

- Income taxes more than 3 years old (if other conditions are met)
- Property taxes in some cases

The Financial Impact: Real Numbers

Example 1: Sarah's Debt Elimination

- Credit cards: $32,000 → **$0**
- Medical bills: $18,000 → **$0**
- Personal loan: $8,000 → **$0**
- Collections: $5,000 → **$0**
- **Total eliminated: $63,000**
- **Time to discharge: 4 months**

Example 2: Michael's Fresh Start

- Credit cards: $45,000 → **$0**
- Payday loans: $3,500 → **$0**
- Deficiency from repossessed car: $12,000 → **$0**
- Medical bills: $22,000 → **$0**
- **Total eliminated: $82,500**
- **Monthly payment savings: $2,100**

What Chapter 7 Cannot Eliminate

Debts That Survive Bankruptcy

Understanding what debts survive Chapter 7 is crucial for determining whether it will actually solve your problems:

Student Loans:

- Federal student loans
- Most private student loans
- **Exception:** Very rare cases of "undue hardship" (difficult to prove)
- **Reality:** 99%+ of student loans survive Chapter 7

Recent Tax Debts:

- Income taxes less than 3 years old
- Payroll taxes if you owned a business
- Fraud-related tax debts
- **Note:** Chapter 13 may be better for tax debt management

Domestic Support Obligations:

- Child support (current and past-due)
- Alimony/spousal support
- Property settlement obligations to ex-spouse (in most cases)

Criminal and Government Debts:

- Criminal fines and restitution
- Court costs and fees
- Government penalties and fines
- Traffic tickets and parking tickets

Certain Secured Debts:

- Mortgage (you can keep house by continuing payments)
- Car loans (you can keep car by continuing payments)
- **Note:** You choose whether to keep these by continuing payments or surrender the property

Recent Large Purchases:

- Luxury goods over $725 purchased within 90 days of filing

- Cash advances over $1,000 within 70 days of filing
- **These may be challenged as non-dischargeable**

Strategic Considerations for Non-Dischargeable Debt

If You Have Significant Non-Dischargeable Debt:

- Calculate what percentage of your total debt will actually be eliminated
- Consider whether Chapter 13 might provide better payment terms
- Evaluate whether bankruptcy is worth it if only some debts are eliminated

Example Analysis:

- Total debt: $75,000
- Student loans: $45,000 (not dischargeable)
- Credit cards: $25,000 (dischargeable)
- Child support: $5,000 (not dischargeable)
- **Result:** Only $25,000 of $75,000 eliminated - may not be worth filing

The Chapter 7 Process: Step by Step

Phase 1: Pre-Filing Preparation (1-4 weeks)

Required Credit Counseling:

- Must complete within 180 days before filing
- Takes 60-90 minutes, costs $25-50
- Available online, by phone, or in person
- Provides certificate required for filing

Document Gathering:

- 6 months of pay stubs

- 2 years of tax returns
- Bank statements (6 months)
- Credit card and loan statements
- Vehicle titles and registrations
- Real estate deeds and mortgage information
- List of all creditors with addresses
- Recent bills and collection notices

Financial Analysis:

- Complete means test calculation
- Choose exemption system (in states that allow choice)
- Identify all assets and their values
- List all income sources
- Calculate monthly expenses

Phase 2: Filing and Initial Response (Day 1-30)

The Filing:

- Submit petition and all supporting documents
- Pay $338 filing fee (or request waiver/payment plan)
- **Automatic stay goes into effect immediately**

Immediate Changes:

- **All collection activity stops** (calls, letters, lawsuits)
- **Wage garnishments halt** immediately
- **Foreclosure proceedings pause**
- **Utility shutoffs prevented** (in most cases)
- **Bank account freezes lifted**

Trustee Assignment:

- Court assigns a Chapter 7 trustee within days
- Trustee reviews your petition for accuracy and completeness
- May request additional documents or clarification

Creditor Notification:

- Court notifies all listed creditors of the bankruptcy
- Creditors must stop collection efforts immediately
- Creditors have deadlines to object or file claims

Phase 3: The 341 Meeting (30-45 days after filing)

What It Is:

- Short meeting with your trustee (usually 10-15 minutes)
- Also called "Meeting of Creditors" though creditors rarely attend
- Conducted under oath but very routine
- Often done by video/phone since COVID

Typical Questions:

- Did you read your petition before signing it?
- Are all your assets and debts listed accurately?
- Have you transferred any property in the past 2 years?
- Do you expect to receive any money (inheritance, tax refund, lawsuit settlement)?
- Have you filed bankruptcy before?

What to Bring:

- Photo ID and Social Security card
- Any documents the trustee requested
- Your attorney (if you have one)

What Happens:

- Trustee verifies information under oath
- Reviews any non-exempt assets
- Asks standard questions about your finances
- May ask follow-up questions about specific issues

Phase 4: Asset Administration (30-60 days)

If You Have Non-Exempt Assets:

- Trustee determines if property is worth selling
- Considers costs of sale, storage, and administration
- Many assets aren't worth the trustee's effort even if technically non-exempt

If You Have Only Exempt Assets (most common):

- Trustee files "no asset" report
- No property is sold
- Case proceeds to discharge

Creditor Objections (rare):

- Creditors have 60 days to object to discharge of specific debts
- Usually involves allegations of fraud or recent large purchases
- Most cases have no objections

Phase 5: Discharge and Completion (90-120 days after filing)

Final Requirements:

- Complete financial management course (required before discharge)
- File certificate with court
- Respond to any trustee requests

The Discharge Order:

- Court issues formal discharge of debts
- You receive official notice by mail
- Creditors receive notice that debts are eliminated
- Case is closed

Post-Discharge:

- You are legally free of discharged debts
- Creditors cannot attempt collection on discharged debts
- Begin rebuilding credit and financial life

Property in Chapter 7: What Really Happens

The Exemption Protection System

How Exemptions Work:

- Exemptions protect specific types and amounts of property
- If your property is exempt, the trustee cannot take it
- You must choose your exemption system when filing
- Exemptions vary by state and can be strategically planned

New York Chapter 7 Exemptions

New York State Exemptions:

- **Homestead:** Up to $179,950 (varies by county)
- **Vehicle:** $5,000 equity
- **Household Goods:** Reasonable necessary amounts
- **Tools of Trade:** $3,750
- **Cash/Bank Accounts:** $6,000
- **Wildcard:** $1,175 (if homestead not used)

- **Retirement Accounts:** Unlimited

Federal Exemptions (alternative choice):

- **Homestead:** $27,900 (individual), $55,800 (joint)
- **Vehicle:** $4,450
- **Household Goods:** $700 per item, $14,875 total
- **Tools of Trade:** $2,800
- **Wildcard:** $1,475 + unused homestead
- **Retirement Accounts:** Unlimited

California Chapter 7 Exemptions

System 1 (CCP § 704) - Homeowner's Choice:

- **Homestead:** $678,000+ (adjusted annually)
- **Vehicle:** $3,625
- **Household Goods:** Reasonable necessary amounts
- **Tools of Trade:** $9,525
- **Jewelry:** $1,850
- **Retirement Accounts:** Unlimited

System 2 (CCP § 703) - Flexible Choice:

- **Homestead:** $31,950
- **Vehicle:** $7,500
- **Household Goods:** $700 per item, $14,875 total
- **Tools of Trade:** $2,800
- **Wildcard:** $1,550 + unused homestead (up to $30,400)
- **Retirement Accounts:** Unlimited

Real Property Protection Examples

Example 1: New York Homeowner *Robert, Queens*

- Home worth $400,000, mortgage $250,000 (equity: $150,000)
- **NY exemption:** $179,950 protects all equity
- **Result:** Keeps home, continues mortgage payments

Example 2: California Renter with Assets *Lisa, San Diego*

- Rents apartment
- Car worth $12,000, loan $5,000 (equity: $7,000)
- Savings: $8,000
- Tools: $3,000
- **Using System 2:** Vehicle protected ($7,500 limit), wildcard protects savings
- **Result:** Keeps all property

Example 3: High-Value Asset Situation *James, Sacramento*

- Home worth $850,000, mortgage $200,000 (equity: $650,000)
- **System 1:** Protects $678,000+ of equity
- **Analysis:** Small amount of equity might be non-exempt
- **Options:** Chapter 13 to protect all equity, or negotiate with trustee

Income Qualification: The Means Test

Understanding the Means Test

The means test determines whether you qualify for Chapter 7 based on your income and expenses. It's designed to ensure that people who can afford to repay their debts use Chapter 13 instead.

Step 1: Income Calculation

Current Monthly Income (CMI):

- Average gross income over past 6 months
- Includes all household income from all sources
- Wages, business income, rental income, benefits, etc.
- Multiplied by 12 for annual figure

Step 2: Median Income Comparison

2025 Approximate Median Incomes:

Household Size New York California1 person $65,000 $68,0002 people $83,000 $87,0003 people $96,000 $97,0004 people $112,000 $114,000

If Below Median:

- You automatically qualify for Chapter 7
- No further means test calculation required
- Most Chapter 7 filers fall into this category

If Above Median:

- Must complete complex means test calculation
- Compares income to allowable expenses
- May still qualify if disposable income is low enough

Step 3: Disposable Income Test (Above Median Only)

Allowable Deductions:

- IRS standard amounts for housing, food, transportation
- Actual amounts for certain expenses (childcare, medical, taxes)
- Secured debt payments (mortgage, car loans)
- Priority debt payments (child support, recent taxes)

Disposable Income Threshold:

- If monthly disposable income is less than $136: qualify for Chapter 7

- If between $136-$227: depends on percentage of unsecured debt it would pay
- If over $227: probably must file Chapter 13

Real Means Test Examples

Example 1: Below Median (Automatic Qualification) *Maria, single, Los Angeles*

- Income: $45,000/year
- California median for 1 person: $68,000
- **Result:** Automatically qualifies, no further testing

Example 2: Above Median but Qualifies *John and Sarah, Buffalo*

- Combined income: $95,000/year
- NY median for 2 people: $83,000
- High mortgage and childcare expenses
- **Disposable income after allowed deductions:** $75/month
- **Result:** Qualifies for Chapter 7 ($75 < $136 threshold)

Example 3: Above Median, Must Use Chapter 13 *Professional couple, Manhattan*

- Combined income: $150,000/year
- Significant disposable income after expenses
- **Result:** Must file Chapter 13 or resolve debts outside bankruptcy

Common Chapter 7 Scenarios

Scenario 1: Medical Bankruptcy

The Situation: Medical debt is the leading cause of personal bankruptcy in America. Even people with insurance can face overwhelming bills.

Typical Profile:

- Large medical bills from serious illness or injury
- Insurance didn't cover everything
- Used credit cards for medical expenses and living costs
- Otherwise financially stable before medical crisis

Chapter 7 Benefits:

- Eliminates all medical debt immediately
- Stops medical collections and lawsuits
- Protects family assets and income
- Allows focus on health recovery, not financial stress

Example: *Janet, age 58, heart attack and surgery*

- Medical bills: $125,000
- Credit cards used during recovery: $18,000
- Lost 6 months of work
- **Result:** All debt eliminated, kept home and retirement accounts

Scenario 2: Job Loss Bankruptcy

The Situation: Long-term unemployment or significant income reduction makes existing debts unaffordable.

Typical Profile:

- Lost job in recession or industry downturn
- Unemployment benefits insufficient to cover debt payments
- Used credit cards and savings to maintain lifestyle
- Found new job but at much lower income

Chapter 7 Benefits:

- Eliminates debt based on old income level
- Allows fresh start with new, lower income

- Stops creditor pressure during job transition
- Preserves limited income for basic needs

Example: *Robert, age 45, manufacturing plant closure*

- Previous income: $65,000
- New income: $35,000
- Accumulated debt during unemployment: $48,000
- **Result:** Debt eliminated, can live comfortably on new income

Scenario 3: Divorce Bankruptcy

The Situation: Divorce often creates overwhelming debt from legal fees, maintaining two households, and dividing assets.

Typical Profile:

- High legal fees for contested divorce
- Credit cards used to establish new household
- Income insufficient to support previous lifestyle
- May have joint debts with ex-spouse

Chapter 7 Benefits:

- Eliminates joint debts (protecting from ex-spouse's non-payment)
- Discharges legal fees and divorce-related expenses
- Provides clean financial start for single life
- Simplifies post-divorce financial planning

Example: *Lisa, age 39, divorced with two children*

- Divorce legal fees: $22,000
- Credit cards for new apartment setup: $15,000
- Medical bills for children: $8,000
- **Result:** All debt eliminated, manageable budget as single parent

Life After Chapter 7 Discharge

Immediate Benefits

Day One After Discharge:

- **Legal freedom** from discharged debts
- **No more collection calls** or letters
- **No more lawsuit threats**
- **Significant reduction in monthly expenses**
- **Mental and emotional relief**

Credit Rebuilding Strategy

Months 1-6:

- Monitor credit reports for accuracy
- Dispute any errors showing discharged debts as still owed
- Begin building emergency fund
- Avoid new debt except for rebuilding credit

Months 6-12:

- Apply for secured credit card
- Use for small purchases, pay in full monthly
- Consider credit-builder loan
- Continue building savings

Months 12-24:

- May qualify for unsecured credit cards
- Could get auto loan (rates initially high)
- Continue responsible credit use

- Build emergency fund to $1,000-2,500

Years 2-4:

- Credit score typically 650-700+ if managed well
- Qualify for better loan terms
- May qualify for FHA mortgage after 2 years
- Build long-term financial stability

Financial Management Post-Bankruptcy

Budgeting Strategy:

- Track all income and expenses
- Live below your means
- Build emergency fund systematically
- Avoid lifestyle inflation

Debt Management:

- Avoid high-interest products (payday loans, etc.)
- Use credit cards only for rebuilding (pay in full)
- Shop for best rates on necessary loans
- Don't co-sign for others' debts

Long-term Planning:

- Start retirement savings
- Consider additional education or training
- Build stable career and income
- Create sustainable financial habits

When Chapter 7 Might Not Be Right

Red Flags for Chapter 7

High Income:

- Fail means test with significant disposable income
- Can afford to repay substantial portion of debt
- Court may find filing abusive

Valuable Non-Exempt Assets:

- Expensive jewelry, art, or collectibles
- Second homes or investment property
- Business assets beyond basic tools
- May be better to use Chapter 13 to protect assets

Recent Financial Misconduct:

- Large purchases within 90 days of filing
- Cash advances within 70 days of filing
- Transferred assets to hide them from creditors
- May face fraud allegations

Non-Dischargeable Debt Majority:

- Mostly student loans, recent taxes, child support
- Chapter 7 won't eliminate most debt
- May not provide meaningful relief

Behind on Secured Debts:

- Want to keep house but behind on mortgage
- Need to catch up on car payments
- Chapter 13 provides better tools for this

Alternative Strategies

If You Don't Qualify for Chapter 7:

- **Chapter 13:** Repay debts over time with court protection
- **Debt settlement:** Negotiate reduced payments outside bankruptcy
- **Credit counseling:** Debt management plan with lower interest
- **Wait and requalify:** Address income or other disqualifying factors

Making the Chapter 7 Decision

Chapter 7 Self-Assessment Checklist

Income Qualification:

- [ ] My income is below state median for my household size
- [ ] OR I can pass the means test calculation
- [ ] I have little disposable income after essential expenses

Debt Composition:

- [ ] Most of my debt is unsecured (credit cards, medical, personal loans)
- [ ] I have little or no non-dischargeable debt (student loans, taxes)
- [ ] My debts are not from recent fraud or misconduct

Asset Situation:

- [ ] My assets fall within exemption limits
- [ ] OR I'm willing to surrender non-exempt property
- [ ] I don't have valuable business or investment assets to protect

Goals and Timing:

- [ ] I want debt relief as quickly as possible
- [ ] I prefer complete discharge over partial repayment
- [ ] I'm ready to commit to responsible financial management

- [ ] I need immediate relief from creditor pressure

Practical Considerations:

- [ ] I'm current on secured debts I want to keep (house, car)
- [ ] OR I'm willing to surrender property I can't afford
- [ ] I haven't filed Chapter 7 in the past 8 years
- [ ] I'm emotionally ready for the bankruptcy process

Your Chapter 7 Success Plan

Pre-Filing Checklist

60 Days Before Filing:

- [ ] Complete credit counseling
- [ ] Gather all required documents
- [ ] Stop using credit cards completely
- [ ] Avoid large purchases or payments to creditors
- [ ] Don't transfer any assets

30 Days Before Filing:

- [ ] Complete means test calculation
- [ ] Choose exemption system (if applicable)
- [ ] Finalize creditor list with accurate addresses
- [ ] Review petition for accuracy and completeness
- [ ] Prepare for immediate post-filing changes

Filing Day:

- [ ] Submit complete, accurate petition
- [ ] Pay filing fee or request payment plan/waiver
- [ ] Notify employer if wages are being garnished

- [ ] Inform bank if accounts are frozen
- [ ] Begin planning for financial management course

Post-Filing Success Strategy

Immediate (0-30 days):

- [ ] Respond promptly to trustee requests
- [ ] Prepare for 341 meeting
- [ ] Monitor that collection activity has stopped
- [ ] Begin emergency fund with small amounts

Short-term (30-120 days):

- [ ] Attend 341 meeting
- [ ] Complete financial management course
- [ ] File course certificate with court
- [ ] Receive discharge order

Long-term (post-discharge):

- [ ] Check credit reports for accuracy
- [ ] Begin credit rebuilding with secured card
- [ ] Build emergency fund systematically
- [ ] Develop sustainable budgeting habits
- [ ] Plan for major financial goals

The Bottom Line: Chapter 7 as a Tool for Recovery

Chapter 7 bankruptcy isn't about giving up - it's about taking control. For people facing overwhelming unsecured debt with limited income, it provides:

Immediate Relief:

- Stop to creditor harassment

- Legal protection from collections
- Elimination of wage garnishment
- Peace of mind and reduced stress

Long-term Benefits:

- Complete discharge of most debts
- Opportunity to rebuild credit responsibly
- Improved cash flow for basic needs
- Fresh start for financial planning

The Key to Success: Chapter 7 works best when you view it as a tool for financial recovery, not just debt elimination. The people who benefit most are those who:

- Learn from the experience
- Develop better financial habits
- Use their fresh start wisely
- Build sustainable long-term financial health

Remember: Chapter 7 bankruptcy is a legal right designed to help people in exactly your situation. There's no shame in using a tool that Congress created specifically to provide relief from overwhelming debt and a pathway to financial recovery.

In the next chapter, we'll dive deep into the Chapter 7 means test - the income qualification system that determines whether you're eligible for this powerful form of debt relief.

7

The Means Test

Who Qualifies for Chapter 7

The Gatekeeper: Understanding Why the Means Test Exists

Imagine you're standing at the entrance to a bridge that leads to financial freedom. The bridge is Chapter 7 bankruptcy - a powerful tool that can eliminate most of your debts in just a few months. But before you can cross that bridge, you must pass through a checkpoint called the **means test**.

The means test is bankruptcy law's way of ensuring that Chapter 7 is reserved for people who genuinely cannot afford to repay their debts. It's designed to prevent abuse while protecting access for those who truly need a fresh start.

Understanding the means test isn't just about checking a box - it's about understanding whether Chapter 7 is the right path for your situation, and if not, what alternatives might work better. In this chapter, we'll walk you through every aspect of the means test, from the basic calculations to complex scenarios, so you can approach this crucial qualification step with confidence.

The Origins: Why Congress Created the Means Test

The Problem Congress Sought to Address

Before 2005, Chapter 7 bankruptcy was available to almost anyone, regardless of income. While this helped many people who genuinely needed relief, it also led to some abuse by high-income individuals who could afford to repay their debts but chose bankruptcy as a quick escape.

The 2005 Bankruptcy Reform

The Bankruptcy Abuse Prevention and Consumer Protection Act (BAPCPA) of 2005 introduced the means test to create a more balanced system:

Goals of the Means Test:

- Ensure Chapter 7 is available to those who truly need it
- Direct people with higher incomes toward Chapter 13 repayment plans
- Reduce bankruptcy system abuse
- Maintain legitimate access to debt relief

The Core Principle: If you have sufficient disposable income to repay a meaningful portion of your debts over time, you should use Chapter 13 rather than Chapter 7.

Means Test Overview: The Two-Step Process

The means test works like a two-step screening process:

Step 1: Initial Income Screening

Compare your average monthly income over the past 6 months to your state's median income for a household of your size.

If your income is BELOW the median:

- You **automatically pass** the means test
- You can file Chapter 7 (subject to other requirements)
- No further calculation needed

If your income is ABOVE the median:

- You must complete **Step 2** of the means test
- You may still qualify, but it requires more complex calculations

Step 2: Disposable Income Calculation

If your income is above the median, calculate your monthly disposable income using allowed expense deductions.

If your disposable income is low enough:

- You still qualify for Chapter 7

If your disposable income is too high:

- You must file Chapter 13 or resolve debts outside bankruptcy

Step 1: The Income Calculation

What Counts as "Current Monthly Income"

The means test uses a specific definition of income called **"Current Monthly Income" (CMI)**:

Time Period: Average of gross income received in the **6 calendar months** before the month you file bankruptcy

Whose Income Counts:

- **Single filers:** Only your income
- **Married filers:** Both spouses' income, even if only one spouse files bankruptcy
- **Separated spouses:** May be able to exclude separated spouse's income in some circumstances

Income Sources That Count

Employment Income:

- Wages, salary, tips, commissions
- Overtime and bonus payments
- Self-employment income (gross, before business expenses)
- Freelance and gig economy income

Business Income:

- Business revenue (before expenses in means test calculation)
- Partnership distributions
- Rental income from investment property

Government Benefits:

- Unemployment compensation
- Workers' compensation
- Disability payments (except Social Security disability)
- Pension and retirement income

Other Income:

- Alimony and child support received
- Interest and dividends
- Rental income
- Regular financial support from family/friends

Income Sources That DON'T Count

Social Security Benefits:

- Social Security retirement
- Social Security disability (SSDI)
- Supplemental Security Income (SSI)

Certain Benefits:

- Veterans' disability compensation

- Victim compensation payments
- War-related benefits

Real Income Calculation Examples

Example 1: Simple W-2 Employee *Jennifer, single, Buffalo,* NY

- **January:** $3,200
- **February:** $3,200
- **March:** $3,400 (overtime)
- **April:** $3,200
- **May:** $3,200
- **June:** $3,200
- **Total 6 months:** $19,400
- **Average monthly:** $3,233
- **Annual CMI:** $38,800

Example 2: Variable Income Worker *Carlos, married, Los Angeles,* CA

Carlos's Income:

Jan-June average: $2,800/month

Spouse's Income:

Jan-June average: $2,200/month

Combined CMI: $5,000/month = $60,000/year

Example 3: Business Owner *Maria, single, Sacramento,* CA

- Business gross receipts: $8,000/month
- Business expenses: $3,500/month
- **CMI for means test:** $8,000/month (gross receipts)
- **Annual CMI:** $96,000

- Note: *Business expenses are deducted later in the calculation*

Step 1: Median Income Comparison

2025 Median Income Figures

New York State:

Household Size Annual Median Income1 person $65,0002 people $83,0003 people $96,0004 people $112,0005 people $121,0006 people $130,000

California:

Household Size Annual Median Income1 person $68,0002 people $87,0003 people $97,0004 people $114,0005 people $123,0006 people $132,000

Note: *These figures are updated periodically by the U.S. Trustee Program and may change.*

Household Size Determination

Who Counts in Your Household:

- You and your spouse (if married and living together)
- Your dependent children living with you
- Other people you financially support (elderly parents, etc.)
- Foster children in your care

Who Doesn't Count:

- Adult children who support themselves
- Roommates or boarders
- Relatives you don't financially support

Real Median Income Comparisons

Example 1: Below Median (Auto-Qualify) *David, single, Albany*, NY

- CMI: $45,000/year

- NY median for 1 person: $65,000
- **Result:** Below median → Automatically qualifies for Chapter 7

Example 2: Above Median (Needs Step 2) *Sarah and Mike, married, San Diego, CA*

- Combined CMI: $125,000/year
- CA median for 2 people: $87,000
- **Result:** Above median → Must complete disposable income test

Example 3: Close to Median *Lisa, single parent with 2 kids, Buffalo, NY*

- CMI: $94,000/year
- NY median for 3 people: $96,000
- **Result:** Below median → Automatically qualifies for Chapter 7

Step 2: The Disposable Income Test

If your income is above the median, you must calculate your **monthly disposable income** using strict IRS standards and actual expenses.

The Calculation Formula

Monthly Disposable Income = Current Monthly Income - Allowed Monthly Deductions

Category 1: IRS National Standards

These are standardized amounts set by the IRS for basic living expenses:

Food, Clothing, and Other Items:

Household Size Monthly Allowance1 person $7092 people $1,2983 people $1,5154 people $1,7755+ people Add $347 per person

Health Care:

- **Under 65:** $75 per person
- **65 and older:** $153 per person

Category 2: IRS Local Standards

These vary by geographic location to account for regional cost differences:

Housing and Utilities:

- Based on your county and household size
- Covers mortgage/rent, property taxes, insurance, utilities
- **Example ranges:** $1,200-$4,500+ per month depending on location

Transportation:

- **Vehicle operation:** Varies by region ($300-$600+ per month)
- **Vehicle ownership:** Up to $568 per vehicle (for up to 2 vehicles)
- **Public transportation:** If you don't own a vehicle

Category 3: Actual Necessary Expenses

For certain categories, you can deduct your actual expenses:

Taxes:

- Federal, state, and local income taxes
- Payroll taxes (Social Security, Medicare)
- Property taxes (if not included in housing allowance)

Mandatory Employment Deductions:

- Union dues
- Required retirement contributions
- Mandatory uniform costs

Insurance:

- Health insurance premiums
- Life insurance (reasonable amounts)
- Disability insurance

Childcare:

- Daycare costs
- After-school care
- Babysitting for work

Elder Care:

- Care for elderly family members
- Adult daycare costs

Special Circumstances:

- Private school tuition (if necessary for special needs)
- Additional medical expenses beyond IRS allowance

Category 4: Debt Service

Secured Debt Payments:

- Mortgage payments (principal, interest, taxes, insurance)
- Car loan payments
- Other secured debt payments

Priority Debt Payments:

- Child support and alimony
- Recent tax debt
- Other non-dischargeable obligations

Category 5: Chapter 13 Administrative Expenses

If you were to file Chapter 13, you could deduct:

- Trustee fees (typically 6-10% of plan payments)
- Attorney fees for Chapter 13 plan

Real Disposable Income Calculations

Example 1: Above Median but Qualifies

Tom and Janet, married, 2 children, Long Island, NY

- Combined CMI: $135,000/year = $11,250/month
- NY median for 4 people: $112,000 (above median)

Monthly Deductions:

- Food/clothing/other (4 people): $1,775
- Healthcare (4 people): $300
- Housing allowance (Nassau County): $3,200
- Transportation (2 vehicles): $1,400
- Taxes and payroll deductions: $2,800
- Childcare: $1,200
- Mortgage payment: $2,500
- Car payments: $650
- **Total deductions:** $12,825

Calculation:

- Monthly income: $11,250
- Monthly deductions: $12,825
- **Disposable income:** -$1,575 (negative)

Result: Qualifies for Chapter 7 (no disposable income)

Example 2: Above Median, Must Use Chapter 13

Professional couple, Manhattan, NY

- Combined CMI: $180,000/year = $15,000/month
- NY median for 2 people: $83,000 (above median)

Monthly Deductions:

- Food/clothing/other (2 people): $1,298
- Healthcare (2 people): $150
- Housing allowance (NYC): $2,500
- Transportation: $800
- Taxes and deductions: $3,500
- Rent: $4,000
- Student loan payments: $800
- **Total deductions:** $13,048

Calculation:

- Monthly income: $15,000
- Monthly deductions: $13,048
- **Disposable income:** $1,952

Result: Must file Chapter 13 (disposable income too high)

Example 3: Business Owner Calculation

Maria, self-employed consultant, Sacramento, CA

- Business gross receipts: $8,000/month
- Business operating expenses: $3,200/month
- Net business income: $4,800/month
- CA median for 1 person: $68,000/year = $5,667/month (below median)

Analysis:

- CMI for means test: $8,000/month (gross receipts)
- Annual CMI: $96,000 (above CA median)
- Must complete Step 2, but business expenses will be deducted

- Likely qualifies for Chapter 7 after business expense deduction

The Disposable Income Thresholds

Once you calculate your monthly disposable income, it's compared to specific thresholds:

The Bright-Line Tests

Less than $136 per month:

- Qualify for Chapter 7
- No further analysis needed

$136 to $227 per month:

- Complex calculation required
- Must compare to percentage of unsecured debt that would be repaid
- May or may not qualify

More than $227 per month:

- Presumed abuse
- Must file Chapter 13 or overcome the presumption

The 25% Rule (Middle Category)

If your disposable income is between $136-$227:

Calculate: Disposable income × 60 months = Total available for unsecured creditors

Compare: Is this amount at least 25% of your unsecured, non-priority debt?

If YES: Must file Chapter 13 **If NO:** Can file Chapter 7

Example:

- Disposable income: $175/month
- Total over 60 months: $10,500

- Unsecured debt: $50,000
- 25% of unsecured debt: $12,500
- Since $10,500 < $12,500, can file Chapter 7

Special Circumstances and Complications

Irregular Income

Seasonal Workers:

- Average income over the 6-month period
- May result in higher or lower CMI depending on timing
- Consider timing of filing to capture lower-income months

Commission-Based Income:

- Include all commissions received in the 6-month period
- May be significantly different from ongoing earning capacity
- Document changes in commission structure

Recent Job Changes:

- Must use actual income received, not new job income
- May result in misrepresentation of current financial reality
- Consider timing of filing

Business Owners and Self-Employed

Gross Receipts Method:

- CMI includes gross business receipts
- Business expenses deducted later in calculation
- Can result in very high CMI initially

Operating Expense Deductions:

- Reasonable and necessary business expenses
- Must be documented and justified
- IRS standards apply for some categories

Timing Considerations:

- Consider seasonal business fluctuations
- Plan filing during lower-income periods if legitimate

Recently Divorced or Separated

Spousal Income Issues:

- Generally must include spouse's income
- Exceptions for separated spouses in some circumstances
- Timing of filing relative to separation/divorce

Support Obligations:

- Child support and alimony payments are deductible
- Received support counts as income
- Must be documented and consistent

Military and Special Income

BAH and Special Pay:

- Basic Allowance for Housing typically counts as income
- Combat pay exclusions may apply
- Special military benefits may be excluded

Disability Income:

- Social Security disability excluded
- VA disability compensation excluded
- Private disability insurance counts as income

Strategies for Means Test Success

Legitimate Pre-Filing Planning

Timing Considerations:

- File during lower-income periods if legitimate
- Consider seasonal income fluctuations
- Account for bonus and overtime timing

Expense Optimization:

- Maximize legitimate actual expenses where allowed
- Ensure all necessary expenses are documented
- Consider timing of major necessary expenses

Income Reduction:

- Reduce overtime if not mandatory
- Consider unpaid leave if job permits
- Avoid unnecessary income during the 6-month period

Documentation Requirements

Income Documentation:

- 6 months of pay stubs
- Tax returns
- Bank statements showing all deposits
- Business records for self-employed

Expense Documentation:

- Receipts for actual expenses claimed
- Insurance premium statements

- Childcare contracts and payments
- Medical expense records

What NOT to Do

Prohibited Manipulations:

- Don't quit your job to reduce income
- Don't hide income or assets
- Don't make unnecessary payments to insiders
- Don't incur debt you can't afford to manipulate the test

Timing Abuse:

- Don't manipulate the 6-month income period inappropriately
- Don't delay necessary income to affect the calculation
- Don't rush filing to avoid legitimate income increases

Common Means Test Mistakes

Calculation Errors

Income Mistakes:

- Including only net income instead of gross
- Forgetting to include spouse's income
- Excluding irregular but actual income
- Miscalculating the 6-month average

Expense Mistakes:

- Using actual expenses where standards apply
- Double-counting expenses in multiple categories
- Including non-allowed expenses

- Inflating reasonable and necessary amounts

Documentation Problems

Insufficient Records:

- Missing pay stubs or incomplete income records
- Lack of expense documentation
- Inconsistent information between documents
- Failure to disclose all income sources

Inconsistent Information:

- Income on means test doesn't match other schedules
- Expenses claimed don't match actual spending patterns
- Business income inconsistent with tax returns

Strategic Errors

Poor Timing:

- Filing during temporarily high-income periods
- Not considering seasonal income variations
- Ignoring upcoming income changes

Inadequate Planning:

- Not maximizing legitimate actual expenses
- Failing to optimize debt service deductions
- Missing available special circumstances adjustments

Working with Professionals

When You Need Help

Complex Situations Requiring Attorney Guidance:

- Income close to median thresholds
- Significant business or self-employment income
- Recent major life changes (divorce, job loss)
- Multiple income sources or irregular income
- Previous bankruptcy filings

Tax Professional Coordination:

- Business owners with complex deductions
- Multiple income sources requiring characterization
- Recent changes in tax situation
- Coordination with tax planning strategies

Choosing the Right Attorney

Experience with Means Test:

- Regular practice in bankruptcy law
- Experience with complex means test calculations
- Knowledge of local trustee practices
- Understanding of IRS standards and local expenses

Red Flags:

- Attorneys who guarantee means test passage
- Pressure to manipulate income or expenses
- Lack of detailed means test analysis
- No discussion of Chapter 13 alternatives

If You Don't Pass the Means Test

Chapter 13 as the Primary Alternative

Advantages of Chapter 13:

- Can still discharge debts (after 3-5 years)
- Keep all property while repaying over time
- Better for people with regular income
- Can catch up on mortgage and car payments

Chapter 13 Payment Calculation:

- Based on actual disposable income
- Often similar to means test calculation
- 3-5 year commitment required

Other Alternatives

Wait and Requalify:

- Address income issues that caused failure
- Consider timing of refiling
- Monitor income changes over time

Debt Settlement:

- Negotiate with creditors outside bankruptcy
- May be appropriate for some high-income situations
- Significant credit damage and tax consequences

Credit Counseling:

- Debt management plans with reduced interest
- Requires full repayment but over longer terms
- May be suitable for moderate income situations

Success Stories: Means Test Challenges Overcome

Case Study 1: The Seasonal Worker

Background: *Roberto, construction worker, Fresno, CA*

- Income varies dramatically by season
- Filed in January after slow winter season
- CMI included low winter months

Challenge:

- Summer income would have failed means test
- Needed to time filing appropriately

Solution:

- Filed during legitimate low-income period
- Documented seasonal income pattern
- Qualified for Chapter 7

Outcome:

- Discharged $35,000 in credit card debt
- Kept work tools and vehicle
- Rebuilt financial stability

Case Study 2: The Business Owner

Background: *Sarah, freelance marketing consultant, Brooklyn, NY*

- High gross receipts, substantial business expenses
- Initial CMI appeared too high for Chapter 7

Challenge:

- Gross business income exceeded median
- Needed to properly document business expenses

Solution:

- Careful documentation of legitimate business expenses
- Proper categorization of business vs. personal expenses
- Showed low net income after necessary business costs

Outcome:

- Qualified for Chapter 7 after proper calculation
- Discharged personal credit card debt
- Maintained business operations

Case Study 3: The Recent Divorce

Background: *Jennifer, recently divorced, San Diego, CA*

- CMI included ex-husband's income from early in 6-month period
- Now supporting herself and children alone

Challenge:

- Married income during part of the 6-month period
- Current income much lower than CMI suggested

Solution:

- Documented separation date and income changes
- Used appropriate calculations for separated spouse
- Showed current financial reality

Outcome:

- Qualified for Chapter 7 based on actual current situation
- Eliminated joint debts from marriage
- Fresh start as single parent

Your Means Test Action Plan

Pre-Filing Preparation (60-90 days)

Income Analysis:

- [ ] Gather 6 months of income documentation
- [ ] Calculate current monthly income accurately
- [ ] Compare to state median for your household size
- [ ] Identify any timing considerations

If Above Median:

- [ ] Gather expense documentation
- [ ] Research IRS standards for your area
- [ ] Calculate actual necessary expenses
- [ ] Estimate disposable income

Documentation Checklist:

- [ ] Pay stubs for past 6 months
- [ ] Tax returns (2 years)
- [ ] Bank statements showing all deposits
- [ ] Business records (if self-employed)
- [ ] Expense receipts and documentation
- [ ] Insurance and healthcare records

Working with the Calculation

Income Accuracy:

- [ ] Include all income sources
- [ ] Use gross amounts, not net
- [ ] Include spouse's income if married
- [ ] Average correctly over 6-month period

Expense Maximization:

- [ ] Use actual expenses where permitted
- [ ] Document all necessary expenses
- [ ] Ensure reasonable and necessary standards
- [ ] Maximize legitimate deductions

If You Don't Initially Qualify

Review Options:

- [ ] Consider Chapter 13 benefits
- [ ] Evaluate timing changes
- [ ] Review calculation for errors
- [ ] Explore other debt relief alternatives

Professional Consultation:

- [ ] Seek experienced bankruptcy attorney guidance
- [ ] Get second opinion on complex calculations
- [ ] Understand all available options
- [ ] Make informed decision about best path forward

The Bottom Line: Means Test as Gateway, Not Barrier

The means test serves as the gateway to Chapter 7 bankruptcy, but it's important to understand its purpose and limitations:

What the Means Test Does:

- Ensures Chapter 7 access for those who need it most
- Directs higher-income debtors toward appropriate repayment plans
- Prevents system abuse while maintaining legitimate access
- Provides objective criteria for qualification

What the Means Test Doesn't Do:

- Prevent all debt relief for higher-income individuals
- Create insurmountable barriers for legitimate cases
- Eliminate discretion for special circumstances
- Make Chapter 13 a punishment for higher income

Key Principles for Success:

1. **Accuracy is essential** - miscalculations can derail your case
2. **Documentation matters** - support all income and expense claims
3. **Timing can be important** - consider when to file for best results
4. **Professional help pays off** - complex calculations benefit from expertise
5. **Alternatives exist** - failing the means test doesn't end all options

Remember: The means test is a tool to ensure the right people get access to the right form of bankruptcy relief. Whether you qualify for Chapter 7 or need to use Chapter 13, both paths can lead to financial recovery and a genuine fresh start.

The goal isn't to "beat" the means test - it's to find the bankruptcy solution that works best for your specific financial situation and provides the most effective path to long-term financial stability.

In the next chapter, we'll explore the property exemptions that determine what you can keep in bankruptcy - one of the most crucial and misunderstood aspects of the bankruptcy process.

8

What You Keep

Property Exemptions in NY and CA

The Greatest Bankruptcy Myth: "They'll Take Everything"

If you've been putting off filing bankruptcy because you're terrified of losing everything you own, you're not alone. This fear - that bankruptcy means losing your home, your car, your furniture, and everything else you've worked for - keeps millions of Americans trapped in cycles of debt they can't escape.

Here's the truth that might surprise you: **Most people who file bankruptcy keep everything they own.**

This protection comes through a system called **exemptions** - laws specifically designed to ensure that bankruptcy provides a genuine fresh start, not destitution. Exemptions protect your essential property, allowing you to maintain basic dignity and the tools you need to rebuild your financial life.

In this chapter, we'll explore exactly how exemptions work, what property is protected in New York and California, how to choose the right exemption system for your situation, and how to strategically plan to maximize what you keep.

Understanding Exemptions: Your Financial Safety Net

What Exemptions Really Mean

An **exemption** is a legal protection that shields specific types and amounts of property from being taken by creditors - including bankruptcy trustees. Think of exemptions as a protective bubble around your essential possessions.

The Core Principle: Exemptions ensure that bankruptcy gives you a genuine fresh start, not a one-way ticket to homelessness and destitution. They reflect society's recognition that certain property is essential for basic human dignity and economic survival.

How Exemptions Work in Practice

If your property is exempt:

- The bankruptcy trustee cannot take it
- You keep it throughout and after your bankruptcy case
- It's protected even if it has significant value (up to exemption limits)

If your property is non-exempt:

- The trustee may sell it to pay creditors
- You receive any proceeds above what creditors are owed
- In Chapter 13, you can keep it by paying creditors its value over time

The Reality: Most Property Is Protected

Statistics from bankruptcy trustees:

- 90%+ of Chapter 7 cases are "no asset" cases (nothing gets sold)
- Most people's property falls within exemption limits
- Trustees often don't pursue low-value non-exempt property due to administrative costs

The Federal vs. State Exemption Choice

How the System Works

Congress created federal exemptions, but allowed states to "opt out" and require their residents to use state exemptions instead. This creates three types of states:

"Opt-Out" States (like California):

- Must use state exemptions only
- Federal exemptions not available
- May offer multiple state exemption systems to choose from

"Choice" States (like New York):

- Can choose between federal or state exemptions
- Must pick one system or the other (no mixing)
- Choice can significantly impact what you keep

Federal-Only States:

- Must use federal exemptions
- No state alternative (rare)

Strategic Importance of Your Choice

The exemption system you choose can mean the difference between keeping or losing significant property:

Example Impact:

- **New York homeowner** with $150,000 home equity:
    - Federal exemptions: Protect $27,900 → **Lose most of home equity**
    - NY state exemptions: Protect $179,950 → **Keep entire home**
- **California renter** with $20,000 in savings:

  - System 1: No wildcard → **Savings at risk**
  - System 2: Large wildcard → **Savings protected**

New York Exemptions: Choosing Your Protection Strategy

New York residents can choose between **federal exemptions** or **New York state exemptions**. Here's how to analyze both options:

New York State Exemptions

Key Protections (2025 approximate amounts):

- **Homestead:** Up to $179,950 - Varies by county; higher in NYC area
- **Vehicle:** $5,000 equity - One vehicle per person
- **Household Goods:** Reasonable amounts - Furniture, appliances, clothing
- **Tools of Trade:** $3,750 - Work equipment, professional tools
- **Cash/Bank Accounts:** $6,000 - Checking, savings, cash
- **Personal Property:** $1,000 - Jewelry, electronics, misc. items
- **Wildcard:** $1,175 - Only if homestead not used
- **Retirement Accounts:** Unlimited - 401k, IRA, pensions, etc.
- **Insurance:** Reasonable amounts - Life insurance cash value

Federal Exemptions (Alternative Choice)

Key Protections (2025 approximate amounts):

- **Homestead:** $27,900 (single), $55,800 (joint) - Lower than NY state
- **Vehicle:** $4,450 - One vehicle
- **Household Goods:** $700 per item, $14,875 total - More generous than NY
- **Tools of Trade:** $2,800 - Lower than NY state

- **Jewelry:** $1,875 - Specific jewelry protection
- **Wildcard:** $1,475 + unused homestead - Very flexible
- **Retirement Accounts:** Unlimited - Same as state
- **Insurance:** $14,875 - Life insurance protection

New York County Variations

The homestead exemption varies significantly by county:

Higher Protection Counties:

- **New York County (Manhattan):** $179,950
- **Kings County (Brooklyn):** $179,950
- **Queens County:** $179,950
- **Bronx County:** $179,950
- **Westchester County:** $179,950

Lower Protection Counties:

- Many upstate counties: $89,975 to $179,950
- Rural counties: May be lower

Choosing Between NY Systems: Decision Framework

Choose New York State Exemptions if:

- You own a home with significant equity
- You live in a high-protection county
- You have substantial cash savings ($6,000+ vs. federal $1,475)
- Your personal property is modest
- You want maximum homestead protection

Choose Federal Exemptions if:

- You rent rather than own

- You have valuable household goods or collections
- You want maximum flexibility with the wildcard exemption
- You have diverse assets that need protection
- Your home equity is modest

Real New York Examples

Example 1: Brooklyn Homeowner *Robert and Maria, married, Brooklyn*

- Home worth $650,000, mortgage $480,000 (equity: $170,000)
- Two cars worth $15,000 and $8,000
- Normal household furnishings
- $3,000 in savings

Analysis:

- **NY state exemptions:** $179,950 homestead protects all equity
- **Federal exemptions:** Only $55,800 homestead → would lose $114,200 in equity
- **Choice:** New York state exemptions (clear winner)

Example 2: Albany Renter *Jennifer, single, rents apartment*

- Car worth $8,000, loan $3,000 (equity: $5,000)
- Household goods worth $12,000
- Jewelry and collections worth $8,000
- $2,500 in savings

Analysis:

- **NY state exemptions:** Car protected, household goods OK, jewelry/collections at risk
- **Federal exemptions:** Car protected, household goods well protected, wildcard protects collections
- **Choice:** Federal exemptions (better protection for personal

property)

Example 3: Syracuse Business Owner *David, self-employed contractor*

- Home worth $180,000, mortgage $120,000 (equity: $60,000)
- Work truck worth $25,000, loan $15,000 (equity: $10,000)
- Tools and equipment worth $8,000
- $4,000 in business checking account

Analysis:

- **NY state exemptions:** Home protected, vehicle partially protected, tools partially protected
- **Federal exemptions:** Home protected, vehicle not fully protected, tools protected
- **Choice:** New York state (better vehicle protection, can use wildcard creatively)

California Exemptions: Choosing Between Two State Systems

California residents cannot use federal exemptions but can choose between **two different state exemption systems.**

System 1 (CCP § 704): The Homeowner's System

Key Protections (2025 approximate amounts):

- **Homestead:** $678,000+ - Adjusted annually for inflation
- **Vehicle:** $3,625 - One vehicle
- **Household Goods:** Reasonable amounts - Basic necessities
- **Tools of Trade:** $9,525 - Higher than System 2
- **Jewelry:** $1,850 - Specific category
- **Bank Deposits:** $1,850 - Very limited
- **Wildcard:** None - No flexible exemption

- **Retirement Accounts:** Unlimited - Same in both systems

System 2 (CCP § 703): The Flexible System

Key Protections (2025 approximate amounts):

- **Homestead:** $31,950 - Much lower than System 1
- **Vehicle:** $7,500 - Higher than System 1
- **Household Goods:** $700 per item, $14,875 total - More generous
- **Tools of Trade:** $2,800 - Lower than System 1
- **Jewelry:** $2,050 - Slightly higher
- **Wildcard:** $1,550 + unused homestead - Up to $30,400 total
- **Retirement Accounts:** Unlimited - Same in both systems

The Wildcard Advantage in System 2

System 2's wildcard exemption is its most powerful feature:

Base Wildcard: $1,550 for any property **Plus Unused Homestead:** If you don't use the full $31,950 homestead exemption, you can apply the unused portion as additional wildcard

Maximum Wildcard: $30,400 (if you don't use any homestead exemption)

What Wildcard Can Protect:

- Cash and bank accounts
- Investment accounts
- Collections and valuables
- Business assets
- Additional vehicle equity
- Any other property not covered by specific exemptions

Choosing Between California Systems: Decision Framework

Choose System 1 (CCP § 704) if:

- You own a home with substantial equity
- You're a long-term homeowner in expensive markets
- Your other assets are modest
- You need maximum homestead protection
- You don't have significant cash or investments

Choose System 2 (CCP § 703) if:

- You rent or have limited home equity
- You have significant cash, savings, or investments
- You own valuable personal property
- You have multiple vehicles or valuable vehicle
- You want flexibility to protect diverse assets

Real California Examples

Example 1: San Francisco Homeowner *Lisa and Tom, married, San Francisco*

- Home worth $1.2 million, mortgage $600,000 (equity: $600,000)
- Two modest cars
- Normal household goods
- $5,000 in savings

Analysis:

- **System 1:** $678,000+ homestead protects most equity
- **System 2:** Only $31,950 homestead → would lose over $500,000 in equity
- **Choice:** System 1 (essential for homeowners with significant equity)

Example 2: Los Angeles Renter *Marcus, single, rents apartment*

- Car worth $15,000, loan $8,000 (equity: $7,000)
- Savings: $25,000
- Home recording studio equipment: $12,000
- Household goods: $8,000

Analysis:

- **System 1:** Car protected, savings mostly at risk, limited protection for equipment
- **System 2:** Car protected ($7,500 limit), wildcard protects savings and equipment
- **Choice:** System 2 (wildcard protects cash and equipment)

Example 3: Sacramento Small Business Owner *Patricia, owns hair salon*

- Home worth $400,000, mortgage $320,000 (equity: $80,000)
- Business equipment: $15,000
- Business checking: $8,000
- Personal car: $12,000 equity

Analysis:

- **System 1:** Home protected, business equipment partially protected
- **System 2:** Home protected (under $31,950), wildcard protects business assets
- **Choice:** System 2 (wildcard protects business assets, home equity low enough)

Retirement Accounts: The Universal Protection

Completely Protected in All Systems

Federal Protection (ERISA Plans):

- 401(k) plans

- 403(b) plans
- Pension plans
- Profit-sharing plans

State and Federal Protection (IRAs):

- Traditional IRAs
- Roth IRAs
- SEP-IRAs
- SIMPLE IRAs

The Bottom Line: Retirement accounts are **never at risk** in bankruptcy. This protection is absolute and applies regardless of the exemption system you choose.

Strategic Implications

Pre-Bankruptcy Planning:

- Don't cash out retirement accounts to pay creditors
- Retirement funds are better protected in qualified accounts than as cash
- Consider maximizing contributions before filing (within legal limits)

Common Mistake: Many people drain their retirement accounts to pay debts before filing bankruptcy, leaving themselves with nothing protected. This is usually a serious strategic error.

Homestead Exemptions: Protecting Your Home

How Homestead Exemptions Work

The homestead exemption protects **equity** in your primary residence, not the entire value of the home.

Equity Calculation:

- Home fair market value

- Minus: All liens and mortgages
- Equals: Your equity (what the exemption protects)

Special Homestead Rules

Recent Purchase Rule: If you acquired your home within **1,215 days** (about 3.3 years) before filing, your homestead exemption may be capped at **$189,050**, regardless of what your state allows.

Intent to Defraud Rule: If you purchased your home with intent to defraud creditors, the exemption may be reduced or eliminated.

Primary Residence Requirement:

- Must be your primary residence, not a vacation or rental property
- Must actually live in the property
- Temporary absences generally don't affect protection

Real Homestead Examples

Example 1: Protected Home (NY) *Sarah, Queens*

- Home value: $500,000
- Mortgage balance: $350,000
- **Equity:** $150,000
- **NY exemption:** $179,950
- **Result:** Home fully protected

Example 2: Partially Protected Home (CA) *Jose, San Jose*

- Home value: $900,000
- Mortgage balance: $200,000
- **Equity:** $700,000
- **System 1 exemption:** $678,000+
- **Result:** Most equity protected, small amount might be at risk

Example 3: At-Risk Home (Federal) *Mike, Buffalo*

- Home value: $300,000
- Mortgage balance: $240,000
- **Equity:** $60,000
- **Federal exemption:** $27,900 (single)
- **Result:** $32,100 of equity at risk if using federal exemptions

Vehicle Exemptions: Keeping Your Transportation

How Vehicle Exemptions Work

Vehicle exemptions protect **equity** in your car, truck, or motorcycle.

Equity Calculation:

- Vehicle fair market value (what you could sell it for)
- Minus: Loan balance owed
- Equals: Your equity (what the exemption protects)

Multiple Vehicle Considerations

Most exemption systems protect one vehicle per person:

- Single person: One vehicle exemption
- Married couple: Two vehicle exemptions (one per spouse)
- Additional vehicles may be at risk unless protected by wildcard

Vehicle Valuation

Common Valuation Sources:

- Kelley Blue Book (KBB)
- Edmunds
- Local used car market

- Actual condition affects value

Factors Affecting Value:

- Mileage and age
- Mechanical condition
- Accident history
- Local market conditions

Real Vehicle Examples

Example 1: Protected Vehicle (CA System 2) *Jennifer, Sacramento*

- 2019 Honda Civic, fair market value: $18,000
- Loan balance: $12,000
- **Equity:** $6,000
- **CA System 2 exemption:** $7,500
- **Result:** Vehicle fully protected

Example 2: Partially Protected Vehicle (NY) *Robert, Buffalo*

- 2020 F-150 truck, fair market value: $35,000
- Loan balance: $25,000
- **Equity:** $10,000
- **NY exemption:** $5,000
- **Result:** $5,000 of equity at risk

Example 3: Multiple Vehicles *Maria and Carlos, married,* Los *Angeles*

- Car 1: $4,000 equity (protected by Maria's exemption)
- Car 2: $6,000 equity (protected by Carlos's exemption)
- Classic car: $15,000 equity (at risk unless protected by wildcard)

Household Goods and Personal Property

What Counts as Household Goods

Typically Protected:

- Furniture (beds, tables, chairs, dressers)
- Appliances (refrigerator, stove, washer, dryer)
- Electronics (TV, computer, phone, stereo)
- Clothing and personal items
- Books and family photos
- Kitchen items and dishes
- Linens and bedding

May Need Special Protection:

- Expensive jewelry
- Art and collectibles
- High-end electronics
- Musical instruments
- Sporting goods

Valuation of Household Goods

Garage Sale Value: Courts typically use "garage sale" or "yard sale" value for used household goods, not replacement cost.

Realistic Valuations:

- Used furniture: Often worth 10-20% of new price
- Electronics: Depreciate rapidly
- Clothing: Minimal resale value
- Most household goods worth less than people think

Protection Strategies

Federal System Advantage:

- $700 per item limit
- $14,875 total limit
- Usually protects all normal household goods

State System Variations:

- "Reasonable amounts" standards
- May need wildcard for valuable items
- Documentation important for high-value items

Tools of Trade: Protecting Your Livelihood

What Qualifies as Tools of Trade

Traditional Tools:

- Mechanic's tools
- Carpenter's equipment
- Plumber's supplies
- Electrician's tools

Professional Equipment:

- Doctor's medical equipment
- Lawyer's law library
- Photographer's cameras
- Musician's instruments

Modern Work Tools:

- Computers and software
- Professional licenses
- Cell phones for business

- Work vehicles

Exemption Limits

Variation by System:

- **CA System 1:** $9,525 (highest)
- **NY State:** $3,750
- **Federal:** $2,800
- **CA System 2:** $2,800

Strategic Considerations

Business vs. Employee:

- Self-employed individuals typically need more tool protection
- Employees may have fewer tools to protect
- Business equipment beyond basic tools may need wildcard protection

Professional Practice:

- Professional licenses generally protected regardless of exemption system
- Office equipment may need careful planning
- Client files and work product typically protected

Wildcard Exemptions: The Ultimate Flexibility

How Wildcard Exemptions Work

Wildcard exemptions can be applied to **any property** you choose to protect. They're the most flexible tool in the exemption toolkit.

Wildcard Amounts by System

Federal System:

- Base wildcard: $1,475
- Plus unused homestead: Up to $13,950 additional
- **Maximum:** $15,425 if no homestead used

California System 2:

- Base wildcard: $1,550
- Plus unused homestead: Up to $30,400 additional
- **Maximum:** $31,950 if no homestead used

New York State:

- Wildcard: $1,175 (only if homestead not used)
- **Maximum:** $1,175

Strategic Wildcard Use

Priority Protection:

1. Cash and bank accounts
2. Investment accounts
3. Valuable collections
4. Business assets
5. Additional vehicle equity
6. High-value personal property

Real Wildcard Examples

Example 1: California System 2 Renter *Alex, Los Angeles, rents apartment*

- Savings account: $18,000
- Investment account: $12,000
- Car equity: $5,000 (protected by vehicle exemption)

- **Wildcard available:** $31,950 (no homestead used)
- **Result:** All savings and investments protected

Example 2: Federal System Strategic Use *Rachel, Albany,* NY

- Home equity: $15,000 (uses $15,000 of $27,900 homestead)
- Unused homestead: $12,900
- Plus base wildcard: $1,475
- **Total wildcard:** $14,375
- **Protects:** $10,000 in savings plus $4,375 in jewelry

Property Valuation: Getting It Right

Why Accurate Valuation Matters

Under-valuation risks:

- Trustee challenges
- Potential fraud allegations
- Loss of credibility

Over-valuation problems:

- May appear non-exempt when actually protected
- Unnecessary stress and planning
- May influence exemption system choice

Valuation Methods

Real Estate:

- Recent appraisal
- Comparative market analysis (CMA)
- County tax assessment (often low)

- Realtor opinion of value

Vehicles:

- Kelley Blue Book
- Edmunds
- Local dealer quotes
- Actual condition adjustments

Personal Property:

- Garage sale/yard sale value
- eBay "sold" listings
- Consignment shop estimates
- Insurance replacement value (usually too high)

Documentation Requirements

What to Keep:

- Appraisals and valuations
- Photos of property condition
- Repair estimates
- Market research
- Professional opinions

Strategic Exemption Planning

Pre-Filing Strategies

Legal Property Repositioning:

- Convert non-exempt assets to exempt assets
- Pay down mortgage to increase protected equity

- Purchase exempt property with non-exempt funds
- Maximize retirement account contributions

Timing Considerations:

- Consider exemption changes over time
- Plan major purchases around exemption limits
- Time filing to maximize protection

What NOT to Do

Prohibited Transfers:

- Don't give property to family/friends to "hide" it
- Don't sell property for less than fair market value
- Don't pay preferential payments to insider creditors
- Don't fraudulently transfer assets

Timing Restrictions:

- Pre-filing transfers may be reversed
- Recent large exemption-based purchases scrutinized
- Intent matters as much as timing

Special Property Situations

Business Assets

Sole Proprietorship:

- Business equipment may qualify as tools of trade
- Business accounts may need wildcard protection
- Inventory typically not well protected
- Accounts receivable may be at risk

Professional Practice:

- Licenses and degrees typically protected
- Office equipment and furniture at risk
- Client files generally protected
- Ongoing income not an "asset"

Inheritance and Windfalls

Timing Matters:

- Property you inherit after filing typically not part of bankruptcy estate
- Property you're entitled to before filing must be disclosed
- Probate proceedings may complicate timing

Strategic Planning:

- Consider timing of filing relative to expected inheritance
- Understand how inheritance affects your case
- Plan for post-filing windfalls

Joint Property

Tenancy by the Entirety:

- Special protection for married couples in some states
- Both spouses must file or property may be fully protected
- Not available in all states

Joint Tenancy:

- Only your share subject to bankruptcy
- May complicate exemption planning
- Co-owner rights must be considered

Common Exemption Mistakes

Planning Errors

Wrong Exemption System Choice:

- Not analyzing all options thoroughly
- Focusing on one asset type to the exclusion of others
- Not considering future needs and goals

Inadequate Valuation:

- Using replacement cost instead of used value
- Not getting professional appraisals when needed
- Overestimating personal property values

Documentation Problems

Insufficient Records:

- Not documenting property values
- Missing ownership documentation
- Inadequate proof of exemption claims

Timing Issues:

- Last-minute property transfers
- Rushed exemption planning
- Not understanding look-back periods

Legal Compliance

Fraudulent Transfers:

- Moving property to avoid creditors
- Selling property for less than fair value

- Not disclosing all property and transfers

Working with Professionals

When You Need Expert Help

Complex Asset Situations:

- Multiple properties
- Business ownership
- High-value collections
- Recent inheritances or windfalls

Close Exemption Calls:

- Property values near exemption limits
- Choice between exemption systems
- Multiple asset types needing protection

Recent Transfers:

- Property moved within 2 years of filing
- Gifts to family members
- Sales below market value

Choosing the Right Professional

Bankruptcy Attorney Qualifications:

- Experience with your specific type of assets
- Knowledge of local exemption practices
- Understanding of pre-filing planning rules
- Familiarity with your chosen court district

Other Professionals:

- **Appraisers:** For real estate and valuable personal property
- **Accountants:** For business asset valuation
- **Financial advisors:** For investment account planning

Your Exemption Action Plan

Pre-Filing Assessment (60-90 days)

Asset Inventory:

- [ ] List all property you own
- [ ] Determine fair market value of each item
- [ ] Identify any joint ownership issues
- [ ] Research recent property transfers

Exemption Analysis:

- [ ] Research available exemption systems
- [ ] Calculate protection under each system
- [ ] Consider strategic property repositioning
- [ ] Plan timing of filing

Valuation Documentation:

- [ ] Obtain property appraisals if needed
- [ ] Research comparable sales
- [ ] Document property condition
- [ ] Gather ownership documentation

System Selection Process

New York Residents:

- [ ] Compare federal vs. state exemptions for your assets

- [ ] Consider homestead protection needs
- [ ] Evaluate wildcard flexibility requirements
- [ ] Make strategic choice based on complete asset picture

California Residents:

- [ ] Compare System 1 vs. System 2 for your situation
- [ ] Analyze homestead vs. wildcard trade-off
- [ ] Consider current and future asset protection needs
- [ ] Choose system that provides best overall protection

Filing Preparation

Documentation Assembly:

- [ ] Gather all property valuations
- [ ] Prepare exemption schedules
- [ ] Document exemption system choice
- [ ] Ensure accuracy and completeness

Final Review:

- [ ] Double-check all exemption calculations
- [ ] Verify property values are reasonable
- [ ] Confirm exemption system choice is optimal
- [ ] Review with attorney if representation

Success Stories: Exemptions That Worked

Case Study 1: The New York Homeowner Choice

Background: *Robert and Linda, married, Westchester County,* NY

- Home worth $480,000, mortgage $320,000 (equity: $160,000)

- Two cars with $8,000 total equity
- Normal household goods
- $4,000 in savings

Exemption Analysis:

- **Federal exemptions:** $55,800 homestead → lose $104,200 home equity
- **NY state exemptions:** $179,950 homestead → keep all home equity

Result:

- Chose NY state exemptions
- Protected entire home
- Kept all other property
- Saved over $100,000 in home equity

Case Study 2: The California Wildcard Strategy

Background: *Maria, single, San Diego, CA, renter*

- Car worth $15,000, loan $8,000 (equity: $7,000)
- Savings account: $22,000
- Art collection: $8,000
- Normal household goods

Exemption Analysis:

- **System 1:** Car protected, savings mostly at risk, art at risk
- **System 2:** Car protected, wildcard ($31,950) protects savings and art

Result:

- Chose California System 2
- Protected all savings and art with wildcard
- Kept vehicle and household goods

- Achieved complete asset protection

Case Study 3: The Business Owner Protection

Background: *James, self-employed electrician, Albany,* NY

- Home worth $150,000, mortgage $80,000 (equity: $70,000)
- Work van worth $25,000, loan $15,000 (equity: $10,000)
- Tools and equipment: $12,000
- Business checking: $6,000

Exemption Analysis:

- **Federal exemptions:** Home protected, van partially protected, tools mostly protected
- **NY state exemptions:** Home protected, van partially protected, tools partially protected, business account protected

Strategic Choice:

- Chose NY state exemptions
- Home fully protected ($70,000 < $179,950)
- Van equity partially protected ($5,000 of $10,000)
- Used cash exemption for business account
- Negotiated with trustee on tools and remaining van equity

Result:

- Kept home and essential business assets
- Maintained ability to earn living
- Minimal loss compared to debt relief gained

The Bottom Line: Exemptions as Your Foundation

Understanding and properly using exemptions is crucial to a successful bankruptcy case. Key principles to remember:

Exemptions Are Your Right:

- Not a loophole or technicality
- Designed to provide genuine fresh start
- Essential for maintaining basic dignity and economic survival

Most People Keep Everything:

- 90%+ of Chapter 7 cases are "no asset" cases
- Exemption limits are often higher than property values
- Trustees consider administrative costs before pursuing property

Planning Makes a Difference:

- Choosing the right exemption system can save thousands
- Proper valuation prevents unnecessary stress
- Strategic pre-filing planning can maximize protection

Professional Help Pays Off:

- Complex asset situations benefit from expert analysis
- Exemption choice can't be changed after filing
- Mistakes can cost significant money and property

The Goal Is Protection, Not Perfection:

- You don't need to protect everything to benefit from bankruptcy
- Sometimes strategic surrender makes sense
- The fresh start is worth more than any single asset

Remember: exemptions exist specifically to ensure that bankruptcy provides a meaningful fresh start, not financial destitution. By understanding and properly using these protections, you can emerge from bankruptcy with the tools and resources you need to rebuild a stable, prosperous financial life.

In the next chapter, we'll walk through the complete Chapter 7 filing process step by step, from initial preparation through final discharge, so you know exactly what to expect throughout your case.

9

The Chapter 7 Filing Process

Your Step-by-Step Roadmap from Decision to Discharge

From Overwhelming to Organized: Your Path Through Chapter 7

Filing for Chapter 7 bankruptcy might seem like navigating a complex maze, but it's actually a well-established, predictable process that millions of Americans have successfully completed. Once you understand the steps and timeline, what initially seems overwhelming becomes manageable - even routine.

Think of Chapter 7 as a structured 3-4 month journey with clear milestones and a definite destination: the legal elimination of your overwhelming debts and a genuine fresh start. This chapter will be your GPS through that journey, showing you exactly what to expect, when to expect it, and how to navigate each phase successfully.

By the end of this process, you'll have transformed from someone drowning in debt to someone with a clean slate and the tools to build a better financial future. Let's walk through exactly how that transformation happens.

The Big Picture: Chapter 7 Timeline Overview

Before diving into the details, here's the bird's-eye view of your Chapter 7 journey:

The Complete Timeline

Pre-Filing Preparation (2-8 weeks before filing): During this initial phase, you'll complete required credit counseling, gather all necessary financial documents, and prepare your bankruptcy forms. This includes collecting six months of pay stubs, tax returns, bank statements, and debt information. You'll also choose your exemption system and ensure all forms are accurate and complete.

Filing and Immediate Relief (Day 0-30): The moment you file your petition, the automatic stay goes into effect, immediately stopping all collection activity, wage garnishments, and foreclosure proceedings. Within days, the court assigns a trustee to your case and sends official notice to all your creditors. This is when you'll experience the first real relief from financial stress.

Meeting of Creditors (Days 30-45): You'll attend a short meeting with your assigned trustee, usually lasting only 10-15 minutes. Despite the name, creditors rarely attend. The trustee will ask routine questions under oath to verify the information in your petition. This meeting is typically conducted by video or phone and is much less intimidating than most people expect.

Asset Administration (Days 45-90): The trustee reviews your assets to determine if any non-exempt property should be sold to pay creditors. In over 90% of cases, this results in a "no asset" determination, meaning you keep all your property. During this period, creditors also have deadlines to file claims or object to your debt discharge.

Final Requirements (Days 60-120): You must complete a mandatory financial management course and file the certificate with the court. The trustee prepares final reports, and any remaining administrative tasks are completed. This phase overlaps with asset administration but focuses on meeting all discharge requirements.

Discharge and Closure (Days 90-120): The court grants your discharge order, permanently eliminating your legal obligation to pay discharged debts. You'll receive official notice by mail, and creditors are notified that they can no longer attempt to collect on discharged debts. Your case is then administratively closed, marking the successful completion of your Chapter 7 bankruptcy.

What This Means for You

From the moment you file:

- All collection activity stops immediately
- Your stress level drops dramatically
- You can focus on rebuilding instead of fighting creditors
- You have a clear path to debt freedom

Most people's experience:

- 90% of Chapter 7 cases are routine with no complications
- Most people keep all their property
- The process is more straightforward than feared
- Life begins improving immediately after filing

Phase 1: Pre-Filing Preparation (2-8 Weeks)

Step 1: Complete Required Credit Counseling

What It Is: A mandatory counseling session that must be completed within **180 days before filing**. This isn't therapy - it's a brief educational session designed to ensure you understand your options.

How It Works:

- **Duration:** 60-90 minutes
- **Format:** Online, phone, or in-person
- **Cost:** $25-$50 (fee waivers available for low income)
- **Provider:** Must be approved by the U.S. Trustee Program

What You'll Cover:

- Budget analysis
- Debt management options
- Alternatives to bankruptcy
- Overview of bankruptcy process

The Certificate: You'll receive a certificate of completion that must be filed with your bankruptcy petition. Without this certificate, your case cannot proceed.

Where to Find Approved Providers:

- U.S. Trustee Program website (justice.gov)
- Search by state and language preferences
- Look for "non-profit" designation
- Verify current approval status

Step 2: Comprehensive Document Gathering

This is often the most time-consuming part of the process, but it's crucial for accuracy and completeness.

Income Documentation (Past 6 Months):

- [ ] Pay stubs from all jobs
- [ ] Self-employment records and bank deposits
- [ ] Social Security award letters
- [ ] Unemployment benefit records
- [ ] Pension and retirement income statements
- [ ] Child support and alimony records
- [ ] Any other income documentation

Tax Documentation:

- [ ] Federal and state tax returns (past 2 years)
- [ ] W-2s and 1099s

- [ ] Tax transcripts from IRS (if available)
- [ ] Unfiled return documentation (if applicable)

Asset Documentation:

- [ ] Real estate deeds and current mortgage statements
- [ ] Vehicle titles and loan information
- [ ] Bank statements (past 6 months, all accounts)
- [ ] Investment account statements
- [ ] Life insurance policies with cash value
- [ ] Retirement account statements (401k, IRA, etc.)
- [ ] Personal property valuations (for high-value items)

Debt Documentation:

- [ ] Credit card statements (most recent)
- [ ] Medical bills and collection notices
- [ ] Personal loan agreements
- [ ] Student loan information
- [ ] Tax debt notices
- [ ] Court judgments and liens
- [ ] Utility and other bills

Monthly Expense Records:

- [ ] Mortgage or rent payments
- [ ] Utility bills (electric, gas, water, garbage)
- [ ] Insurance premiums (health, auto, life, home)
- [ ] Transportation costs (car payment, insurance, gas, maintenance)
- [ ] Food and household expenses
- [ ] Medical and dental expenses

- [ ] Childcare and education costs
- [ ] Other necessary living expenses

Step 3: Complete Bankruptcy Forms

The bankruptcy petition consists of multiple forms that provide a complete financial picture:

Core Forms:

- **Voluntary Petition (Form 101):** Basic case information
- **Schedules A/B:** Real and personal property
- **Schedule C:** Property exemptions
- **Schedules D/E/F:** Creditors and claims
- **Schedules G/H:** Executory contracts and co-debtors
- **Schedule I:** Current income
- **Schedule J:** Current expenses
- **Statement of Financial Affairs:** Financial history

Means Test Forms:

- **Form 122A-1:** Chapter 7 Statement of Current Monthly Income
- **Form 122A-2:** Chapter 7 Means Test Calculation (if required)

Additional Requirements:

- **Creditor Matrix:** List of all creditors with current addresses
- **Certificate of Credit Counseling**
- **Payment Advices:** 60 days of pay stubs

Step 4: Choose Your Exemptions

For New York Residents: Review both federal and state exemption options and choose the system that best protects your property.

For California Residents: Choose between System 1 (CCP § 704) and System 2 (CCP § 703) based on your asset composition.

Critical Decision: Your exemption choice cannot be changed after filing, so this decision requires careful analysis.

Step 5: Final Pre-Filing Review

Accuracy Check:

- [ ] All forms completed accurately and consistently
- [ ] All creditors listed with current addresses
- [ ] All assets disclosed and properly valued
- [ ] All income sources included
- [ ] Exemptions properly claimed

Timing Considerations:

- [ ] Avoided large purchases in past 90 days
- [ ] No cash advances in past 70 days
- [ ] No preferential payments to family/friends
- [ ] No recent asset transfers

Preparation for Immediate Changes:

- [ ] Notified employer about potential garnishment stop
- [ ] Prepared for collection activity to cease
- [ ] Arranged for automatic stay notification to creditors

Phase 2: Filing and Immediate Relief (Day 0-30)

Day 0: The Filing

The Moment of Filing: When your petition is electronically filed with the bankruptcy court, several things happen immediately:

Immediate Legal Effects:

- **Automatic stay** goes into effect instantly
- All collection activity must stop
- Wage garnishments halt
- Foreclosure proceedings pause
- Utility shutoffs prevented (usually)
- Lawsuits suspended

Required Payment:

- **Filing fee:** $338 (as of 2025)
- **Fee waiver:** Available for income below 150% of poverty guidelines
- **Payment plan:** Available in some circumstances

Immediate Tasks:

- [ ] Notify your employer if wages were being garnished
- [ ] Inform your bank if accounts were frozen
- [ ] Stop using all credit cards immediately
- [ ] Begin tracking expenses for Schedule J updates

Days 1-10: Trustee Assignment and Initial Review

Trustee Assignment: The court will assign a **Chapter 7 trustee** to your case within a few days. The trustee's role is to:

- Review your petition for accuracy and completeness
- Identify any non-exempt assets
- Ensure compliance with bankruptcy laws
- Administer the case fairly

Initial Trustee Review: Your trustee will examine your petition and may request additional documentation or clarification. Common requests include:

- Bank statements
- Property valuations
- Income verification
- Explanation of unusual transactions

Creditor Notification: The court sends official notice to all listed creditors, informing them of:

- The bankruptcy filing
- The automatic stay
- Deadlines for filing claims or objections
- The meeting of creditors date

Days 10-30: The Breathing Room Period

What's Happening:

- Collection activity remains stopped
- Creditors receive official notice
- Trustee continues reviewing your case
- You prepare for the Meeting of Creditors

Your Experience: For most people, this is the first peaceful period they've had in months or years:

- No more collection calls
- No more threatening letters
- No more wage garnishments
- Ability to focus on the future instead of fighting the past

Common Questions During This Period:

"Can I use my bank accounts?" Yes, but be careful with accounts at banks where you owe money, as they might freeze accounts.

"Can I get paid?" Yes, continue working and receiving income normally. This doesn't affect your case.

"Can I pay my regular bills?" Yes, continue paying ongoing expenses like rent, utilities, and groceries.

"What about my car payment?" If you want to keep the car, continue making payments. If not, you can surrender it and eliminate the debt.

Phase 3: The Meeting of Creditors (341 Meeting) - Days 30-45

What the 341 Meeting Really Is

Despite its formal name, the "Meeting of Creditors" is usually a brief, routine administrative hearing. It's called a "341 Meeting" after Section 341 of the Bankruptcy Code.

Reality Check:

- **Duration:** Usually 5-15 minutes
- **Attendees:** You, your attorney (if you have one), and the trustee
- **Creditors:** Rarely attend (despite the name)
- **Format:** Often conducted by video/phone since COVID
- **Atmosphere:** Professional but not adversarial

Before the Meeting: Preparation

Required Documents to Bring:

- [ ] Photo ID (driver's license, passport, etc.)
- [ ] Social Security card or W-2 showing full SSN
- [ ] Any additional documents the trustee requested
- [ ] Bank statements (if requested)
- [ ] Property valuations (if requested)

What to Expect:

In-Person 341 Meetings:

- Arrive 15-30 minutes early to check in with the trustee's staff and locate the correct courtroom or meeting room
- Bring a valid photo ID and Social Security card for verification
- Wait in the designated seating area until your case is called by name and case number
- Approach the table where you'll sit directly across from or next to the trustee
- Raise your right hand to be sworn in under oath before answering any questions
- Have original documents readily accessible in an organized folder to provide if requested

Zoom 341 Meetings:

- Test your internet connection, camera, and microphone at least 30 minutes before the scheduled time
- Join the Zoom meeting 10-15 minutes early and wait in the virtual waiting room until admitted
- Ensure you're in a quiet, well-lit space with a professional background
- Have your photo ID and Social Security card ready to hold up to the camera for verification
- Listen for your case to be called and unmute yourself when instructed
- Raise your right hand on camera to be sworn in under oath
- Have all documents scanned and saved on your computer for easy screen sharing if requested

Phone 341 Meetings:

- Call the designated number at the exact scheduled time (not early, as you may be blocked from joining)

- Have a quiet, private location with good cell reception or landline connection
- Keep your photo ID and Social Security card nearby for verification purposes over the phone
- Listen carefully for your case to be called, as audio quality may vary
- Speak clearly when taking the oath and answering questions
- Have all documents organized and ready to read specific information aloud if requested by the trustee

During the Meeting: Typical Questions

The trustee will ask standard questions to verify the information in your petition:

Identity and Petition Review:

- "Please state your name and current address for the record."
- "Did you sign the petition and schedules filed in this case?"
- "Did you read the petition and schedules before you signed them?"
- "Are the contents true and correct to the best of your knowledge?"

Assets and Exemptions:

- "Do you own any real estate?"
- "Have you listed all of your assets?"
- "Do you believe the value of your assets as listed is accurate?"
- "Are you entitled to any tax refunds?"

Financial Transactions:

- "Have you made any transfers of property or payments to creditors in the past year?"
- "Have you given any gifts in excess of $600 in the past year?"
- "Do you have any pending lawsuits or insurance claims?"

Income and Expenses:

- "Has your income changed since filing?"
- "Are your monthly expenses as listed accurate?"
- "Do you expect to receive any money from any source?"

Previous Bankruptcies:

- "Have you filed bankruptcy before?"
- "Have you received credit counseling and debtor education?"

After the Meeting: What Happens Next

If Everything Goes Smoothly:

- Trustee files a "no asset" report (most common)
- Case proceeds toward discharge
- No further hearings required

If Issues Arise:

- Trustee may request additional documentation
- Asset investigation may continue
- Additional meetings may be scheduled (rare)

Creditor Deadlines:

- **60 days** after the meeting: Deadline for creditors to object to discharge
- **30 days** after the meeting: Deadline to file claims (in asset cases)

Real 341 Meeting Examples

Example 1: Simple Case *Jennifer, single, credit card debt*

- **Duration:** 8 minutes
- **Questions:** Standard verification questions only
- **Outcome:** No asset case, proceeded to discharge

Example 2: Business Owner Case *Robert, self-employed contractor*

- **Duration:** 15 minutes
- **Questions:** Additional questions about business assets and recent transactions
- **Follow-up:** Requested business bank statements
- **Outcome:** After document review, proceeded to discharge

Example 3: High-Asset Case *Maria and Carlos, significant home equity*

- **Duration:** 20 minutes
- **Questions:** Detailed questions about property values and exemptions
- **Follow-up:** Real estate appraisal ordered
- **Outcome:** Chapter 13 conversion to protect equity

Phase 4: Asset Administration (Days 45-90)

The Trustee's Asset Review

No Asset Cases (90%+ of Chapter 7 filings):

- All property is exempt or of minimal value
- Trustee files "Report of No Distribution"
- Case proceeds directly to discharge
- No property is sold

Asset Cases (Less than 10% of filings):

- Some non-exempt property exists
- Trustee evaluates whether sale is worthwhile
- Administrative costs considered
- Property may be sold or abandoned

What Makes an Asset Case

Non-Exempt Property:

- Property that exceeds exemption limits
- Property not covered by any exemption
- Recently acquired property (depending on timing)

Economic Viability:

- Property must be worth more than the cost to sell it
- Trustee considers storage, insurance, legal fees
- Small amounts of non-exempt equity often not pursued

Real Asset Case Example: *David, vintage car collection*

- Owned three classic cars worth $45,000 total
- Vehicle exemption only protected $5,000
- Trustee sold cars for $40,000
- David received $5,000 (his exemption)
- Creditors received $35,000 after expenses

Creditor Claims and Objections

Claim Filing:

- Creditors must file formal claims to receive payment
- Deadline typically 90 days after Meeting of Creditors
- Many creditors don't file claims (especially in no-asset cases)

Discharge Objections:

- Creditors can object to discharge of specific debts
- Must be filed within 60 days of Meeting of Creditors
- Usually involves allegations of fraud or recent purchases

- Most cases have no objections

Common Objection Situations:

- Large purchases within 90 days of filing
- Cash advances within 70 days of filing
- Luxury goods or services
- Debts incurred without intent to repay

Your Role During This Phase

Stay Available:

- Respond promptly to trustee requests
- Provide any additional documentation
- Update contact information if you move

Continue Normal Life:

- Keep working and earning income
- Pay ongoing expenses normally
- Begin planning for post-discharge life

Avoid New Problems:

- Don't incur new debt
- Don't make large purchases without trustee approval
- Don't transfer property

Phase 5: Final Requirements (Days 60-120)

Complete the Financial Management Course

Requirement: You must complete a second educational course before receiving your discharge. This is different from the pre-filing credit counseling.

Timing:

- Must be completed after filing but before discharge
- Most people complete it 60-90 days after filing
- Certificate must be filed with the court

Course Details:

- **Duration:** 2 hours (can be broken into sessions)
- **Cost:** $25-$50 (fee waivers available)
- **Format:** Online, phone, or in-person
- **Provider:** Must be approved by U.S. Trustee Program

Course Content:

- Personal financial management
- Budget development
- Credit management
- Using credit responsibly
- Money management tools

Trustee's Final Report

No Asset Cases:

- Trustee files final report confirming no assets to distribute
- Usually a simple, one-page document
- Filed 60-90 days after Meeting of Creditors

Asset Cases:

- Detailed accounting of property sold and funds distributed
- May take longer depending on complexity
- Must account for all funds received and distributed

Pre-Discharge Requirements Checklist

- [ ] Meeting of Creditors completed
- [ ] Financial management course completed
- [ ] Course certificate filed with court
- [ ] All trustee requests satisfied
- [ ] No pending objections or issues
- [ ] Required time periods elapsed

Phase 6: Discharge and Case Closure (Days 90-120)

The Discharge Order

What It Is: A court order that legally eliminates your obligation to pay discharged debts. This is the goal of your entire bankruptcy case.

When It's Granted:

- Usually 60-90 days after the Meeting of Creditors
- All requirements must be completed
- No successful objections pending
- Time periods for objections expired

What It Covers:

- All debts listed in your petition (with exceptions)
- Most unsecured debts are eliminated
- Legal obligation to pay is permanently ended
- Creditors cannot attempt collection on discharged debts

What Happens After Discharge

Immediate Effects:

- You receive official discharge notice by mail

- Creditors receive notice that debts are discharged
- Any remaining collection activity must stop permanently
- You're legally free from discharged debt obligations

Continuing Obligations:

- **Non-discharged debts:** Still owe student loans, recent taxes, child support, etc.
- **Secured debts:** Still responsible if you kept the property
- **New debts:** Any obligations incurred after filing

Case Closure

Final Steps:

- Trustee files final report and account
- Court reviews all filings
- Case is administratively closed
- File becomes part of permanent court record

Your New Status:

- Debt-free from all discharged obligations
- Protected from collection on old debts
- Ready to begin rebuilding credit and financial life
- Clean slate for future financial planning

Common Process Questions and Concerns

"What if I made a mistake on my forms?"

Minor Errors:

- Can usually be corrected with amended schedules
- Common corrections include updated addresses, forgotten

creditors, or valuation adjustments

- File amendments as soon as errors are discovered

Major Omissions:

- Failure to list assets or income can be more serious
- May require reopening the case
- Could affect discharge if deemed fraudulent
- Always better to disclose and correct than hide

"What if I forgot to list a creditor?"

Before Discharge:

- File amended schedule to add the creditor
- Creditor receives notice and can file claim
- Debt typically still gets discharged

After Discharge:

- May require reopening the case
- More complex but usually still results in discharge
- Some courts have different procedures

"What if my income changes during the case?"

Income Increases:

- Generally doesn't affect Chapter 7 eligibility once filed
- May need to update Schedule I
- Trustee typically not concerned unless extreme

Income Decreases:

- Update schedules if significant
- May affect ongoing expenses and planning

- Usually doesn't impact the case negatively

"What if I need to move during the case?"

Notification Requirements:

- Must notify court and trustee of address change
- Update all creditors with new address
- File change of address with court

Different Districts:

- Case remains in original filing district
- May need to travel for hearings
- Consider local attorney if representation needed

"What happens if creditors continue calling?"

Understanding the Law:

- Automatic stay prohibits collection activity
- Violation can result in sanctions against creditor
- You have the right to notify them of the bankruptcy

Steps to Take:

1. Inform creditor of bankruptcy case number and filing date
2. Send written notice if calls continue
3. Document violations
4. Report persistent violations to your attorney or the court

Pro Se vs. Attorney Representation

Filing Without an Attorney (Pro Se)

Advantages:

- Lower upfront costs
- Direct control over your case
- Educational experience

Challenges:

- Complex forms and procedures
- Risk of errors that could affect your case
- No guidance on exemption strategies
- Handling trustee and creditor issues alone

Best Suited For:

- Simple cases with limited assets
- No asset cases with straightforward debts
- People comfortable with legal procedures
- Cases with no complications

Working with an Attorney

Advantages:

- Expert guidance on forms and strategy
- Exemption optimization
- Representation at meetings and hearings
- Problem resolution experience

Costs:

- Typical range: $1,200-$2,500 in NY/CA
- Often includes all standard services
- Payment plans may be available
- Often pays for itself through better exemption planning

Best Suited For:

- First-time filers
- Cases with significant assets
- Complex income situations
- People who want professional guidance

Regional Variations: NY and CA Specifics

New York District Differences

Southern District (Manhattan, Bronx, Westchester):

- High volume court with efficient procedures
- Video 341 meetings common
- Trustees experienced with high-cost-of-living issues
- Generally faster processing times

Eastern District (Brooklyn, Queens, Long Island):

- Largest caseload in the state
- Mix of video and in-person meetings
- Diverse trustee panel
- Some local procedure variations

Northern District (Albany, Syracuse, Utica):

- Smaller, more personal court
- Often in-person meetings
- Trustees familiar with regional economic issues
- More flexible scheduling

Western District (Buffalo, Rochester):

- Similar to Northern District
- Strong local legal community

- Trustees understand manufacturing/industrial economy
- Generally accommodating procedures

California District Differences

Northern District (San Francisco, Oakland, San Jose):

- Tech economy expertise
- High cost of living considerations
- Video meetings prevalent
- Innovation in court procedures

Central District (Los Angeles, Orange County):

- Largest bankruptcy court in the nation
- Highly systematized procedures
- Video meetings standard
- Fast-moving dockets

Eastern District (Sacramento, Fresno, Bakersfield):

- Agricultural and government economy focus
- Mix of meeting formats
- Regional cost-of-living awareness
- More personal attention possible

Southern District (San Diego):

- Military and border economy expertise
- Efficient procedures
- Video meetings common
- Smaller, manageable dockets

Your Chapter 7 Success Strategy

Pre-Filing Excellence

Documentation Strategy:

- [ ] Start gathering documents 60-90 days before filing
- [ ] Organize systematically by category
- [ ] Make copies of everything
- [ ] Create a filing system for ongoing use

Accuracy Focus:

- [ ] Double-check all forms before filing
- [ ] Verify all creditor information
- [ ] Confirm all asset valuations
- [ ] Review exemption choices carefully

Timeline Management:

- [ ] Complete credit counseling early
- [ ] Allow adequate time for form preparation
- [ ] Don't rush the filing process
- [ ] Plan for potential delays

During the Process

Trustee Relations:

- [ ] Respond promptly to all requests
- [ ] Be completely honest and forthcoming
- [ ] Provide clear, organized documentation
- [ ] Maintain professional communication

Creditor Management:

- [ ] Refer all collection attempts to your attorney or the court

- [ ] Document any automatic stay violations
- [ ] Update creditors with accurate contact information
- [ ] Don't engage in negotiations during the case

Personal Management:

- [ ] Focus on the future, not past financial problems
- [ ] Begin planning post-discharge financial strategies
- [ ] Avoid new debt during the process
- [ ] Maintain employment and income stability

Post-Discharge Planning

Credit Rebuilding:

- [ ] Check credit reports for accuracy
- [ ] Begin secured credit card applications
- [ ] Create realistic budget for new financial life
- [ ] Start emergency fund even with small amounts

Financial Education:

- [ ] Apply lessons learned from financial management course
- [ ] Consider additional financial education resources
- [ ] Develop sustainable spending habits
- [ ] Plan for major future expenses

Measuring Success: What to Expect

Immediate Success Indicators (0-30 days)

Relief Factors:

- Collection calls stopped

- Wage garnishments halted
- Stress levels decreased
- Sleep improved
- Ability to focus on other life areas

Process Indicators:

- Petition filed successfully
- Automatic stay in effect
- Trustee assigned and responsive
- No immediate complications

Short-term Success (30-120 days)

Case Progress:

- 341 Meeting completed successfully
- No creditor objections
- Trustee satisfied with documentation
- Financial management course completed

Personal Progress:

- Improved financial habits developing
- Better relationship with money
- Increased confidence about financial future
- Reduced anxiety about debt

Long-term Success (Post-Discharge)

Legal Success:

- Discharge granted for all eligible debts
- Protected property retained

- No ongoing bankruptcy complications
- Case closed successfully

Financial Success:

- Living within means on current income
- Building emergency fund
- Responsible credit use beginning
- Long-term financial planning in place

Life Success:

- Reduced financial stress
- Improved family relationships
- Better work performance
- Optimism about the future

The Bottom Line: Chapter 7 as a Structured Solution

Chapter 7 bankruptcy isn't chaos - it's a carefully structured legal process designed to provide relief efficiently and fairly. Understanding this structure helps you navigate the process with confidence rather than fear.

Key Principles for Success:

Preparation Matters:

- Thorough preparation prevents problems
- Accurate documentation speeds the process
- Good organization reduces stress
- Professional help can optimize outcomes

The Process Is Predictable:

- Each phase has clear goals and timelines
- Most cases follow standard patterns

- Trustees and courts want routine success
- Complications are the exception, not the rule

Relief Is Real and Lasting:

- Automatic stay provides immediate relief
- Discharge provides permanent protection
- Fresh start enables genuine recovery
- Success is measured by life improvement, not perfection

Your Role Is Active but Limited:

- Honesty and cooperation ensure success
- Responsive communication prevents problems
- Financial discipline supports long-term goals
- Professional guidance optimizes outcomes

Remember: Chapter 7 bankruptcy is not something that happens to you - it's something you actively use to solve your financial problems and create a better future. By understanding and engaging with the process, you transform from a victim of overwhelming debt into someone taking control of their financial destiny.

In the next chapter, we'll explore life after Chapter 7 discharge: how to rebuild your credit, manage your finances responsibly, and create the sustainable financial stability that bankruptcy was designed to make possible.

10

Life After Chapter 7

Rebuilding with Confidence

The New You: Standing at the Starting Line

Congratulations. You've done something that required tremendous courage: you acknowledged that your debt situation was unsustainable, navigated the bankruptcy process, and successfully obtained your Chapter 7 discharge. You are now legally free from the debts that were drowning you just a few months ago.

But if you're like most people who've just completed Chapter 7, you might be feeling a complex mix of emotions: relief, uncertainty, hope, and maybe even a little fear. What happens now? How do you rebuild? Will anyone ever trust you financially again? How do you make sure you never end up in this situation again?

This chapter is your guide to the next phase of your financial journey. We'll show you exactly how to rebuild your credit, manage your finances responsibly, protect yourself from future financial crises, and create the stable, sustainable financial life that bankruptcy was designed to make possible.

The truth is, many people find that their financial life after Chapter 7 becomes better than it ever was before - not despite the bankruptcy, but because of the fresh start and hard-won wisdom it provided.

Understanding Your New Legal Status

What Your Discharge Actually Means

When you received your Chapter 7 discharge order, something powerful happened: **your legal obligation to pay discharged debts was permanently eliminated.** This isn't temporary relief - it's permanent legal protection.

Your Discharge Protects You From:

- Any attempts to collect discharged debts
- Lawsuits on discharged debts
- Wage garnishments for old debts
- Bank account seizures for discharged obligations
- Harassment or pressure tactics from old creditors

Important Legal Reality: If a creditor violates your discharge by attempting to collect a discharged debt, they can face serious legal penalties. Your discharge order isn't just a piece of paper - it's a federal court order with real enforcement power.

What Debts Are Gone Forever

Typically Discharged (Gone Forever):

- Credit card balances that existed when you filed
- Medical bills from before your filing date
- Personal loans and payday loans
- Collection accounts and charge-offs
- Most utility bills and service debts
- Deficiency balances from repossessed vehicles

- Most court judgments for money

Debts That Survived Your Bankruptcy:

- Student loans (in most cases)
- Recent tax debts
- Child support and alimony
- Criminal fines and restitution
- Debts you reaffirmed (like a car loan you kept)
- Any debts incurred after your filing date

The Immediate Financial Impact

Your Monthly Cash Flow: For most people, Chapter 7 creates an immediate and dramatic improvement in monthly cash flow. If you were paying $800/month in minimum credit card payments before bankruptcy, that $800 is now available for:

- Building an emergency fund
- Improving your living situation
- Investing in your career or education
- Creating financial stability

Real Example: *Sarah, before bankruptcy:*

- Take-home income: $3,200/month
- Minimum debt payments: $950/month
- Available for living expenses: $2,250/month

Sarah, after discharge:

- Take-home income: $3,200/month
- Minimum debt payments: $0/month
- Available for living expenses: $3,200/month
- **Improvement: $950/month more for building her future**

Your Credit Report After Discharge

What to Expect Immediately

The Bankruptcy Notation: Your credit report will show your Chapter 7 bankruptcy for **10 years** from the filing date. This might sound scary, but remember: your credit was likely already severely damaged before you filed.

Discharged Accounts: All accounts included in your bankruptcy should now show:

- **Balance: $0**
- **Status: "Included in bankruptcy" or "Discharged"**
- **No more late payments** accumulating
- **No more increasing balances**

Checking Your Credit Reports

Get Your Free Reports: You're entitled to free credit reports from all three bureaus annually at www.annualcreditreport.com. After bankruptcy, check all three reports to ensure accuracy.

What to Look For:

- [ ] Discharged debts showing $0 balances
- [ ] Accurate bankruptcy filing information
- [ ] No new collection accounts that shouldn't be there
- [ ] Correct personal information

Common Errors to Dispute:

- Discharged debts still showing balances owed
- Accounts marked as "past due" after discharge
- Multiple listings for the same debt
- Incorrect dates or amounts

The Credit Score Recovery Timeline

Immediately After Discharge: Your credit score might actually improve slightly because:

- Your debt-to-income ratio drops dramatically
- You stop accumulating new late payments
- Your credit utilization drops to zero on discharged accounts

Month-by-Month Expectations:

Months 1-6 Post-Discharge:

- Score may fluctuate as credit reports update
- Focus on checking reports for accuracy
- Begin planning credit rebuilding strategy
- **Typical score range:** 450-550

Months 6-12:

- May qualify for secured credit cards
- Score begins steady upward trend
- New positive payment history starts building
- **Typical score range:** 500-600

Months 12-18:

- Often receive unsecured credit offers (review carefully)
- May qualify for auto loans (higher rates initially)
- Credit mix begins to diversify
- **Typical score range:** 550-650

Years 2-3:

- Credit score continues improving with responsible use
- May qualify for better loan terms

- Could be eligible for FHA mortgage
- **Typical score range:** 620-720

Years 4-7:

- Credit score approaches or exceeds pre-bankruptcy levels
- Access to conventional credit products
- May qualify for conventional mortgages
- **Typical score range:** 650-750+

Your Credit Rebuilding Strategy

Phase 1: Foundation Building (Months 1-6)

Priority #1: Secured Credit Cards

Secured credit cards are your best initial tool for rebuilding credit. Here's how they work:

- You make a security deposit ($200-$500)
- This deposit becomes your credit limit
- You use the card like any credit card
- Your payments are reported to credit bureaus
- After 12-18 months, many convert to unsecured cards

Choosing the Right Secured Card:

- [ ] Reports to all three credit bureaus
- [ ] No annual fee (if possible)
- [ ] Reasonable fees and terms
- [ ] Path to "graduate" to unsecured card
- [ ] FDIC-insured bank

How to Use a Secured Card:

- Make small purchases ($20-50/month)
- Pay the full balance every month
- Never exceed 30% of your credit limit
- Set up automatic payments to ensure you're never late

Priority #2: Authorized User Strategy

If you have family members with good credit, ask them to add you as an authorized user on their account:

- You benefit from their payment history
- You don't need to use the card
- Their good credit helps rebuild your profile
- Choose accounts with long, positive payment histories

Priority #3: Credit Builder Loans

Some credit unions and online lenders offer "credit builder loans":

- You make monthly payments into a savings account
- The loan is "paid off" when you complete all payments
- You receive the money at the end
- Payments are reported to credit bureaus
- Builds credit while forcing you to save

Phase 2: Diversification (Months 6-18)

Unsecured Credit Cards: As your score improves, you may receive offers for unsecured cards:

- Start with smaller credit limits
- Avoid cards with excessive fees
- Continue paying balances in full
- Don't apply for multiple cards at once

Auto Loans: If you need a vehicle, an auto loan can help rebuild credit:

- Shop around for the best rates
- Consider credit unions for better terms
- Make larger down payments if possible
- Choose affordable payments you can handle easily

Retail Credit: Store credit cards are often easier to qualify for:

- Use for purchases you'd make anyway
- Pay off immediately
- Avoid high interest rates
- Don't open too many accounts

Phase 3: Optimization (Months 18+)

Credit Mix: A diverse mix of credit types can help your score:

- Credit cards (revolving credit)
- Auto loan (installment credit)
- Perhaps a small personal loan
- Don't overextend for the sake of variety

Credit Limit Increases: As you demonstrate responsible use:

- Request credit limit increases on existing cards
- This improves your credit utilization ratio
- Don't increase spending when limits increase
- Use increases to keep utilization low

Strategic Account Management:

- Keep old accounts open (they help your credit history length)
- Use cards occasionally to keep them active
- Consider upgrading secured cards to unsecured

- Monitor your credit score regularly

Financial Management After Bankruptcy

Creating Your Post-Bankruptcy Budget

The 50/30/20 Rule (Modified for Post-Bankruptcy):

- **50% for needs:** Housing, food, transportation, utilities, minimum debt payments
- **30% for wants:** Entertainment, dining out, hobbies, discretionary spending
- **20% for financial security:** Emergency fund, retirement, additional debt payments

Post-Bankruptcy Modifications: Consider adjusting to 50/20/30 initially, putting more toward financial security:

- **50% for needs:** Same essential expenses
- **20% for wants:** Reduced discretionary spending while rebuilding
- **30% for financial security:** Aggressive emergency fund building

Building Your Emergency Fund

Why It's Critical: An emergency fund prevents future debt when unexpected expenses arise. Without one, you're vulnerable to the same cycle that led to bankruptcy.

Emergency Fund Targets:

- **Immediate goal:** $500-$1,000
- **Short-term goal:** $2,500-$5,000
- **Long-term goal:** 3-6 months of essential expenses

Building Strategy:

- Start with $25-$50 per month if that's all you can afford
- Use automatic transfers to a separate savings account

- Save any windfalls (tax refunds, bonuses, gifts)
- Gradually increase contributions as income allows

Where to Keep Emergency Funds:

- High-yield savings account
- Money market account
- Short-term CDs (for portion you won't need immediately)
- Keep it separate from checking to avoid temptation

Smart Spending Habits

The 24-Hour Rule: For any purchase over $100, wait 24 hours before buying. This prevents impulse purchases and gives you time to consider if you really need the item.

Needs vs. Wants Analysis: Before any significant purchase, ask:

- Do I need this or just want it?
- Can I afford this without going into debt?
- Is there a cheaper alternative that meets my needs?
- Will I still want this in a month?

Subscription Audit: Review all recurring subscriptions monthly:

- Cancel services you don't regularly use
- Look for cheaper alternatives
- Avoid auto-renewal traps
- Consider sharing services with family when appropriate

Housing After Bankruptcy

Renting with a Bankruptcy on Your Record

The Reality: Many landlords will rent to people with discharged bankruptcies, especially when you can demonstrate current financial stability.

Strategies for Renting:

- **Be honest** about your bankruptcy on applications
- **Explain the circumstances** that led to filing
- **Emphasize your current stability** (steady income, discharge completion)
- **Offer a larger security deposit** if needed
- **Provide references** from previous landlords, employers, or other character references
- **Show proof of income** and current financial responsibility

What Landlords Want to See:

- Stable employment history
- Income that's 2.5-3 times the rent
- No recent evictions
- Current bills paid on time
- Responsible attitude toward financial obligations

Alternative Strategies:

- Consider smaller, private landlords who may be more flexible
- Look into "second chance" rental programs
- Consider having a co-signer initially
- Rent in areas with lower demand where landlords are more flexible

Buying a Home After Chapter 7

Timeline for Home Ownership:

- **FHA loans:** Available 2 years after discharge with good payment history

- **VA loans:** Available 2 years after discharge for qualified veterans
- **USDA loans:** Similar to FHA timing and requirements
- **Conventional loans:** Typically require 4 years after discharge

Preparing for Homeownership:

- **Build credit score** to 620+ for FHA, 640+ for conventional
- **Save for down payment** (3.5% for FHA, 5-20% for conventional)
- **Establish payment history** on all bills and new credit
- **Stable employment** for at least 2 years
- **Low debt-to-income ratio** (typically under 43%)

FHA Loans After Bankruptcy: FHA loans are often the best option for post-bankruptcy homebuyers:

- Lower down payment requirements (3.5%)
- More lenient credit score requirements
- Consideration of extenuating circumstances
- Competitive interest rates
- Available through most lenders

Employment Considerations

How Bankruptcy Affects Employment

Private Sector Employment:

- Most private employers **cannot** discriminate based solely on bankruptcy
- Some financial industry positions may have restrictions
- Security clearance positions may require disclosure
- Most employers care more about job skills than financial history

Government Employment:

- Federal positions may require disclosure
- Some positions involving financial responsibility may be affected
- Generally not an automatic disqualification
- Each case evaluated individually

Professional Licenses:

- Most professional licenses are not affected by bankruptcy
- Some financial services licenses may require disclosure
- Real estate licenses typically not affected
- Check with your specific licensing board if concerned

Disclosure Strategies

When Asked Directly:

- Be honest about your bankruptcy
- Briefly explain the circumstances
- Emphasize lessons learned and current financial responsibility
- Focus on your qualifications and job skills

Application Questions:

- Answer honestly if specifically asked about bankruptcy
- Don't volunteer information if not asked
- Focus on your professional qualifications
- Be prepared to discuss if it comes up in interviews

Insurance and Banking After Bankruptcy

Banking Relationships

Checking and Savings Accounts: Most banks will open accounts for people with discharged bankruptcies:

- Credit unions often more accommodating
- Online banks typically less restrictive
- Some banks may require secured accounts initially
- ChexSystems issues usually resolve over time

If You Have Banking Problems:

- Try credit unions instead of major banks
- Consider second-chance banking programs
- Look into online banks with fewer restrictions
- Use prepaid cards temporarily if necessary

Insurance Considerations

Auto Insurance:

- Bankruptcy may initially affect rates
- Shop around for the best rates
- Consider usage-based insurance programs
- Maintain continuous coverage to avoid higher rates

Life Insurance:

- Term life insurance typically not affected
- Whole life policies may be more expensive initially
- Health is usually the primary factor
- Compare quotes from multiple companies

Health Insurance:

- Bankruptcy doesn't affect health insurance eligibility
- Continue existing coverage if possible
- Explore marketplace options if needed
- Don't go without health insurance - medical debt was likely part of

your original problem

Protecting Your Fresh Start

Avoiding Financial Traps

High-Risk Products to Avoid:

Payday Loans:

- Extremely high interest rates (300-400% APR)
- Designed to trap borrowers in debt cycles
- Use emergency fund or credit union loans instead

Title Loans:

- Risk losing your vehicle
- High fees and interest rates
- Often predatory toward vulnerable populations

Rent-to-Own:

- Extremely expensive way to purchase items
- Can cost 2-3 times retail price
- Save money and buy used instead

Subprime Auto Dealers:

- Often target bankruptcy filers with terrible terms
- Excessive interest rates and fees
- Shop around for better financing options

Recognizing Predatory Lending

Red Flags:

- Guaranteed approval regardless of credit

- Pressure to sign immediately
- Fees that seem excessive
- Terms that seem too good to be true
- Requests for upfront fees
- High-pressure sales tactics

Better Alternatives:

- Credit union loans
- Secured credit cards for building credit
- Save up to buy items with cash
- Traditional bank financing

Building Long-Term Wealth

Retirement Savings: Even small amounts matter:

- Take advantage of employer 401(k) matches
- Start with even $25-50 per month to IRAs
- Increase contributions annually
- Remember: retirement accounts are protected in bankruptcy

Education and Career Development: Invest in yourself:

- Take advantage of employer training programs
- Consider community college courses
- Develop skills that increase earning potential
- Network within your industry

Gradual Wealth Building:

- Focus on increasing income over time
- Avoid lifestyle inflation as income grows
- Build assets that appreciate (education, skills, eventually real estate)

- Be patient - wealth building takes time

Emotional and Psychological Recovery

Processing the Bankruptcy Experience

Common Post-Bankruptcy Emotions:

- **Relief** from the end of financial stress
- **Embarrassment** about needing bankruptcy
- **Anxiety** about making financial mistakes again
- **Optimism** about the future possibilities
- **Determination** to rebuild responsibly

Healthy Perspective:

- Bankruptcy was a tool to solve a problem, not a personal failing
- You took responsible action to address an unsustainable situation
- Many successful people have filed bankruptcy
- Your worth as a person isn't determined by your credit score

Rebuilding Financial Confidence

Start Small:

- Make and keep small financial commitments
- Pay all bills on time, every time
- Build savings gradually but consistently
- Celebrate small victories along the way

Education and Knowledge:

- Read about personal finance
- Understand how credit scores work

- Learn about investing and wealth building
- Stay informed about financial best practices

Support Systems:

- Consider joining financial support groups
- Work with a financial counselor if helpful
- Surround yourself with financially responsible people
- Don't be ashamed to ask for help when needed

Relationships and Money

Family Communication:

- Be open about your financial situation and goals
- Include family members in budgeting decisions
- Teach children about responsible money management
- Set family financial goals together

Social Situations:

- Don't let financial limitations prevent social connections
- Suggest low-cost activities with friends
- Be honest about your budget limitations
- Remember that true friends care about you, not your spending power

One Year Later: Measuring Your Progress

Financial Metrics to Track

Credit Score Improvement:

- Check your score monthly (many credit cards provide free scores)
- Aim for 50-100 point improvements annually

- Track improvements across all three bureaus

Emergency Fund Growth:

- Month 3: $250-500
- Month 6: $500-1,000
- Month 12: $1,000-2,500
- Year 2: $2,500-5,000

Debt Management:

- Any new debt should be manageable and purposeful
- Credit utilization should stay below 30%
- All bills paid on time, every time

Income and Career:

- Focus on increasing earning potential
- Track any promotions or raises
- Invest in education or skills development

Lifestyle Improvements

Stress Reduction:

- Better sleep without financial anxiety
- Improved relationships without money stress
- Ability to focus on other life goals
- Overall better mental and physical health

Financial Habits:

- Automatic savings transfers
- Regular budget reviews
- Careful spending decisions
- Long-term financial planning

Future Planning:

- Emergency fund providing security
- Credit rebuilding on track
- Clear financial goals for the next 2-5 years
- Understanding of how to avoid past mistakes

Success Stories: Real People, Real Recovery

Sarah's Story: From Medical Debt to Homeownership

Background: Sarah, a nurse in Buffalo, filed Chapter 7 after $67,000 in medical debt from cancer treatment bankrupted her despite having health insurance.

Immediate Post-Bankruptcy (Months 1-6):

- Used secured credit card for small purchases
- Built emergency fund with $100/month
- Focused on health recovery and work stability

Year One:

- Credit score improved from 480 to 620
- Emergency fund reached $1,500
- Qualified for unsecured credit card

Year Two:

- Credit score reached 680
- Emergency fund at $3,000
- Qualified for FHA loan pre-approval

Year Three:

- Purchased home with FHA loan
- Credit score at 720

- Teaching other cancer survivors about financial recovery

Key Lessons:

- Medical bankruptcy doesn't define your future
- Consistent small steps create significant progress
- Health and financial recovery can happen simultaneously

Marcus's Story: From Business Failure to Financial Stability

Background: Marcus, a small business owner in Sacramento, filed Chapter 7 after his restaurant failed during the pandemic, leaving him with $95,000 in business and personal debt.

Immediate Strategy:

- Took job as restaurant manager while planning comeback
- Used Chapter 7 to eliminate personal guarantees on business debt
- Focused on rebuilding personal credit separate from business plans

Rebuilding Phase:

- Started with secured credit card and credit union membership
- Built emergency fund aggressively ($300/month)
- Took community college courses in business management

Two Years Later:

- Credit score improved to 650
- Emergency fund at $8,000
- Qualified for car loan at reasonable rate

Three Years Later:

- Opened new restaurant with better business structure
- Separated personal and business finances completely
- Teaching other entrepreneurs about financial planning

Key Lessons:

- Business failure doesn't mean personal failure
- Better financial education prevents future problems
- Bankruptcy can provide the fresh start needed for eventual success

Jennifer's Story: Single Mom to Financial Security

Background: Jennifer, a single mother in Queens, filed Chapter 7 after divorce left her with $45,000 in joint credit card debt and a much-reduced income.

Immediate Challenges:

- Finding rental housing with bankruptcy on record
- Managing tight budget as single parent
- Rebuilding credit while supporting two children

Strategic Approach:

- Found apartment with smaller landlord willing to work with her
- Used automatic savings to build emergency fund ($50/month)
- Got secured credit card and became authorized user on her mother's account

One Year Progress:

- Credit score improved from 510 to 590
- Emergency fund at $800
- All bills current and paid on time

Three Years Later:

- Credit score at 680
- Emergency fund at $4,000
- Qualified for FHA loan and bought first home

Current Status:

- Homeowner with stable housing costs
- Teaching financial literacy to other single parents
- Planning for children's college education

Key Lessons:

- Single parents can achieve financial stability after bankruptcy
- Small, consistent steps lead to major improvements
- Community support and education accelerate recovery

Your Personal Recovery Plan

Months 1-3: Foundation

Financial Tasks:

- [ ] Check all three credit reports for accuracy
- [ ] Dispute any errors on credit reports
- [ ] Open basic checking and savings accounts
- [ ] Apply for secured credit card
- [ ] Set up automatic savings transfer ($25-100/month)

Habit Development:

- [ ] Create and follow monthly budget
- [ ] Pay all bills on time, every time
- [ ] Track all expenses for budget refinement
- [ ] Avoid new debt except for credit rebuilding

Personal Development:

- [ ] Process the bankruptcy experience emotionally
- [ ] Set realistic financial goals for the next year
- [ ] Begin financial education (books, podcasts, courses)

- [ ] Build support network of financially responsible people

Months 3-6: Building Momentum

Credit Building:

- [ ] Use secured credit card for small purchases monthly
- [ ] Pay credit card balance in full every month
- [ ] Consider becoming authorized user on family member's account
- [ ] Monitor credit score monthly

Financial Growth:

- [ ] Increase emergency fund contributions if possible
- [ ] Review and optimize budget monthly
- [ ] Look for ways to increase income
- [ ] Avoid financial traps and predatory lending

Life Improvements:

- [ ] Focus on career development and stability
- [ ] Improve living situation within budget
- [ ] Build healthy financial habits
- [ ] Celebrate small victories and progress

Months 6-12: Expanding Options

Credit Expansion:

- [ ] Apply for unsecured credit card if qualified
- [ ] Consider credit-builder loan from credit union
- [ ] Continue perfect payment history on all accounts
- [ ] Keep credit utilization below 30%

Financial Security:

- [ ] Build emergency fund to $1,000-2,500
- [ ] Consider increasing retirement contributions
- [ ] Explore ways to increase earning potential
- [ ] Begin considering major financial goals (home, car, etc.)

Long-term Planning:

- [ ] Set 2-year and 5-year financial goals
- [ ] Research homeownership requirements if interested
- [ ] Consider additional education or training
- [ ] Build stronger financial foundation

Years 2-5: Long-term Stability

Major Financial Goals:

- [ ] Consider homeownership (FHA loan after 2 years)
- [ ] Build emergency fund to 3-6 months expenses
- [ ] Maximize retirement savings
- [ ] Consider other investments as appropriate

Credit Optimization:

- [ ] Maintain excellent payment history
- [ ] Optimize credit mix and utilization
- [ ] Request credit limit increases on existing accounts
- [ ] Monitor credit for identity theft or errors

Wealth Building:

- [ ] Focus on increasing income over time
- [ ] Invest in education and career development
- [ ] Build assets that appreciate in value
- [ ] Help others who are facing financial difficulties

The Long View: Bankruptcy as a Turning Point

What Success Really Looks Like

Financial Success Metrics:

- Living within your means comfortably
- Emergency fund providing genuine security
- Credit score allowing access to mainstream financial products
- Ability to handle unexpected expenses without debt
- Progress toward long-term financial goals

Life Success Indicators:

- Reduced stress and anxiety about money
- Better relationships due to reduced financial tension
- Ability to be generous with others
- Confidence in financial decision-making
- Sense of control over your financial future

Common Long-term Outcomes

Five Years Post-Bankruptcy:

- Most people have credit scores in the 650-750 range
- Many own homes with FHA or conventional loans
- Emergency funds providing real security
- Stable career progression and income growth
- Confidence and knowledge about money management

Ten Years Post-Bankruptcy:

- Bankruptcy notation removed from credit reports

- Full access to conventional financial products
- Often better financial position than before bankruptcy
- Strong financial habits and decision-making skills
- Ability to help others facing financial difficulties

The Bigger Picture

Bankruptcy as Education: Many people find that bankruptcy, while difficult, provided valuable financial education they never received elsewhere. It forced them to:

- Understand their true financial position
- Learn about credit and debt management
- Develop budgeting and planning skills
- Recognize and avoid financial traps
- Build genuine financial security rather than just managing debt

Bankruptcy as Motivation: The fresh start often provides powerful motivation to:

- Make different financial choices
- Build real wealth rather than just maintaining debt payments
- Develop financial literacy and responsibility
- Create security for family and future
- Help others avoid similar financial problems

Your New Financial Identity

From Debt Management to Wealth Building

Before Bankruptcy: Many people spend years simply managing debt - making minimum payments, juggling due dates, and never making real progress toward financial goals.

After Bankruptcy: With debt eliminated, you can focus on building rather than just managing. Every dollar that previously went to minimum payments can now go toward:

- Emergency funds that provide real security
- Retirement savings that compound over time
- Education and skills that increase earning power
- Assets that appreciate and build wealth

The Knowledge Advantage

Hard-Won Wisdom: Going through bankruptcy provides financial education that many people never receive:

- Understanding the true cost of debt
- Recognizing predatory lending practices
- Appreciating the value of emergency funds
- Learning to distinguish between needs and wants
- Developing skills for long-term financial planning

Teaching Others: Many bankruptcy filers become valuable resources for friends and family facing financial difficulties. Your experience and recovery can help others:

- Recognize when debt has become unmanageable
- Understand their options before crisis points
- Learn from your mistakes and successes
- Build better financial habits from the beginning

Final Thoughts: Your Bankruptcy Success Story

Chapter 7 bankruptcy isn't the end of your financial story - it's the end of the chapter where debt controlled your life and the beginning of the chapter where you control your finances.

What You've Accomplished:

- You recognized an unsustainable situation and took action
- You navigated a complex legal process successfully
- You eliminated overwhelming debt and gained a fresh start
- You have the opportunity to build genuine financial security

What You're Building:

- Financial habits that will serve you for life
- Security that comes from genuine savings and planning
- Confidence that comes from understanding and controlling your finances
- A future where your financial decisions support your life goals

Your Ongoing Commitment:

- To live within your means and build emergency funds
- To use credit responsibly as a tool, not a crutch
- To continue learning about financial management and wealth building
- To help others when they face financial difficulties

Remember: You didn't file bankruptcy because you failed at money management - you filed because you succeeded at recognizing a problem and taking decisive action to solve it. That same wisdom and courage that got you through bankruptcy will serve you well as you build your new financial life.

Your fresh start isn't just about eliminating debt - it's about creating the stable, secure, and prosperous financial future that you and your family deserve. The hardest part is behind you. The best part is ahead of you.

Welcome to your new financial life.

In the next chapter, we'll begin exploring Chapter 13 bankruptcy - the reorganization option that allows people with regular income to keep their property while repaying debts over time.

11

Chapter 13 Basics

Reorganize, Repay, Rebuild

Chapter 13: The Path Less Traveled but Often More Powerful

While Chapter 7 bankruptcy gets most of the attention - and rightfully so, as it's the most common form of consumer bankruptcy - Chapter 13 is often the more powerful tool for people who want to keep valuable property, catch up on missed payments, or who simply don't qualify for Chapter 7 due to higher income.

Think of Chapter 13 as bankruptcy with a payment plan. Instead of liquidating assets to pay creditors (as Chapter 7 does in theory), Chapter 13 allows you to keep all your property while reorganizing your debts into an affordable payment plan lasting 3 to 5 years. At the end of the plan, any remaining eligible debts are discharged, giving you the same fresh start as Chapter 7 - just with a different route to get there.

But Chapter 13 isn't just "Chapter 7 with payments." It has unique powers that Chapter 7 doesn't have: it can stop foreclosure and let you catch up on missed mortgage payments over time, it can reduce car loan balances in certain situations, and it can even eliminate second mortgages in some cases. For the right person in the right situation, Chapter 13 can be life-changing.

In this chapter, we'll explore exactly how Chapter 13 works, who it helps most, what makes it different from Chapter 7, and how to determine if it might be the right path for your situation.

Understanding Chapter 13: The Wage Earner's Plan

What Chapter 13 Really Is

Chapter 13 bankruptcy, officially called "reorganization bankruptcy" or the "wage earner's plan," is a court-supervised payment plan that allows people with regular income to:

- **Keep all their property** (even non-exempt property)
- **Reorganize their debts** into affordable monthly payments
- **Stop foreclosure** and catch up on missed mortgage payments
- **Prevent repossession** and catch up on car payments
- **Discharge remaining eligible debts** after completing the plan

The Core Concept: Instead of selling property to pay creditors (Chapter 7's approach), Chapter 13 uses your future income to pay creditors over time while you keep your property.

How Chapter 13 Works: The Big Picture

Step 1: Propose a Payment Plan You create a plan to repay all or part of your debts over 3-5 years based on what you can afford after essential living expenses.

Step 2: Get Court Approval The bankruptcy court reviews your plan to ensure it meets legal requirements and is feasible based on your income and expenses.

Step 3: Make Monthly Payments You make one monthly payment to a court-appointed trustee, who distributes the money to your creditors according to your plan.

Step 4: Complete the Plan After making all required payments for 3-5 years, you receive a discharge that eliminates any remaining eligible debt.

Step 5: Keep Your Property Throughout the entire process, you keep all your property - your house, cars, savings, everything - as long as you stay current on the plan.

Chapter 13 vs. Chapter 7: A Side-by-Side Comparison

Duration:

- **Chapter 7:** 3-4 months
- **Chapter 13:** 3-5 years

Property Protection:

- **Chapter 7:** Keep exempt property only
- **Chapter 13:** Keep all property

Income Requirements:

- **Chapter 7:** Must pass means test (lower income generally required)
- **Chapter 13:** Must have regular income to fund plan

Monthly Payments:

- **Chapter 7:** None after filing (except ongoing secured debts)
- **Chapter 13:** Monthly plan payments for 3-5 years

Foreclosure Protection:

- **Chapter 7:** Temporary delay only
- **Chapter 13:** Can catch up on missed payments over time

Debt Discharge:

- **Chapter 7:** Immediate discharge of eligible debts
- **Chapter 13:** Discharge after completing payment plan

Flexibility:

- **Chapter 7:** Little flexibility once filed
- **Chapter 13:** Can modify plan if circumstances change

Who Chapter 13 Is Designed For

The Ideal Chapter 13 Candidate

Chapter 13 works best for people who have:

Regular, Predictable Income:

- Steady employment (W-2 or self-employed)
- Pension or retirement income
- Social Security or disability benefits
- Regular alimony or child support
- Any other reliable monthly income

Valuable Property to Protect:

- Home with significant equity
- Multiple vehicles
- Business assets or equipment
- Investment accounts or valuable collections
- Any property that exceeds exemption limits

Ability to Pay Something Toward Debts:

- Enough income after essential expenses to fund a meaningful payment plan
- Willingness to commit to 3-5 years of payments
- Discipline to stick to a budget and payment schedule

Common Chapter 13 Scenarios

Scenario 1: The Homeowner Facing Foreclosure *Robert and Linda, married, Sacramento*

- Behind $18,000 on mortgage payments

- Foreclosure sale scheduled in 30 days
- Combined income: $75,000/year
- Want to keep their home of 15 years

How Chapter 13 Helps:

- Filing immediately stops foreclosure
- Can spread the $18,000 arrearage over 5 years ($300/month)
- Resume regular mortgage payments going forward
- Discharge other unsecured debts to free up money for mortgage

Scenario 2: The High-Income Debt Overwhelm *Maria, single, Long Island*

- Income: $95,000/year (above NY median)
- Credit card debt: $65,000
- Failed Chapter 7 means test
- Current on mortgage and car

How Chapter 13 Helps:

- Can file Chapter 13 regardless of income level
- Pay portion of unsecured debt over 5 years
- Keep all property and maintain lifestyle
- Discharge remaining debt after plan completion

Scenario 3: The Asset Protection Case *David, business owner, Buffalo*

- Owns home with $40,000 non-exempt equity
- Business equipment worth $25,000
- Investment account with $15,000
- Would lose significant property in Chapter 7

How Chapter 13 Helps:

- Keep all property including non-exempt assets

- Pay creditors the value of non-exempt property over time
- Maintain business operations throughout the case
- Discharge remaining debts after plan completion

Scenario 4: The Tax Debt Management *Jennifer, self-employed,* Los Angeles

- Owes IRS $35,000 in back taxes
- Current on mortgage and other bills
- Steady income but can't afford IRS payment plan
- Needs protection from IRS collection actions

How Chapter 13 Helps:

- Stop IRS levies and wage garnishments immediately
- Pay tax debt over 5 years without penalties or interest
- Maintain business operations without IRS pressure
- Discharge other debts to free up money for taxes

The Chapter 13 Payment Plan: How It Really Works

What Goes Into Your Monthly Payment

Your Chapter 13 payment isn't arbitrary - it's calculated based on your actual financial situation and legal requirements. The payment must cover:

Priority Debts (Must Be Paid in Full):

- Recent income taxes
- Payroll taxes if you owned a business
- Child support and alimony
- Certain other government debts

Secured Debt Arrears (Catch-Up Payments):

- Missed mortgage payments

- Missed car payments
- Other secured debt arrears

Administrative Expenses:

- Trustee fees (typically 6-10% of your payment)
- Attorney fees (often paid through the plan)

Unsecured Debts (Whatever You Can Afford):

- Credit cards
- Medical bills
- Personal loans
- Collection accounts

Payment Calculation Example

Jennifer and Mark, married, San Diego

- Combined take-home income: $6,500/month
- Essential expenses: $5,200/month
- Available for debt payment: $1,300/month

Their Chapter 13 Plan:

- Priority debts (taxes): $400/month
- Mortgage arrears: $350/month
- Trustee fees: $130/month
- Attorney fees: $75/month
- Unsecured creditors: $345/month
- **Total payment: $1,300/month**

After 5 Years:

- All priority debts paid in full
- Caught up on mortgage completely

- Paid about 25% to unsecured creditors
- Remaining $45,000 in credit card debt discharged

The "Best Interests" Test

Chapter 13 includes a crucial protection for creditors called the "best interests test." This requires that unsecured creditors receive **at least as much** as they would have received in a Chapter 7 liquidation.

What This Means: If you have $20,000 in non-exempt property that would be sold in Chapter 7, your Chapter 13 plan must pay unsecured creditors at least $20,000 over the life of the plan.

Real Example: *David owns a classic car worth $15,000 that's not exempt*

- In Chapter 7: Car would be sold, creditors get $15,000
- In Chapter 13: David keeps car but must pay creditors at least $15,000 over 3-5 years
- David chooses Chapter 13 to keep the car and pays $300/month for 5 years

Chapter 13's Unique Powers

Power 1: Stopping Foreclosure and Catching Up

The Immediate Relief: The moment you file Chapter 13, the automatic stay stops foreclosure proceedings - even if the sale is scheduled for the next day.

The Long-Term Solution: Unlike Chapter 7, which only provides temporary foreclosure relief, Chapter 13 allows you to catch up on missed payments over the life of your plan.

How It Works:

- Continue making regular monthly mortgage payments
- Spread past-due payments over 3-5 years as part of your plan
- Interest on arrears typically stops accruing
- Successfully complete the plan = keep your home

Real Example: *Sarah, Queens*, NY

- $24,000 behind on mortgage
- In Chapter 13: Pays $400/month for 5 years to catch up
- Much more affordable than trying to pay $24,000 lump sum
- Keeps home she's lived in for 20 years

Power 2: Cramming Down Car Loans

In certain situations, Chapter 13 allows you to reduce your car loan balance to the actual value of the vehicle - a process called "cramdown."

Cramdown Requirements:

- You've owned the car for **910 days or more** (about 2.5 years)
- The car is worth **less than you owe** on the loan
- The loan was used to purchase the vehicle (not a refinance)

How Cramdown Works:

- Car value becomes the new loan balance
- Remaining debt becomes unsecured and may be discharged
- Interest rate may also be reduced to market rates

Cramdown Example: *Michael, Buffalo*, NY

- Owes $18,000 on car loan
- Car is worth $12,000
- Owned for 3 years (qualifies for cramdown)
- **Result:** New loan balance of $12,000, $6,000 discharged

Power 3: Stripping Second Mortgages

If your home is "underwater" (you owe more on your first mortgage than the home is worth), Chapter 13 can eliminate second mortgages entirely.

Requirements for Lien Stripping:

- Home value is **less than** the first mortgage balance
- Second mortgage is **completely unsecured** by home value
- Must complete the Chapter 13 plan successfully

Lien Stripping Example: *Carlos and Elena, Los Angeles*

- Home value: $450,000
- First mortgage: $480,000
- Second mortgage: $75,000
- **Result:** Second mortgage treated as unsecured debt and potentially discharged

Power 4: Protecting Co-Signers

Chapter 13 provides special protection for co-signers on consumer debts, which Chapter 7 doesn't offer.

Co-Debtor Stay:

- Creditors cannot pursue co-signers while your Chapter 13 case is active
- Protection lasts as long as you're paying the debt through your plan
- Particularly valuable for family members who co-signed loans

Strategic Use: This protection can be crucial when family members have co-signed for:

- Student loans
- Car loans
- Personal loans
- Credit cards

Plan Length: 3 Years vs. 5 Years

How Plan Length Is Determined

Your plan length depends primarily on your income relative to your state's median income:

3-Year Plans:

- Available if your income is **below** the state median
- Minimum plan length is 36 months
- Can voluntarily extend to 5 years if beneficial

5-Year Plans:

- Required if your income is **above** the state median
- Maximum plan length is 60 months
- Cannot be shorter than 5 years

Strategic Considerations for Plan Length

Advantages of 3-Year Plans:

- Get out of bankruptcy sooner
- Less long-term commitment
- Lower total payments to creditors
- Faster path to discharge

Advantages of 5-Year Plans:

- Lower monthly payments
- More time to catch up on secured debts
- Better for complex financial situations
- May allow higher percentage to unsecured creditors

Real Comparison: *Lisa, single, Los Angeles, income $55,000 (below CA median)*

- **3-year option:** $800/month for 36 months = $28,800 total
- **5-year option:** $500/month for 60 months = $30,000 total
- Lisa chooses 3-year plan for faster completion despite higher

monthly payment

What Chapter 13 Can and Cannot Do

What Chapter 13 Can Accomplish

Debt Management:

- Reorganize all debts into one affordable payment
- Stop all collection activity immediately
- Discharge remaining eligible debt after plan completion
- Pay priority debts over time without penalties

Property Protection:

- Keep all property regardless of exemption status
- Stop foreclosure and catch up on mortgage over time
- Prevent car repossession and catch up on payments
- Protect business assets and maintain operations

Family Protection:

- Protect co-signers from collection efforts
- Maintain family stability during financial crisis
- Keep children in same schools and communities
- Preserve family assets and heirlooms

Special Powers:

- Cram down car loans to vehicle value
- Strip second mortgages if home is underwater
- Cure defaults on secured debts over time
- Modify payment terms on some contracts

What Chapter 13 Cannot Do

Non-Dischargeable Debts:

- Cannot eliminate student loans (except in rare hardship cases)
- Cannot discharge recent income taxes in most cases
- Cannot eliminate child support or alimony
- Cannot discharge criminal fines or restitution

Income Requirements:

- Cannot help if you don't have regular income
- Cannot work if your income is too irregular to support payments
- Cannot assist if your expenses exceed your income significantly

Commitment Requirements:

- Cannot provide relief if you can't commit to 3-5 years of payments
- Cannot work if you're unwilling to live under court supervision
- Cannot succeed without financial discipline and budgeting

Property Limitations:

- Cannot keep property if you can't afford ongoing payments
- Cannot protect property if you can't afford plan payments
- Cannot maintain lifestyle that exceeds your income

The Chapter 13 Process Overview

Phase 1: Filing and Plan Proposal (Month 1)

Initial Filing:

- File bankruptcy petition and supporting documents
- Propose initial payment plan
- Automatic stay goes into effect immediately

- Begin making plan payments within 30 days

Plan Requirements: Your plan must address:

- How you'll pay priority debts in full
- How you'll catch up on secured debt arrears
- How much unsecured creditors will receive
- How you'll maintain ongoing obligations

Phase 2: Plan Confirmation (Months 1-3)

Trustee Review:

- Trustee reviews your plan for feasibility
- May recommend modifications
- Ensures plan meets legal requirements
- Considers creditor objections

Creditor Input:

- Creditors can object to plan terms
- Court resolves disputes between parties
- Plan may be modified to address concerns
- Must satisfy "best interests" test

Confirmation Hearing:

- Court approves or denies your plan
- May be continued if modifications needed
- Once confirmed, plan becomes binding
- Payments continue throughout plan period

Phase 3: Plan Execution (Years 1-5)

Monthly Payments:

- Make payments to trustee, not directly to creditors
- Trustee distributes funds according to plan
- Must maintain employment and income
- Report significant income changes to court

Ongoing Obligations:

- Stay current on post-filing mortgage payments
- Maintain insurance on property
- Pay ongoing living expenses
- Comply with all plan terms

Plan Modifications:

- Can request modifications if circumstances change
- May need court approval for major changes
- Income changes may require plan adjustments
- Missed payments may lead to dismissal

Phase 4: Plan Completion and Discharge (Years 3-5)

Final Requirements:

- Complete all plan payments
- Take financial management course
- Maintain compliance with all plan terms
- Stay current on ongoing obligations

Discharge:

- Receive discharge of remaining eligible debts
- Protection from collection on discharged debts
- Retain all property
- Case closed successfully

Chapter 13 Eligibility Requirements

Income Requirements

Regular Income: You must have regular income sufficient to:

- Pay essential living expenses
- Fund a meaningful payment plan
- Support dependents
- Maintain property you want to keep

Sources of Regular Income:

- Employment (W-2 or self-employed)
- Social Security benefits
- Pension or retirement income
- Disability benefits
- Alimony or child support
- Rental income
- Any other predictable income source

Debt Limits

Chapter 13 has maximum debt limits (adjusted periodically):

Current Debt Limits (2025):

- **Secured debt:** $2,750,000
- **Unsecured debt:** $1,100,000
- **Total debt:** Cannot exceed these limits

What Counts as Debt:

- All scheduled debt regardless of disputes

- Contingent and unliquidated claims
- Both personal and business debts
- Secured and unsecured obligations

Previous Bankruptcy Restrictions

Time Limits Between Filings:

- **Chapter 13 to Chapter 13:** 2 years from previous filing
- **Chapter 7 to Chapter 13:** 4 years from previous filing
- **Chapter 13 to Chapter 7:** 6 years (with exceptions)

Previous Dismissals:

- Limited automatic stay if case dismissed within past year
- May need to prove good faith
- Additional restrictions may apply

Is Chapter 13 Right for You?

Chapter 13 Self-Assessment

Income and Employment:

- [ ] I have regular, predictable income
- [ ] My income is sufficient for essential expenses plus debt payments
- [ ] I am willing to live on a court-supervised budget for 3-5 years
- [ ] My employment is stable and likely to continue

Property and Assets:

- [ ] I have valuable property I want to protect
- [ ] My property exceeds exemption limits available in Chapter 7
- [ ] I am behind on mortgage or car payments but want to keep the property

- [ ] I have business assets that are essential to my livelihood

Debt Situation:

- [ ] My debts are within Chapter 13 limits
- [ ] I have significant secured debts I want to reorganize
- [ ] I don't qualify for Chapter 7 due to income or other factors
- [ ] I have priority debts that need to be paid over time

Personal Commitment:

- [ ] I am willing to commit to 3-5 years of monthly payments
- [ ] I understand the discipline required for successful completion
- [ ] I am prepared to live under court supervision
- [ ] I have realistic expectations about the process

When Chapter 13 Is Clearly Better Than Chapter 7

Homeowner Facing Foreclosure: Chapter 13's ability to stop foreclosure and allow catch-up payments over time makes it clearly superior for homeowners who want to save their homes.

High Income/Failed Means Test: If you don't qualify for Chapter 7 due to income, Chapter 13 provides debt relief that's otherwise unavailable.

Valuable Non-Exempt Property: If you would lose significant property in Chapter 7, Chapter 13 allows you to keep everything while paying creditors over time.

Co-Signer Protection Needed: Chapter 13's co-debtor stay protects family members and friends who co-signed your debts.

When Chapter 7 Might Be Better

Simple Debt Elimination: If you qualify for Chapter 7, have no property to protect, and want quick debt relief, Chapter 7's 3-4 month timeline is appealing.

Unstable Income: If your income is irregular or likely to change significantly, Chapter 7's lack of ongoing payment requirements may be better.

Limited Commitment Ability: If you cannot realistically commit to 3-5 years of payments, Chapter 7's shorter timeline may be more suitable.

Common Chapter 13 Misconceptions

"Chapter 13 Is for Rich People"

Reality: Chapter 13 is often used by working-class families to save their homes from foreclosure or protect essential property. The median income for Chapter 13 filers is often lower than people expect.

"You Have to Pay Back All Your Debts"

Reality: While you pay more to creditors than in Chapter 7, you often pay only a fraction of your unsecured debt. Many plans pay 10-25% to unsecured creditors, with the remainder discharged.

"Chapter 13 Is Harder on Your Credit"

Reality: Chapter 13 stays on your credit report for 7 years compared to Chapter 7's 10 years. Many creditors view Chapter 13 favorably because it shows effort to repay debts.

"You Can't Have Any Luxury in Chapter 13"

Reality: While you must live within your budget, Chapter 13 doesn't require poverty. You can include reasonable recreation and entertainment expenses in your budget.

"Chapter 13 Always Takes 5 Years"

Reality: Plan length depends on your income relative to state median. Many people qualify for 3-year plans, and some complete plans early.

Success Stories: Chapter 13 in Action

The Foreclosure Save: Robert and Maria's Story

Background: Robert and Maria, married with two children, Buffalo, NY. Combined income $68,000. Behind $22,000 on mortgage, foreclosure scheduled in 45 days.

The Crisis:

- Robert lost overtime work during economic downturn
- Used credit cards to maintain lifestyle
- Fell behind on mortgage when credit cards maxed out
- Facing loss of family home of 12 years

Chapter 13 Solution:

- Filed Chapter 13 three weeks before foreclosure sale
- Plan payment: $650/month for 5 years
- Mortgage arrears: $367/month for 5 years
- Unsecured creditors: $200/month (about 15% of debt)
- Trustee and attorney fees: $83/month

Outcome:

- Stopped foreclosure and kept family home
- Caught up on all mortgage payments over 5 years
- Discharged $45,000 in credit card debt
- Completed plan successfully and received discharge
- Family remained stable throughout process

Key Lessons:

- Chapter 13 can save homes even when foreclosure is imminent
- Monthly payments often less than previous debt obligations
- Family stability preserved during financial recovery

The Asset Protection: David's Business Rescue

Background: David, self-employed contractor, Sacramento. Income $85,000. Owns home, work trucks, and expensive tools. Accumulated debt during economic downturn.

The Challenge:

- Home equity: $45,000 (partially non-exempt)
- Work trucks: $30,000 equity
- Tools and equipment: $20,000
- Would lose significant property in Chapter 7
- Needed to maintain business operations

Chapter 13 Strategy:

- Protected all business assets
- Plan payment: $1,200/month for 5 years
- Paid creditors value of non-exempt property over time
- Maintained business operations throughout case
- Discharged remaining unsecured debt

Business Benefits:

- Continued earning income throughout case
- Protected essential business assets
- Maintained client relationships
- Avoided business interruption
- Emerged with stronger financial foundation

Final Results:

- Successfully completed 5-year plan
- Kept all property and business assets

- Discharged $38,000 in remaining debt
- Business more profitable after discharge
- Built emergency fund to prevent future crises

The High-Income Relief: Jennifer's Professional Recovery

Background: Jennifer, attorney, Manhattan. Income $120,000. Failed Chapter 7 means test. Accumulated debt during period of reduced income and family medical crisis.

The Situation:

- Income above NY median for single person
- Credit card debt: $78,000
- Student loans: $45,000 (non-dischargeable)
- Current on mortgage and other obligations
- Needed debt relief while maintaining professional standing

Chapter 13 Approach:

- 5-year plan required due to above-median income
- Plan payment: $1,400/month
- Priority debts (taxes): $200/month
- Unsecured creditors: $1,000/month (about 40% of debt)
- Trustee fees: $200/month

Professional Considerations:

- Maintained law practice throughout case
- No impact on professional licensing
- Continued earning full income
- Plan structured around professional obligations
- Completed plan ahead of schedule

Long-term Success:

- Discharged $35,000 in credit card debt
- Maintained professional career
- Built substantial emergency fund
- Purchased new home two years after discharge
- Now helps other professionals with financial planning

Your Chapter 13 Decision Framework

Financial Analysis Questions

Income Stability:

- Is my income regular and predictable?
- Will my income likely continue for 3-5 years?
- Can I afford plan payments plus living expenses?
- Do I have backup income sources if needed?

Property Evaluation:

- What property do I want to protect?
- How much would I lose in Chapter 7?
- Is the property worth the 3-5 year commitment?
- Can I maintain property during the plan?

Debt Composition:

- How much of my debt is secured vs. unsecured?
- Do I have significant priority debts?
- Am I behind on important secured debts?
- Will Chapter 13 provide meaningful debt relief?

Personal Commitment:

- Am I willing to live under court supervision?
- Can I commit to 3-5 years of payments?
- Do I have the discipline for long-term budgeting?
- Am I prepared for the emotional journey?

The Mathematical Test

Calculate Your Chapter 13 Payment:

1. **Monthly income:** (gross monthly income)
2. **Minus allowable expenses:** (IRS standards + actual necessary expenses)
3. **Equals disposable income:** (available for debt payments)
4. **Add priority debts:** (taxes, child support, etc.)
5. **Add secured arrears:** (missed mortgage/car payments)
6. **Add administrative costs:** (trustee and attorney fees)
7. **Remainder for unsecured:** (credit cards, medical bills)

Example Calculation:

- Monthly gross income: $7,000
- Allowable expenses: $5,500
- **Disposable income: $1,500**
- Priority debts: $300/month
- Mortgage arrears: $400/month
- Administrative costs: $200/month
- **Unsecured creditors: $600/month**

Making the Final Decision

Chapter 13 Makes Sense If:

- You can afford the calculated payment
- You have valuable property to protect
- You need Chapter 13's special powers (foreclosure prevention, cramdown, etc.)
- You don't qualify for Chapter 7
- You can commit to the long-term process

Chapter 7 Might Be Better If:

- You qualify for Chapter 7 and have no property at risk
- You want quick debt relief without long-term payments
- Your income is irregular or uncertain
- You cannot afford Chapter 13 payment calculations

The Bottom Line: Chapter 13 as a Powerful Tool

Chapter 13 bankruptcy is often misunderstood, but for the right person in the right situation, it can be more powerful than Chapter 7. It's particularly valuable for:

Homeowners: Who want to save their homes from foreclosure while reorganizing other debts.

Asset Owners: Who have valuable property they'd lose in Chapter 7 but want to keep.

High-Income Earners: Who don't qualify for Chapter 7 but still need debt relief.

Strategic Debtors: Who can benefit from Chapter 13's special powers like cramdown and lien stripping.

The Key to Success: Chapter 13 requires commitment, discipline, and realistic expectations. But for those who complete it successfully, it provides not just debt relief but a structured path to long-term financial stability.

Remember: Chapter 13 isn't punishment - it's reorganization. It's a tool that allows you to keep what's important to you while getting the debt relief you need to build a better financial future.

In the next chapter, we'll dive deep into how Chapter 13 payment plans actually work - how they're calculated, what gets paid first, and how to ensure your plan is both affordable and confirmable.

12

The Repayment Plan

How Chapter 13 Actually Works

The Repayment Plan: Your Financial GPS for the Next 3-5 Years

If Chapter 13 bankruptcy is a journey from overwhelming debt to financial stability, then your repayment plan is your GPS - it shows you exactly where you're going, how long it will take to get there, and what route you'll follow. Unlike the quick sprint of Chapter 7, Chapter 13 is a marathon with a carefully planned pace that allows you to keep your property while systematically addressing your debts.

But here's what many people don't understand: your Chapter 13 repayment plan isn't designed to punish you or make you pay back every penny you owe. It's designed to be **affordable based on your actual income and necessary expenses**, while providing creditors with a fair distribution of whatever you can reasonably pay.

In this chapter, we'll pull back the curtain on how Chapter 13 repayment plans actually work. You'll learn how payments are calculated, which debts get paid first, how to ensure your plan is both affordable and legally compliant, and what to do when life inevitably throws you curveballs during your 3-5 year journey.

Understanding the Repayment Plan Framework

What a Chapter 13 Plan Actually Is

Your Chapter 13 repayment plan is a **court-approved budget** that accomplishes several things simultaneously:

- **Organizes your debts** into categories with different treatment rules
- **Establishes a monthly payment** you can actually afford
- **Prioritizes certain debts** that must be paid in full
- **Addresses secured debt arrears** over time
- **Provides something to unsecured creditors** based on what you can afford
- **Creates a clear timeline** for completing your bankruptcy

Think of it as a contract between you, your creditors, and the bankruptcy court that says: "Here's exactly how I'll use my disposable income over the next 3-5 years to address my debts fairly and get a fresh start."

The Legal Requirements Your Plan Must Meet

Feasibility: Your plan must be something you can actually accomplish based on your income and expenses. The court won't approve a plan that sets you up for failure.

Good Faith: Your plan must represent an honest effort to repay creditors based on your circumstances. You can't hide income or inflate expenses to avoid paying what you can afford.

Best Interests Test: Unsecured creditors must receive at least as much as they would have received if you filed Chapter 7 instead.

Legal Minimums:

- Priority debts must be paid in full

- Secured debt arrears must be addressed
- Administrative expenses must be covered
- Plan must last 3-5 years depending on your income

The Debt Hierarchy: Who Gets Paid First

Priority Debts: First in Line (Must Be Paid 100%)

Why Priority Debts Come First: These are debts that Congress has determined are so important to society that they cannot be discharged in bankruptcy and must be paid in full.

Common Priority Debts:

Recent Income Taxes:

- Federal and state income taxes less than 3 years old
- Taxes for which returns were filed less than 2 years ago
- Taxes assessed less than 240 days ago
- **Payment benefit:** No additional penalties or interest in most cases

Payroll Taxes:

- Employee withholdings you collected but didn't pay to government
- Your portion of Social Security and Medicare taxes
- Unemployment taxes
- **Reality check:** These are serious debts that the IRS aggressively pursues

Domestic Support Obligations:

- Current and past-due child support
- Current and past-due alimony/spousal support
- **Important:** These continue to accrue during your case

Real Priority Debt Example: *Jennifer, self-employed consultant, Sacramento*

- Owes IRS $28,000 for 2021-2022 taxes
- Owes state $8,000 for same period
- Behind $12,000 on child support
- **Total priority debt:** $48,000
- **Must pay in full over plan:** $800/month for 5 years

Secured Debts: Keeping Your Property

What Makes a Debt "Secured": The creditor has a lien on specific property. If you don't pay, they can repossess or foreclose on that property.

Two Components of Secured Debt Treatment:

Ongoing Payments:

- Continue making regular monthly payments outside the plan
- Must stay current to keep the property
- Interest rates typically remain the same

Arrears (Past-Due Amounts):

- Missed payments are paid through the plan over 3-5 years
- Interest on arrears typically stops accruing
- Allows you to catch up without losing property

Secured Debt Strategy Example: *Robert and Maria, Buffalo, NY*

- **Mortgage:** $1,850/month (continue paying outside plan)
- **Mortgage arrears:** $22,000 behind (pay $367/month through plan)
- **Car payment:** $425/month (continue outside plan)
- **Car arrears:** $3,200 behind (pay $53/month through plan)

Administrative Expenses: The Cost of the Process

Trustee Fees:

- Typically 6-10% of your plan payment
- Covers trustee's administration of your case
- Built into your monthly payment automatically

Attorney Fees:

- Often paid through the plan rather than upfront
- Typically $3,000-$5,500 total
- Allows you to get representation even if you can't pay attorney fees before filing

Other Administrative Costs:

- Court filing fees
- Required courses and counseling
- Appraisal or valuation costs if needed

Unsecured Debts: What's Left Over

The Bottom of the Priority List: Unsecured creditors get whatever you can afford after paying priority debts, secured arrears, and administrative expenses.

Common Unsecured Debts:

- Credit card balances
- Medical bills
- Personal loans
- Collection accounts
- Deficiency balances from repossessions
- Most court judgments

The Reality: Many Chapter 13 plans pay only 10-25% to unsecured creditors, with the remainder discharged at the end of the plan.

Calculating Your Monthly Payment

Step 1: Determine Your Disposable Income

Current Monthly Income (CMI):

- Average gross income over past 6 months
- All household income from all sources
- Same calculation as Chapter 7 means test

Allowable Monthly Expenses:

- IRS national and local standards for basic living expenses
- Actual necessary expenses for certain categories
- Secured debt payments to maintain property
- Administrative expenses for the Chapter 13 case

Disposable Income Formula: Monthly Disposable Income = Current Monthly Income - Allowable Monthly Expenses

Step 2: Add Required Payments

Your monthly payment must cover:

Priority Debt Payments:

- Total priority debt ÷ plan length (36 or 60 months)
- Example: $36,000 in taxes ÷ 60 months = $600/month

Secured Debt Arrears:

- Total arrears ÷ plan length
- Example: $18,000 mortgage arrears ÷ 60 months = $300/month

Administrative Expenses:

- Trustee fees (6-10% of total payment)
- Attorney fees spread over plan length
- Example: $4,500 attorney fees ÷ 60 months = $75/month

Remainder for Unsecured Creditors:

- Whatever's left of your disposable income
- Sometimes $0 if priority and secured debts consume all available income

Real Payment Calculation Example

David and Sarah, married, San Diego, CA

- Combined gross income: $8,500/month
- Allowable expenses: $6,800/month
- **Disposable income: $1,700/month**

Required Payments:

- Priority debts (taxes): $450/month
- Mortgage arrears: $350/month
- Car arrears: $100/month
- Administrative costs (trustee + attorney): $200/month
- **Subtotal required: $1,100/month**

Remaining for unsecured creditors: $600/month Total plan payment: $1,700/month

What This Accomplishes:

- Pays $27,000 in taxes over 5 years
- Catches up on $21,000 in mortgage arrears
- Catches up on $6,000 in car arrears
- Pays $36,000 to unsecured creditors (about 30% of $120,000 owed)
- **Discharges remaining $84,000 in unsecured debt**

Plan Length: 3 Years vs. 5 Years

How Plan Length Is Determined

3-Year Plans (Below Median Income):

- Available if your income is below your state's median
- Can voluntarily extend to 5 years if beneficial
- Must pay at least what unsecured creditors would receive in Chapter 7

5-Year Plans (Above Median Income):

- Required if your income is above your state's median
- Must commit all disposable income for full 5 years
- Generally results in higher payments to creditors

Strategic Considerations

Advantages of Shorter Plans:

- Get out of bankruptcy supervision sooner
- Pay less total money to creditors
- Less long-term commitment required
- Lower risk of income changes affecting the plan

Advantages of Longer Plans:

- Lower monthly payments
- More time to catch up on secured debt arrears
- May allow completion when shorter plan wouldn't be affordable
- Spreads attorney fees over longer period

Real Comparison: *Lisa, single, income $62,000 (below CA median of $68,000)*

3-Year Option:

- Monthly payment: $900
- Total paid: $32,400

- Completed in 36 months

5-Year Option:

- Monthly payment: $650
- Total paid: $39,000
- Completed in 60 months

Lisa chooses the 3-year plan despite higher monthly payments because she wants to complete bankruptcy sooner and pay less total money.

Making Your Monthly Payments

The Trustee Payment System

How Payments Work:

- You make one monthly payment to the Chapter 13 trustee
- Trustee distributes money to creditors according to your plan
- You don't pay creditors directly (except ongoing secured debts)
- Trustee handles all the accounting and distribution

Payment Methods:

Payroll Deduction (Most Common):

- Automatic deduction from your paycheck
- Ensures payments are never late
- Required in many districts
- Reduces risk of dismissal for missed payments

Direct Payment:

- You send payment directly to trustee
- Monthly responsibility to make timely payments
- More risk if you forget or have cash flow issues

- Some trustees prefer this for self-employed debtors

When Payments Start:

- Usually within 30 days of filing
- Continue even before plan confirmation
- Must maintain payments throughout the entire case

Staying Current on Ongoing Obligations

What You Pay Outside the Plan:

Ongoing Mortgage Payments:

- Regular monthly mortgage payments
- Property taxes and insurance
- HOA fees if applicable
- Must stay current to keep your home

Ongoing Car Payments:

- Regular monthly car payments
- Insurance and registration
- Must stay current to keep your vehicle

Post-Filing Living Expenses:

- Utilities and housing costs
- Food and necessary expenses
- Insurance premiums
- Other essential living costs

The Two-Payment Reality: Most Chapter 13 debtors effectively have two payment obligations:

1. **Plan payment** to the trustee
2. **Ongoing payments** for secured debts and living expenses

Plan Modifications: When Life Changes

Why Modifications May Be Necessary

Income Changes:

- Job loss or reduction in hours
- New employment with different pay
- Spouse's income changes
- Disability or retirement

Expense Changes:

- Unexpected medical bills
- Family changes (new baby, divorce)
- Home or car repairs
- Changes in insurance costs

Debt Changes:

- New priority debts (recent taxes)
- Secured debt payoffs
- Discovery of additional creditors

Types of Plan Modifications

Payment Amount Changes:

- Increase or decrease monthly payment
- Adjust payment to creditor categories
- Extend or shorten plan length (within limits)

Creditor Treatment Changes:

- Add newly discovered creditors

- Address new priority debts
- Modify secured debt treatment

Plan Structure Changes:

- Change from 3-year to 5-year plan
- Modify administrative expense treatment
- Adjust timing of payments

The Modification Process

Step 1: Recognize the Need

- Don't wait until you've missed payments
- Contact your attorney as soon as circumstances change
- Document the reasons for needed changes

Step 2: File Motion to Modify

- Formal request to the court
- Explanation of changed circumstances
- Proposed new plan terms

Step 3: Notice to Creditors

- All creditors notified of proposed changes
- Opportunity to object to modifications
- Hearing scheduled if there are objections

Step 4: Court Approval

- Judge reviews modification request
- Considers feasibility and good faith
- Approves or denies the modification

Real Modification Example

Jennifer, Buffalo, NY - Job Loss Scenario

- **Original plan:** $850/month for 5 years
- **Crisis:** Lost job, new job pays $800/month less
- **Modification request:** Reduce payment to $400/month, extend plan to maximum 60 months
- **Outcome:** Court approved modification, Jennifer completed modified plan successfully

Plan Confirmation: Getting Court Approval

The Confirmation Process

Initial Plan Filing:

- Plan filed with initial bankruptcy petition
- May be modified before confirmation hearing
- Trustee and creditors review proposed terms

Trustee Recommendation:

- Trustee analyzes plan feasibility
- Reviews compliance with legal requirements
- Makes recommendation to court

Creditor Input:

- Creditors can object to plan terms
- Common objections involve payment amounts or feasibility
- Must be resolved before confirmation

Confirmation Hearing:

- Usually 20-75 days after filing
- Court reviews plan and any objections
- Debtor may need to testify about feasibility

- Judge confirms or denies the plan

Requirements for Confirmation

Legal Standards:

Feasibility:

- Plan must be workable based on your income and expenses
- Court considers your payment history and employment stability
- Must show ability to complete the plan successfully

Good Faith:

- Plan represents honest effort to repay creditors
- Not filed primarily to delay creditors
- Fair treatment of all creditor classes

Best Interests Test:

- Unsecured creditors must receive at least what they'd get in Chapter 7
- Calculated based on your non-exempt property value
- Protects creditors from unfair treatment

Compliance with Law:

- Meets all Chapter 13 requirements
- Proper treatment of different debt types
- Appropriate plan length for your income level

Common Confirmation Issues

Feasibility Problems:

- Income insufficient to support proposed payments
- Unrealistic expense budgets

- Unstable employment history

Treatment Issues:

- Inadequate payments to priority creditors
- Improper secured debt treatment
- Unfair discrimination between creditors

Documentation Problems:

- Missing required financial information
- Inconsistent income or expense reporting
- Inadequate proof of changed circumstances

Managing Your Plan Successfully

Keys to Plan Success

Budget Discipline:

- Live within the confirmed plan budget
- Track expenses carefully
- Avoid unnecessary debt
- Build small emergency fund if possible

Payment Consistency:

- Never miss trustee payments
- Stay current on ongoing secured debts
- Pay attention to payment due dates
- Contact trustee immediately if problems arise

Communication:

- Report income changes promptly
- Notify court of address changes

- Respond quickly to trustee requests
- Keep attorney informed of any issues

Long-term Perspective:

- Focus on successful completion
- Remember the benefits of plan completion
- Stay motivated during difficult periods
- Celebrate milestones along the way

Warning Signs to Watch For

Financial Red Flags:

- Struggling to make plan payments
- Using credit cards for living expenses
- Behind on ongoing mortgage or car payments
- New debt accumulating

Life Changes:

- Job loss or significant income reduction
- Major unexpected expenses
- Family changes affecting budget
- Health issues affecting income or expenses

Legal Issues:

- Missed trustee payments
- Creditor complaints or motions
- Trustee requests for additional information
- Court notices or deadlines

What Happens If You Can't Complete Your Plan

Conversion to Chapter 7:

- May be possible if you qualify
- Eliminates remaining unsecured debt quickly
- May lose property you were protecting in Chapter 13

Hardship Discharge:

- Available in rare circumstances
- Must show circumstances beyond your control
- Very difficult to obtain

Voluntary Dismissal:

- You can dismiss your case voluntarily
- Loses all bankruptcy protection
- Creditors can resume collection activities

Involuntary Dismissal:

- Court dismisses case for non-compliance
- Usually due to missed payments or plan violations
- May be able to refile if circumstances improve

Special Plan Provisions

Cramdown of Secured Debts

How Cramdown Works in Your Plan: When you have a car loan that qualifies for cramdown:

- **Secured portion:** Equal to car's current value
- **Unsecured portion:** Remainder of loan balance
- **Plan treatment:** Pay secured portion with interest, unsecured portion may be discharged

Cramdown Example: *Michael, Sacramento, CA*

- Car loan balance: $22,000
- Car current value: $14,000
- **Plan treatment:** $14,000 paid as secured debt, $8,000 treated as unsecured debt
- **Interest rate:** Reduced to current market rate
- **Result:** Saves Michael approximately $8,000 plus interest

Lien Stripping Procedures

Second Mortgage Elimination: When your home's value is less than your first mortgage:

- Second mortgage becomes unsecured debt
- Paid through plan like other unsecured debt
- Lien permanently removed after plan completion

Lien Strip Example: *Carlos and Elena, Los Angeles*

- Home value: $480,000
- First mortgage: $520,000
- Second mortgage: $85,000
- **Result:** Second mortgage treated as unsecured debt, potentially discharged

Priority Debt Management

Tax Debt Payment Strategy:

- Spread tax payments over plan length
- No additional penalties or interest
- Maintain compliance with current tax obligations
- Often much better than IRS payment plans

Child Support Catch-Up:

- Past-due support paid through plan
- Current support continues outside plan
- Protects wages from additional garnishment
- Helps maintain family relationships

Plan Completion and Discharge

Final Plan Requirements

Payment Completion:

- All plan payments made in full
- No outstanding balances to trustee
- Compliance with all plan terms throughout case

Current Obligations:

- Ongoing mortgage payments current
- Ongoing car payments current
- All post-petition taxes filed and paid
- Child support obligations current

Final Education:

- Complete financial management course
- File certificate with court
- Usually required before discharge

The Chapter 13 Discharge

What Gets Discharged:

- Remaining balances on unsecured debts included in plan
- Some debts that wouldn't be discharged in Chapter 7

- Certain tax debts older than 3 years
- Some divorce-related property settlement debts

What Survives Discharge:

- Student loans (except rare hardship cases)
- Recent tax debts
- Child support and alimony
- Criminal fines and restitution
- Debts incurred after filing

Discharge Benefits:

- Permanent elimination of discharged debts
- Legal protection from collection efforts
- Fresh start with significantly reduced debt load
- Ability to rebuild credit and financial stability

Life After Plan Completion

Immediate Benefits:

- No more trustee payments
- Freedom from court supervision
- Significant reduction in total debt burden
- Improved monthly cash flow

Credit Impact:

- Chapter 13 notation remains for 7 years from filing
- Often easier to rebuild credit than after Chapter 7
- Demonstrates commitment to repaying debts
- May qualify for conventional credit sooner

Financial Lessons:

- Improved budgeting and money management skills
- Understanding of credit and debt consequences
- Appreciation for financial stability and emergency funds
- Knowledge to avoid future financial problems

Your Plan Success Strategy

Pre-Confirmation Preparation

60 Days Before Filing:

- [ ] Calculate realistic disposable income
- [ ] Identify all priority and secured debts
- [ ] Determine appropriate plan length
- [ ] Choose experienced Chapter 13 attorney

30 Days Before Filing:

- [ ] Finalize plan payment amount
- [ ] Ensure plan meets all legal requirements
- [ ] Prepare for immediate payment obligations
- [ ] Set up payroll deduction if required

During Your Plan

Monthly Habits:

- [ ] Make all trustee payments on time
- [ ] Stay current on ongoing secured debts
- [ ] Track expenses and stay within budget
- [ ] Report any income changes immediately

Annual Reviews:

- [ ] Review plan performance with attorney
- [ ] Assess need for modifications
- [ ] File required annual reports
- [ ] Celebrate milestones and progress

Preparing for Completion

Final Year:

- [ ] Ensure all payments are current
- [ ] Complete financial management course
- [ ] Verify compliance with all plan terms
- [ ] Prepare for post-discharge financial planning

After Discharge:

- [ ] Update credit reports to reflect discharge
- [ ] Begin credit rebuilding strategies
- [ ] Build emergency fund for future stability
- [ ] Apply lessons learned to future financial decisions

Common Plan Pitfalls and How to Avoid Them

Payment Problems

The Problem: Missing trustee payments or falling behind on ongoing obligations **The Solution:** Set up automatic payments, communicate early about problems, request modifications when needed

Prevention Strategies:

- Use payroll deduction for trustee payments
- Set up automatic payments for mortgage and car
- Build small buffer in budget for unexpected expenses

- Monitor payment accounts regularly

Income Reporting Issues

The Problem: Failing to report income changes or new income sources **The Solution:** Report all income changes within 14 days, update schedules as required

What to Report:

- Job changes or promotions
- New income sources
- Changes in spouse's income
- Bonus or overtime income
- Tax refunds or windfalls

Budget Inflation

The Problem: Gradually increasing spending beyond plan budget **The Solution:** Regular budget reviews, strict spending discipline, focus on plan completion goals

Warning Signs:

- Using credit cards for living expenses
- Struggling to make required payments
- Accumulating new debt during the plan
- Living paycheck to paycheck despite plan relief

The Bottom Line: Your Roadmap to Success

A Chapter 13 repayment plan isn't just a payment schedule - it's a comprehensive financial rehabilitation program that provides structure, protection, and a clear path to debt freedom. Success requires:

Realistic Planning:

- Base your plan on accurate income and expense projections

- Include reasonable buffers for unexpected circumstances
- Choose appropriate plan length for your situation

Consistent Execution:

- Make all payments on time, every time
- Stay current on ongoing obligations
- Live within your confirmed budget

Proactive Management:

- Communicate changes promptly
- Request modifications when needed
- Monitor your progress regularly

Long-term Perspective:

- Focus on successful completion, not perfection
- Remember the benefits you're working toward
- Use the experience to build lasting financial skills

The Reward: Successful Chapter 13 completion provides not just debt relief, but financial education, improved money management skills, and the satisfaction of having met your obligations while protecting what matters most to you.

Your Chapter 13 plan is your roadmap from financial crisis to financial stability. Follow it consistently, communicate openly about challenges, and keep your eyes on the destination: a genuine fresh start with the property and stability you've worked to protect.

In the next chapter, we'll explore how Chapter 13 specifically handles mortgages and car loans - the secured debts that are often the reason people choose Chapter 13 over Chapter 7.

13

Mortgages and Cars

Secured Debts in Chapter 13

The Property Protection Chapter

For most people considering Chapter 13 bankruptcy, the decision comes down to one crucial question: "How can I keep my house and car?" Unlike Chapter 7, which offers limited tools for dealing with secured debts, Chapter 13 was specifically designed to help people keep their essential property while reorganizing their finances.

This is where Chapter 13 truly shines. It provides powerful tools that simply don't exist anywhere else in the legal system: the ability to stop foreclosure dead in its tracks and catch up on missed payments over time, the power to reduce car loan balances to the actual value of your vehicle, and even the ability to eliminate second mortgages entirely in certain situations.

If you're behind on your mortgage, facing foreclosure, struggling with an underwater car loan, or trying to protect property that has special meaning to you, Chapter 13 might be the most powerful tool available to you. In this chapter, we'll explore exactly how Chapter 13 handles secured debts, what options are available to you, and how to use these tools strategically to protect what matters most.

Understanding Secured Debt in Bankruptcy

What Makes a Debt "Secured"

A **secured debt** is a loan that's backed by specific collateral. If you don't pay, the creditor has the legal right to take that collateral through repossession or foreclosure. This gives secured creditors much more power than unsecured creditors, but it also means the debt is tied to property you may desperately want to keep.

Common Secured Debts:

- **Mortgages:** Secured by your home
- **Car loans:** Secured by your vehicle
- **Home equity loans/lines of credit:** Secured by your home
- **Purchase money security interests:** Furniture, appliances, electronics bought on credit
- **Judgment liens:** Court judgments that attach to your property

How Chapter 13 Changes the Game

Chapter 7's Limited Options: In Chapter 7, you basically have two choices with secured debt:

1. **Keep the property and keep paying** (stay current on payments)
2. **Surrender the property** (give it back and discharge any deficiency)

Chapter 13's Powerful Tools: Chapter 13 offers much more sophisticated options:

1. **Cure and maintain:** Catch up on missed payments over time while staying current going forward
2. **Cramdown:** Reduce loan balances to current property value
3. **Lien stripping:** Eliminate second mortgages and other junior liens
4. **Rate modification:** Sometimes reduce interest rates to current market rates

5. **Term extension:** Spread payments over the life of your plan

The Two-Payment Structure

Understanding Your Obligations: In Chapter 13, secured debts typically involve two separate payment streams:

Ongoing Payments (Outside the Plan):

- Regular monthly mortgage payments
- Regular monthly car payments
- Continue as if bankruptcy never happened
- Must stay current to keep the property

Arrearage Payments (Through the Plan):

- Past-due amounts paid through your Chapter 13 plan
- Spread over 3-5 years
- Often without additional interest or penalties
- Administered by the bankruptcy trustee

Saving Your Home: Mortgage Treatment in Chapter 13

The Foreclosure Emergency

The Crisis Timeline: When you fall behind on mortgage payments, foreclosure follows a predictable but accelerating timeline:

- **30-60 days:** Late notices and fees
- **90+ days:** Default notices and acceleration demands
- **120+ days:** Foreclosure proceedings begin
- **6-18 months:** Foreclosure sale (timing varies by state)

Chapter 13's Immediate Relief: The moment you file Chapter 13, the **automatic stay** stops foreclosure proceedings completely, even if the sale is scheduled for the next day. This immediate protection gives you breathing room to propose a plan for catching up.

How Mortgage Arrears Work in Chapter 13

The Cure and Maintain Approach: Chapter 13 allows you to "cure" your mortgage default by paying past-due amounts over time while "maintaining" current payments going forward.

Arrears Calculation Example: *Jennifer and Mark, married, Sacramento*

- Monthly mortgage payment: $2,450
- Missed payments: 8 months
- Late fees and costs: $3,200
- **Total arrears:** $22,800 ($19,600 + $3,200)
- **Plan treatment:** $380/month for 5 years to cure arrears
- **Ongoing obligation:** Continue $2,450/month outside the plan

Interest on Arrears: In most cases, **interest stops accruing on mortgage arrears** once they're included in your Chapter 13 plan. This can save thousands of dollars compared to trying to catch up outside of bankruptcy.

Pre-Foreclosure vs. Post-Foreclosure Filing

Before Foreclosure Sale:

- Automatic stay stops foreclosure immediately
- Can cure all defaults through the plan
- Resume normal mortgage relationship after completion
- Keep all ownership rights and equity

After Foreclosure Sale:

- Generally too late to save the home
- Property ownership has transferred to new owner
- Chapter 13 cannot reverse completed foreclosures

- **Timing is crucial - don't wait until the last minute**

Real Foreclosure Save Example

Background: Robert and Linda, Buffalo, NY

- Home value: $195,000
- Mortgage balance: $148,000
- Monthly payment: $1,385
- Behind: $16,650 (12 months of payments)
- Foreclosure sale scheduled in 30 days

Chapter 13 Solution:

- Filed bankruptcy 3 weeks before sale
- Automatic stay stopped foreclosure immediately
- Plan payment included $277/month for 5 years to cure arrears
- Continued $1,385/month mortgage payments outside plan

Outcome:

- Saved family home of 18 years
- Children remained in same school district
- Total cost: $277/month vs. impossible lump sum
- Successfully completed plan and kept home

Second Mortgages and Home Equity Lines

When You Can Strip Second Mortgages: If your home's current value is **less than** what you owe on your first mortgage, Chapter 13 can treat second mortgages as unsecured debt.

Lien Stripping Requirements:

- Home value must be less than first mortgage balance
- Second mortgage must be completely "underwater"

- Must complete the entire Chapter 13 plan
- Lien is permanently removed after plan completion

Lien Stripping Example: *Carlos and Elena,* Los *Angeles*

- Home current value: $420,000
- First mortgage balance: $445,000
- Second mortgage balance: $75,000
- **Result:** Second mortgage treated as unsecured debt in plan
- **Potential savings:** $75,000 plus interest

Partial Lien Stripping: If there's some equity to support the second mortgage but not the full amount, you may be able to reduce the second mortgage to the available equity amount.

Strategic Timing: Lien stripping depends on current home values. If home values are rising, it may be worth waiting. If they're falling, acting quickly may be beneficial.

Keeping Your Vehicle: Car Loan Treatment

The Transportation Necessity

Why Vehicle Protection Matters: For most Americans, a reliable vehicle isn't a luxury - it's essential for:

- Getting to work and maintaining employment
- Transporting children to school and activities
- Medical appointments and emergencies
- Basic errands and life activities

Chapter 13's Vehicle Protection: Unlike Chapter 7, which offers limited help if you're behind on car payments, Chapter 13 provides powerful tools to keep your vehicle while addressing payment problems.

Curing Car Loan Arrears

How Car Arrears Work: Similar to mortgages, you can catch up on missed car payments through your Chapter 13 plan while continuing regular payments outside the plan.

Car Arrearage Example: *Michael, single, San Diego*

- Monthly car payment: $485
- Behind: 4 months = $1,940
- Late fees: $280
- **Total arrears:** $2,220
- **Plan treatment:** $37/month for 5 years
- **Ongoing payment:** Continue $485/month outside plan

Cramdown: Reducing Your Car Loan Balance

What Is Cramdown? Cramdown allows you to reduce your car loan balance to the current fair market value of the vehicle, treating the rest as unsecured debt.

Cramdown Requirements:

- You must have owned the vehicle for **910 days or more** (about 2.5 years)
- The loan must be for the **purchase of the vehicle** (not a refinance)
- The vehicle must be worth **less than the loan balance**
- You must complete your Chapter 13 plan successfully

Cramdown Calculation Example: *Sarah, Buffalo, NY*

- Current loan balance: $19,500
- Vehicle current value: $12,000
- **Secured portion:** $12,000 (must be paid with interest)
- **Unsecured portion:** $7,500 (treated like credit card debt)
- **Interest rate:** Often reduced to current market rate
- **Savings:** $7,500 plus interest over life of loan

Vehicle Valuation for Cramdown

Valuation Sources:

- **Kelley Blue Book (KBB):** Most commonly accepted
- **Edmunds:** Alternative valuation source
- **Local dealer quotes:** Sometimes used for unique vehicles
- **Professional appraisals:** For high-value or unusual vehicles

Which Value to Use:

- **Retail value:** What you'd pay at a dealer
- **Private party value:** What you'd pay from individual
- **Trade-in value:** What dealer would give you in trade
- **Courts typically use retail or private party value**

Condition Adjustments:

- **Excellent condition:** Above average value
- **Good condition:** Average value
- **Fair condition:** Below average value
- **Poor condition:** Significant reductions

Multiple Vehicle Situations

Primary Vehicle:

- Usually gets full protection under cramdown rules
- Essential for work and family transportation
- Courts generally supportive of keeping

Secondary Vehicle:

- May face more scrutiny from trustee and court
- Must justify necessity (spouse's work, teen driver, etc.)

- May need to show it's more economical than alternatives

Luxury or Recreational Vehicles:

- Boats, RVs, motorcycles face higher scrutiny
- Must show they're necessary, not luxury items
- May be required to surrender if payments strain budget

Real Vehicle Cramdown Success

Background: David, Sacramento, CA

- 2019 pickup truck essential for construction work
- Original loan: $45,000
- Current balance: $32,000
- Current truck value: $22,000
- Owned for 3 years (qualifies for cramdown)

Cramdown Result:

- Secured debt: $22,000 at 6% interest
- Unsecured debt: $10,000 (may be discharged)
- New payment: $350/month vs. original $525/month
- **Total savings:** Over $15,000 including interest

Work Impact:

- Kept essential work vehicle
- Maintained employment and income
- Used savings to stabilize other financial areas

Strategic Decisions: Keep, Surrender, or Replace

The Keep vs. Surrender Analysis

Factors Supporting Keeping Property:

Financial Factors:

- Current on payments or can afford catch-up through plan
- Property value supports the debt amount
- Ongoing payments fit within post-bankruptcy budget
- Property is essential for employment or family stability

Personal Factors:

- Emotional attachment or family significance
- Stability for children and family
- Specialized needs (wheelchair accessible, etc.)
- Community ties and established relationships

Factors Supporting Surrender:

Financial Factors:

- Payments are unaffordable even with Chapter 13 help
- Property is significantly underwater
- Better alternatives available at lower cost
- Maintenance and upkeep costs are excessive

Strategic Factors:

- Surrender creates more money for other priorities
- Simpler budget and financial management
- Opportunity to relocate or downsize appropriately
- Freedom from long-term payment obligations

Real Decision-Making Examples

Example 1: The Underwater Home *Jennifer, single, Las Vegas*

- Home value: $180,000
- Mortgage balance: $285,000
- Monthly payment: $2,150 (50% of income)
- **Decision:** Surrender home, rent affordable apartment
- **Result:** $1,500/month savings, much more manageable budget

Example 2: The Family Home Save *Robert and Maria, Buffalo*

- Home value: $195,000
- Mortgage balance: $148,000
- Children established in school district
- Behind on payments due to temporary income loss
- **Decision:** Use Chapter 13 to catch up and keep home
- **Result:** Family stability maintained, payments manageable

Example 3: The Vehicle Strategy *Michael, Los Angeles*

- Car 1: 2018 Civic, reliable, moderate payment
- Car 2: 2019 truck, expensive, rarely used
- **Decision:** Keep Civic through cramdown, surrender truck
- **Result:** Reduced transportation costs, eliminated unnecessary debt

When Replacement Makes Sense

Vehicle Replacement Strategy: Sometimes it makes sense to surrender an expensive vehicle and purchase a more affordable replacement:

Surrender Scenarios:

- Current vehicle payment too high for budget
- Vehicle unreliable or requiring expensive repairs
- Significantly underwater on loan
- Don't qualify for beneficial cramdown

Replacement Considerations:

- Must get court approval for major purchases during Chapter 13
- Should choose reliable, affordable transportation
- Consider certified pre-owned vehicles with warranties
- Focus on necessity, not luxury features

Ongoing Payment Management

Staying Current on Secured Debts

The Critical Importance: While Chapter 13 helps you catch up on past-due amounts, you must **stay current on ongoing payments** to keep your property. This means:

For Your Home:

- Regular monthly mortgage payments
- Property taxes and insurance
- HOA fees and assessments
- Maintenance and basic repairs

For Your Vehicle:

- Monthly loan payments
- Insurance premiums
- Registration and licensing
- Basic maintenance and repairs

Payment Modification During Chapter 13

Loan Modification Options: You may be able to negotiate loan modifications even while in Chapter 13:

Mortgage Modifications:

- Interest rate reductions
- Term extensions
- Principal reductions (rare)
- Conversion from adjustable to fixed rate

Auto Loan Modifications:

- Interest rate adjustments
- Term extensions
- Payment deferrals for temporary hardship

Court Approval Required: Any modification of secured debt terms during Chapter 13 requires court approval to ensure it doesn't interfere with your plan.

Insurance Requirements

Maintaining Adequate Coverage:

Homeowner's Insurance:

- Required by mortgage lender
- Must maintain sufficient coverage levels
- Liability protection essential
- Consider umbrella policies for high-value homes

Auto Insurance:

- Required by law and lender
- Comprehensive and collision coverage required
- Liability limits must meet lender requirements
- Consider gap coverage for newer vehicles

Insurance Lapses: Allowing insurance to lapse can result in:

- Lender purchasing expensive "force-placed" insurance

- Potential default on loan terms
- Complications with Chapter 13 plan
- Risk of losing property protection

Special Situations and Advanced Strategies

Business Vehicle Protection

Commercial Vehicle Considerations: If your vehicle is essential for business operations:

Enhanced Protection:

- Courts more likely to approve cramdown
- Business necessity supports higher payments
- May qualify for faster depreciation schedules
- Essential tool protection under exemptions

Documentation Requirements:

- Business use records and mileage logs
- Income dependence on vehicle use
- Cost comparison with alternatives
- Professional necessity documentation

Investment Property in Chapter 13

Rental Property Challenges: Investment properties face special scrutiny in Chapter 13:

Income Considerations:

- Rental income must be reported and may affect plan
- Vacancy and maintenance risks considered
- Cash flow analysis required

- May need to demonstrate profitability

Strategic Options:

- Keep if genuinely profitable and manageable
- Surrender if drain on resources
- Sell through plan if equity available
- Convert to primary residence if applicable

Tax Consequences of Debt Relief

Forgiven Debt Income: When debt is forgiven or discharged, it may create taxable income:

Chapter 13 Discharge:

- Generally not taxable income
- Insolvency exception typically applies
- Different rules for business vs. personal debt
- Consult tax professional for complex situations

Cramdown Tax Issues:

- Generally no immediate tax consequence
- May affect depreciation basis for business vehicles
- Future sale may trigger different tax treatment

Common Secured Debt Mistakes

Filing Too Late

The Foreclosure Timing Problem: Many people wait until the last possible moment to file Chapter 13, creating unnecessary stress and complications:

Better Approach:

- File as soon as you know you can't catch up on your own

- Don't wait for formal foreclosure proceedings
- Earlier filing provides more options and flexibility
- Reduces stress and allows better planning

Unrealistic Payment Plans

The Affordability Trap: Some people propose Chapter 13 plans they can't actually afford:

Common Mistakes:

- Underestimating ongoing maintenance costs
- Failing to budget for property taxes and insurance
- Ignoring other essential expenses
- Overestimating future income stability

Better Strategy:

- Create realistic budgets including all property costs
- Build in small buffers for unexpected expenses
- Consider downsizing if payments are truly unaffordable
- Get professional help with budget analysis

Ignoring Property Condition

The Maintenance Reality: Keeping property means ongoing responsibility for maintenance and repairs:

Hidden Costs:

- Deferred maintenance coming due
- Major systems nearing replacement (HVAC, roof, etc.)
- Vehicle maintenance and repair needs
- Property tax increases and insurance changes

Planning Approach:

- Assess condition honestly before committing to keep property
- Budget for predictable maintenance and repairs
- Consider age and condition in keep/surrender decision
- Build emergency fund for unexpected problems

Success Strategies for Secured Debt Management

Pre-Filing Planning

60-90 Days Before Filing:

- [ ] Assess all secured property honestly
- [ ] Calculate true cost of keeping each asset
- [ ] Research current values for cramdown potential
- [ ] Evaluate alternatives (rental, different vehicle, etc.)
- [ ] Consult with experienced Chapter 13 attorney

30 Days Before Filing:

- [ ] Finalize keep/surrender decisions
- [ ] Ensure ongoing payments are current if possible
- [ ] Gather all loan documents and statements
- [ ] Document business use of vehicles if applicable
- [ ] Prepare realistic budget including property costs

During Your Chapter 13 Case

Monthly Habits:

- [ ] Make all ongoing secured debt payments on time
- [ ] Maintain required insurance coverage
- [ ] Keep property in good repair

- [ ] Monitor payment accounts for any issues

Annual Reviews:

- [ ] Assess property values for potential modifications
- [ ] Review insurance coverage and adjust as needed
- [ ] Plan for predictable maintenance and repairs
- [ ] Consider refinancing opportunities as credit improves

Preparing for Plan Completion

Final Year Strategies:

- [ ] Assess refinancing opportunities
- [ ] Plan for post-discharge property management
- [ ] Build emergency fund for future repairs
- [ ] Consider property improvements that add value

Post-Discharge Planning:

- [ ] Refinance if beneficial rates available
- [ ] Establish property maintenance schedules
- [ ] Build long-term wealth through property appreciation
- [ ] Help others facing similar secured debt challenges

Real Success Stories: Secured Debt Saves

The Foreclosure Prevention: Maria's Story

Background: Maria, single mother, Sacramento, CA. Nurse earning $68,000/year. Behind on mortgage due to medical leave for surgery.

Crisis Situation:

- Home value: $385,000
- Mortgage balance: $298,000

- Monthly payment: $2,180
- Behind: $17,440 (8 months)
- Foreclosure sale scheduled in 6 weeks

Chapter 13 Solution:

- Filed 4 weeks before sale
- Plan included $291/month for 5 years to cure arrears
- Continued $2,180/month mortgage outside plan
- Discharged $28,000 in medical debt that caused the crisis

Long-term Outcome:

- Successfully completed 5-year plan
- Kept family home and neighborhood stability
- Children remained in same schools
- Home value increased to $465,000 during plan
- Built $167,000 in equity by plan completion

The Vehicle Cramdown: David's Business Rescue

Background: David, self-employed electrician, Buffalo, NY. Needed work truck but underwater on loan due to rapid depreciation.

Vehicle Situation:

- 2018 Ford F-250 work truck
- Original loan: $52,000
- Current balance: $38,000
- Current truck value: $28,000
- Essential for electrical contracting business

Cramdown Strategy:

- Owned truck for over 3 years (qualified for cramdown)

- Reduced secured debt to $28,000
- $10,000 became unsecured debt
- Interest rate reduced from 8.5% to 5.5%
- New payment: $425/month vs. original $615/month

Business Benefits:

- Kept essential work vehicle
- Reduced monthly overhead by $190
- Used savings to purchase additional tools
- Expanded business during Chapter 13 plan
- Built emergency fund for future vehicle needs

The Strategic Surrender: Jennifer's Fresh Start

Background: Jennifer, divorced, Long Island, NY. Struggling with underwater home and expensive car after divorce settlement.

Property Analysis:

- Home value: $420,000
- Mortgage balance: $485,000
- Monthly payment: $3,200 (65% of income)
- Car loan: $650/month for luxury SUV
- Total property payments: $3,850/month

Strategic Decision:

- Surrendered underwater home (saved $3,200/month)
- Surrendered expensive SUV (saved $650/month)
- Rented affordable apartment ($1,800/month)
- Purchased reliable used car ($285/month)
- **Net monthly savings: $1,965**

Life Improvement:

- Moved to better school district
- Children adjusted well to new home
- Built substantial emergency fund
- Eliminated commute stress
- Achieved work-life balance
- Purchased appropriate home 3 years later with FHA loan

Your Secured Debt Action Plan

Assessment Phase

Property Evaluation:

- [ ] List all secured debts and current property values
- [ ] Calculate total monthly payments including insurance, taxes, maintenance
- [ ] Assess condition and future maintenance needs
- [ ] Determine business necessity or personal importance
- [ ] Research alternatives (rental, different vehicles, etc.)

Financial Analysis:

- [ ] Calculate cramdown potential for vehicles
- [ ] Assess lien stripping opportunities for real estate
- [ ] Determine affordability within Chapter 13 budget
- [ ] Compare keep vs. surrender scenarios financially
- [ ] Consider strategic timing for maximum benefit

Decision Framework

Keep Property If:

- Payments are affordable within Chapter 13 budget
- Property is essential for employment or family stability
- Cramdown or lien stripping provides significant benefit
- Property condition is good with manageable maintenance needs
- Emotional or strategic value justifies the cost

Surrender Property If:

- Payments are unaffordable even with Chapter 13 help
- Property is significantly underwater with no recovery prospects
- Maintenance costs are excessive or unpredictable
- Better alternatives available at substantially lower cost
- Surrender provides significant budget relief for other priorities

Implementation Strategy

For Kept Property:

- [ ] Ensure all ongoing payments remain current
- [ ] Maintain required insurance coverage
- [ ] Budget for predictable maintenance and repairs
- [ ] Monitor for refinancing opportunities as credit improves
- [ ] Build emergency fund for unexpected property expenses

For Surrendered Property:

- [ ] Stop payments only after court approval
- [ ] Arrange for peaceful surrender to avoid deficiency claims
- [ ] Secure alternative housing or transportation before surrender
- [ ] Use savings from surrender to strengthen overall financial position
- [ ] Plan for eventual replacement when financially stable

The Bottom Line: Secured Debt as Your Foundation

Secured debts - your mortgage and car loans - often represent the foundation of your financial life. Your home provides shelter and stability for your family. Your vehicle provides transportation essential for employment and daily life. Chapter 13's powerful tools for protecting secured property make it uniquely valuable for people who have assets worth protecting.

Key Principles for Success:

Be Realistic About Affordability: Don't try to keep property you truly can't afford. Chapter 13 helps with temporary problems, not permanently unaffordable situations.

Use Chapter 13's Special Powers: Take advantage of cramdown, lien stripping, and other tools that can save you thousands of dollars while protecting essential property.

Plan for the Long Term: Property ownership means ongoing responsibilities. Budget for maintenance, repairs, insurance, and taxes throughout your plan and beyond.

Make Strategic Decisions: Sometimes surrendering property is the smartest choice, even when you could keep it. Focus on building overall financial stability, not just keeping property.

Remember the Goal: The goal isn't to keep every piece of property you own - it's to build a stable, sustainable financial life that supports your family's needs and goals.

Chapter 13's secured debt tools are powerful, but they're most effective when used as part of a comprehensive financial strategy focused on long-term stability and success.

In the next chapter, we'll explore how to modify your Chapter 13 plan when life inevitably changes during your 3-5 year journey - because flexibility and adaptation are key to successful plan completion.

14

Changing Your Plan

Modifications in Chapter 13

Life Happens: Why Your Plan Might Need to Change

When you filed your Chapter 13 bankruptcy, you probably thought you had everything figured out. You calculated your income, budgeted your expenses, and proposed a payment plan that seemed both affordable and legally compliant. But here's the reality that catches many people off guard: **life rarely cooperates with our carefully laid plans.**

Over the course of 3-5 years, the unexpected becomes almost inevitable. You might lose your job, get sick, have a baby, get divorced, or face a dozen other life changes that affect your ability to make your plan payments. The good news? Chapter 13 was designed with this reality in mind. Unlike most legal obligations, Chapter 13 plans can be **modified** when circumstances genuinely change.

Plan modification isn't a sign of failure - it's a built-in safety valve that helps ensure you can complete your bankruptcy successfully despite life's curveballs. In this chapter, we'll explore when modifications are appropriate, how the process works, what changes are possible, and how to navigate modifications successfully while protecting your case.

Understanding Plan Modifications

What Is a Plan Modification?

A **plan modification** is a formal change to the terms of your confirmed Chapter 13 plan. It's essentially a legal way to update your bankruptcy to reflect changed circumstances in your life.

Modifications Can Change:

- Your monthly payment amount
- The length of your plan (within legal limits)
- How different types of creditors are treated
- The percentage paid to unsecured creditors
- Which debts are included in your plan
- How secured debts are handled

What Modifications Cannot Do:

- Extend your plan beyond 60 months total
- Reduce priority debt payments below required amounts
- Violate the "best interests" test for unsecured creditors
- Be used to manipulate the system unfairly

Pre-Confirmation vs. Post-Confirmation Modifications

Pre-Confirmation Modifications:

- Changes made before your plan is approved by the court
- Relatively easy to make
- Common as you fine-tune your plan during the early months
- No formal motion required, just file an amended plan

Post-Confirmation Modifications:

- Changes made after your plan has been approved
- Require formal court procedures
- Need to show "substantial change in circumstances"
- More complex but still very doable

When Modifications Are Appropriate

Income Changes: The Most Common Trigger

Job Loss or Reduction in Hours: Losing your job or having your hours cut is one of the most common reasons for plan modification.

Real Example: *David, Buffalo, NY - Manufacturing Worker*

- **Original plan:** $650/month based on $55,000/year income
- **Crisis:** Plant closed, new job pays $38,000/year
- **Modification:** Reduced payment to $400/month, extended plan to 60 months
- **Outcome:** Successfully completed modified plan

Income Increases: Sometimes your income goes up significantly, which may actually require a modification to pay more to creditors.

Real Example: *Jennifer, Sacramento, CA - Nurse*

- **Original plan:** $800/month based on $65,000/year income
- **Change:** Promoted to supervisor, income increased to $85,000/year
- **Required modification:** Increased payment to $1,200/month
- **Result:** Paid more to creditors, completed plan faster

Self-Employment Income Fluctuations: If you're self-employed, your income may vary significantly from your original projections.

Family Changes: Life's Major Transitions

Marriage or Divorce: Getting married or divorced can dramatically affect your household budget and income.

Marriage Modification Example: *Lisa, single, Long Island,* NY

- **Original situation:** Single mother, $45,000 income, $500/month plan
- **Change:** Married, combined household income $95,000
- **Modification:** Increased payment to $1,100/month, shortened plan
- **Benefit:** Faster debt elimination, better family financial foundation

New Children: Having a baby creates new expenses and may qualify for increased expense deductions.

Divorce During Chapter 13:

- May need to separate joint plan into individual cases
- Income and expenses typically change significantly
- Child support obligations may change priority debt treatment
- Property division may affect secured debt treatment

Health Issues: Medical Emergencies and Chronic Conditions

Temporary Disability: Short-term medical issues that affect your ability to work may qualify for temporary payment reduction.

Permanent Disability: If you become permanently disabled, you may qualify for:

- Significant payment reduction
- Early discharge in extreme cases
- Conversion to Chapter 7 if you qualify

Family Medical Emergencies:

- Spouse's illness affecting household income
- Child's medical needs requiring specialized care

- Caring for elderly parents

Medical Emergency Example: *Robert and Maria, San Diego, CA*

- **Original plan:** $950/month based on dual income
- **Crisis:** Maria diagnosed with cancer, unable to work for 8 months
- **Emergency modification:** Reduced payment to $400/month temporarily
- **Recovery modification:** Gradually increased payments as Maria returned to work
- **Final outcome:** Completed plan successfully with supportive court

Economic Changes: External Factors Beyond Your Control

Economic Recession:

- Industry-wide layoffs or pay cuts
- Reduced hours across multiple jobs
- Business income decline for self-employed

Cost of Living Changes:

- Significant increases in housing, utilities, or other essential expenses
- Changes in health insurance costs
- Increased childcare or eldercare expenses

Natural Disasters:

- Hurricane, earthquake, or flood damage
- Loss of income due to business closure
- Increased living expenses due to displacement

The Modification Process: Step by Step

Step 1: Recognize the Need Early

Don't Wait Until You're Behind: The best time to request a modification is **before** you miss any payments. Waiting until you're already behind makes the process more complicated and risky.

Early Warning Signs:

- Struggling to make monthly payments
- Using credit cards for living expenses
- Borrowing money to make plan payments
- Stress about upcoming payment dates
- Major life changes affecting income or expenses

Step 2: Document the Changed Circumstances

Gather Supporting Evidence:

For Income Changes:

- Layoff notice or termination letter
- New employment offer or pay stubs
- Medical documentation for disability
- Business records showing income decline

For Expense Changes:

- Medical bills and treatment records
- Childcare contracts and costs
- Divorce decree and support orders
- Insurance premium changes

For Family Changes:

- Birth certificates for new children
- Marriage certificate or divorce decree

- Death certificates if applicable
- Custody agreements affecting expenses

Step 3: Calculate the Proposed New Payment

Work with Your Attorney: Your bankruptcy attorney should help calculate:

- New disposable income based on changed circumstances
- Minimum payment required under bankruptcy law
- How the change affects different creditor classes
- Whether plan length needs to be adjusted

Consider All Options:

- Temporary vs. permanent payment changes
- Plan length adjustments
- Treatment of different debt types
- Impact on unsecured creditor payments

Step 4: File the Motion to Modify

Required Documentation:

- Motion explaining the changed circumstances
- Updated income and expense schedules
- Proposed modified plan
- Supporting documentation for the changes

Notice to Parties:

- All creditors must be notified of the proposed modification
- Trustee reviews the proposal
- Creditors have opportunity to object

Step 5: Address Objections and Get Court Approval

Common Objections:

- Trustee concerns about feasibility
- Creditor objections to reduced payments
- Questions about the permanence of changes
- Requests for additional documentation

Court Hearing:

- May be required if there are objections
- Opportunity to explain circumstances to the judge
- Court considers fairness to all parties
- Judge approves, denies, or requires further modifications

Types of Modifications: What's Possible

Payment Amount Changes

Temporary Payment Reductions: For short-term problems (3-6 months):

- Medical leave or temporary disability
- Seasonal employment variations
- Short-term family emergencies
- Economic disruptions with expected recovery

Permanent Payment Adjustments: For long-term or permanent changes:

- Permanent job loss requiring lower-paying work
- Chronic health conditions affecting work capacity
- Family changes creating lasting budget impacts
- Retirement or other permanent income reductions

Payment Increase Modifications: Sometimes required when income increases significantly:

- Job promotions or new higher-paying positions
- Marriage bringing additional household income
- Business income recovery or growth
- Inheritance or other windfalls

Plan Length Modifications

Extending Plan Length:

- Maximum of 60 months total from original filing
- Allows lower monthly payments
- Spreads obligations over longer period
- May increase total amount paid to creditors

Shortening Plan Length:

- Available when income increases significantly
- Accelerates debt elimination
- May reduce total interest paid
- Requires ability to afford higher monthly payments

Creditor Treatment Changes

Adding New Creditors:

- Creditors discovered after plan confirmation
- New priority debts (recent taxes, support obligations)
- Post-petition debts that qualify for inclusion

Modifying Secured Debt Treatment:

- Changes in property values affecting cramdown

- Refinancing opportunities during the plan
- Property surrender decisions
- Insurance or maintenance cost changes

Adjusting Unsecured Creditor Payments:

- Changes based on new disposable income calculations
- Addition of new unsecured debts
- Modifications to percentage paid to unsecured creditors

Common Modification Scenarios

Scenario 1: Job Loss and Re-employment

Background: *Michael, married, Sacramento*, CA

- Original income: $75,000/year
- Original plan: $900/month for 5 years
- Crisis: Laid off from manufacturing job

Immediate Response:

- Filed emergency motion within 2 weeks of layoff
- Requested temporary payment suspension
- Court granted 3-month payment moratorium

Re-employment Modification:

- Found new job at $52,000/year (30% reduction)
- Filed permanent modification after 3 months
- New plan: $550/month for remaining term
- Extended plan to 60 months to accommodate reduction

Successful Outcome:

- Avoided dismissal during unemployment

- Completed modified plan successfully
- Maintained home and family stability throughout crisis

Scenario 2: Medical Emergency

Background: *Sarah, single, Buffalo,* NY

- Original income: $48,000/year as teacher
- Original plan: $600/month for 3 years
- Crisis: Diagnosed with chronic illness requiring treatment

Medical Impact:

- Unable to work for 6 months
- Ongoing medical expenses not covered by insurance
- Reduced work capacity requiring part-time schedule

Modification Strategy:

- Emergency reduction to $200/month during treatment
- Permanent modification to $350/month for part-time work
- Plan extended to 60 months
- Medical expenses added as priority debts

Long-term Success:

- Maintained health insurance through employment
- Completed plan despite health challenges
- Built support network through modification process

Scenario 3: Family Changes

Background: *Jennifer, divorced, Long Island,* NY

- Original plan based on dual income: $1,200/month
- Crisis: Divorce proceeding, loss of spouse's income

- New responsibility: Primary custody of two children

Divorce Complications:

- Spouse filed separate bankruptcy
- Joint debts needed to be split between cases
- Child support became priority debt
- Childcare costs increased significantly

Complex Modification:

- Split joint case into individual cases
- Reduced payment to $450/month
- Added child support as priority debt
- Extended plan to maximum 60 months
- Modified secured debt treatment for house

Positive Resolution:

- Maintained family home for children's stability
- Successfully completed individual plan
- Built new financial foundation as single parent

Emergency Modifications: When Speed Matters

Crisis Situations Requiring Immediate Action

Emergency Circumstances:

- Sudden job loss with no savings
- Medical emergency affecting ability to work
- Natural disaster impacting home or employment
- Death of spouse or primary income earner

Emergency Modification Process:

- File motion immediately upon crisis
- Request temporary payment suspension or reduction
- Provide preliminary documentation with more to follow
- Ask for expedited hearing if necessary

Emergency Relief Options:

- **Payment moratorium:** Temporary suspension of all payments
- **Reduced payments:** Significant temporary reduction
- **Case suspension:** Pause the entire case temporarily
- **Emergency conversion:** Switch to Chapter 7 if appropriate

Working with Trustees in Emergencies

Trustee Communication: Most Chapter 13 trustees are reasonable about genuine emergencies:

- Call the trustee's office immediately when crisis occurs
- Explain the situation honestly and completely
- Ask about informal arrangements pending formal modification
- Provide documentation as quickly as possible

Interim Agreements: Many trustees will agree to:

- Accept reduced payments temporarily
- Defer payment deadlines for short periods
- Work with you on payment arrangements
- Support reasonable modification requests

Hardship Discharge: The Last Resort

When Plans Cannot Be Completed

Hardship Discharge Requirements: In very rare circumstances, you may qualify for early discharge without completing your plan:

Legal Requirements:

- Failure to complete plan due to circumstances "for which the debtor should not justly be held accountable"
- Modification of the plan is not practicable
- Value paid to unsecured creditors equals at least what they would have received in Chapter 7
- Generally limited to catastrophic circumstances

Common Hardship Situations:

- Permanent total disability preventing employment
- Terminal illness affecting ability to complete plan
- Catastrophic events destroying income capacity
- Family tragedies requiring long-term caregiving

Hardship Discharge Limitations:

- Much more limited than regular Chapter 13 discharge
- Some debts that would be discharged in completed Chapter 13 survive
- Rarely granted by courts
- Requires substantial documentation and proof

Alternative to Hardship Discharge: Conversion to Chapter 7

When Conversion Makes Sense:

- You qualify for Chapter 7 under current circumstances
- Cannot complete Chapter 13 plan due to permanent changes
- Would receive better relief under Chapter 7

- Want to eliminate obligations more quickly

Conversion Process:

- File motion to convert case to Chapter 7
- Must qualify under Chapter 7 requirements at time of conversion
- Lose Chapter 13 protections (co-debtor stay, etc.)
- Subject to Chapter 7 property exemptions and liquidation

Strategic Considerations:

- Timing of conversion relative to plan completion
- Property protection differences between chapters
- Impact on co-debtors and family members
- Credit reporting differences between chapters

Avoiding Common Modification Mistakes

Timing Mistakes

Waiting Too Long:

- Don't wait until you've missed multiple payments
- File modification requests as soon as problems become apparent
- Early action preserves more options and court goodwill

Acting Too Quickly:

- Don't file modifications for temporary or minor changes
- Consider whether the problem might resolve itself
- Evaluate costs and benefits of modification process

Documentation Problems

Insufficient Evidence:

- Provide complete documentation of changed circumstances
- Include medical records, employment letters, financial statements
- Show the change is genuine and beyond your control

Inconsistent Information:

- Ensure all documentation supports your modification request
- Avoid discrepancies between different documents
- Be honest about all aspects of your situation

Strategic Errors

Unrealistic Proposals:

- Don't propose payment amounts you still can't afford
- Consider long-term sustainability, not just current crisis
- Build small buffer into modified payment if possible

Ignoring Creditor Impact:

- Consider how modification affects different creditor classes
- Understand objections that may be raised
- Propose fair and reasonable adjustments

Working with Professionals During Modifications

Attorney Representation

Why Attorney Help Is Crucial:

- Complex legal requirements for modifications
- Need to calculate proper payment amounts under bankruptcy law
- Interaction with trustee and creditors requires experience
- Court procedures and documentation requirements

What to Expect from Your Attorney:

- Evaluation of whether modification is appropriate
- Calculation of new payment amounts
- Preparation of all required documentation
- Representation at hearings and negotiations with parties

Cost Considerations:

- Modification legal fees often modest ($500-1,500)
- May be payable through the modified plan
- Cost usually justified by successful plan completion
- Early attorney involvement prevents more expensive problems

Working with Your Trustee

Trustee's Role in Modifications:

- Reviews proposed modifications for legal compliance
- Makes recommendations to the court
- Continues to administer payments under modified plan
- Monitors compliance with modified terms

Building Positive Trustee Relationships:

- Communicate honestly about problems and proposed solutions
- Provide complete and accurate financial information
- Respond promptly to trustee requests and concerns
- Maintain professionalism throughout the process

Success Strategies for Plan Modifications

Preparation and Documentation

Before Filing Modification:

- [ ] Gather all documentation supporting the change
- [ ] Calculate realistic new payment amounts
- [ ] Consider long-term sustainability of proposed changes
- [ ] Discuss strategy with experienced bankruptcy attorney

Documentation Checklist:

- [ ] Income verification (pay stubs, termination letters, etc.)
- [ ] Medical records (if health-related modification)
- [ ] Family documentation (birth certificates, divorce decrees, etc.)
- [ ] Expense documentation (new costs or changed expenses)
- [ ] Financial statements showing current situation

Communication Strategy

With Your Attorney:

- Provide complete and honest information about circumstances
- Ask questions about options and likely outcomes
- Follow attorney advice about timing and strategy
- Stay involved throughout the modification process

With Your Trustee:

- Communicate proactively about problems
- Provide requested information promptly and completely
- Ask about informal arrangements if formal modification takes time
- Maintain professional relationship throughout case

With Your Family:

- Explain the modification process and likely timeline
- Involve family in budget adjustments if appropriate

- Manage expectations about outcomes and timeframes
- Use modification as opportunity for financial education

Long-term Planning

Building Flexibility:

- Create small emergency fund if possible during plan
- Develop backup plans for income interruption
- Build marketable skills to improve employment security
- Maintain health insurance and emergency resources

Monitoring and Adjustment:

- Review budget and plan performance regularly
- Identify potential problems before they become crises
- Stay informed about legal requirements and options
- Plan for successful completion despite obstacles

The Psychology of Plan Modifications

Dealing with Modification Stress

Common Emotional Responses:

- **Shame:** Feeling like you've failed at your plan
- **Anxiety:** Worry about court approval and consequences
- **Frustration:** Anger at circumstances beyond your control
- **Relief:** Gratitude for having modification options available

Healthy Perspective:

- Modifications are built into Chapter 13 for good reasons
- Life changes are normal and expected over 3-5 years

- Using available legal tools is smart, not shameful
- Focus on successful completion, not perfect execution

Family and Social Considerations

Explaining Modifications to Family:

- Help family understand that modifications are normal
- Involve older children in age-appropriate financial discussions
- Use modifications as teaching moments about adaptability
- Maintain optimism about successful plan completion

Dealing with Social Stigma:

- Remember that financial difficulties are common
- Focus on your commitment to meeting obligations
- Take pride in using legal tools responsibly
- Help others understand that modifications show responsibility

Real Success Stories: Modifications That Worked

The Manufacturing Layoff: David's Adaptation

Background: David, married with two children, Buffalo, NY. Automotive parts manufacturing worker with 15 years experience.

Original Plan:

- Income: $65,000/year
- Plan payment: $800/month for 5 years
- Protecting family home from foreclosure
- 18 months into plan when crisis hit

The Crisis:

- Plant closure due to industry consolidation

- Six months unemployment with minimal benefits
- Family faced losing home they'd fought to save

Modification Strategy:

- Emergency motion filed within 2 weeks of layoff
- Temporary payment reduction to $200/month
- Court granted 6-month modification period
- Used time to retrain in HVAC field

Successful Resolution:

- Found new career in HVAC with union training program
- New income: $58,000/year (90% of original)
- Modified plan: $700/month for remaining term
- Successfully completed plan and kept family home

Key Lessons:

- Early action prevented case dismissal
- Temporary modifications provided breathing room
- Career change led to stable long-term employment
- Family stability maintained throughout crisis

The Medical Challenge: Sarah's Determination

Background: Sarah, single mother, Sacramento, CA. Elementary school teacher supporting two young children.

Original Situation:

- Income: $52,000/year teaching
- Plan payment: $650/month for 3 years
- Minimal emergency savings due to prior financial crisis

Health Crisis:

- Diagnosed with autoimmune condition requiring treatment
- Unable to work full-time for 8 months
- Significant medical expenses not covered by insurance
- Risk of losing teaching position and benefits

Complex Modification Process:

- Emergency reduction to $150/month during treatment
- Added medical expenses as priority debts
- Extended plan to 60 months maximum
- Negotiated part-time teaching arrangement

Innovative Solutions:

- Qualified for disability accommodations at work
- Used summers for additional recovery time
- Built support network through parent community
- Developed online tutoring income stream

Inspiring Outcome:

- Maintained health benefits throughout treatment
- Returned to full-time teaching after recovery
- Increased plan payments as health improved
- Completed modified plan successfully
- Now advocates for teachers with chronic illness

The Divorce Recovery: Jennifer's New Beginning

Background: Jennifer, Long Island, NY. Married with joint Chapter 13 plan to save family home and address business debt.

Family Crisis:

- Husband's affair and abandonment of family

- Loss of spouse's $45,000 annual income
- Primary custody of three children ages 8-16
- Emotional trauma affecting work performance

Legal Complications:

- Joint Chapter 13 plan needed to be split
- Spouse filed separate bankruptcy in different state
- Joint debts required complex allocation
- Home mortgage became unaffordable on single income

Strategic Modification Approach:

- Separated joint case into individual cases
- Surrendered family home to eliminate mortgage burden
- Relocated to affordable rental in good school district
- Modified plan to $380/month for 5 years

Rebuilding Process:

- Used modification time to complete nursing degree
- Increased income from $35,000 to $65,000
- Children adapted well to new living situation
- Built emergency fund during final plan years

Empowering Results:

- Successfully completed individual Chapter 13 plan
- Purchased appropriate home with FHA loan 2 years later
- Achieved financial independence and stability
- Became mentor for other single mothers facing bankruptcy
- Children learned resilience and financial responsibility

Your Modification Action Plan

Early Warning System

Monthly Plan Health Check:

- [ ] Review budget performance and payment ability
- [ ] Identify any concerning trends or potential problems
- [ ] Assess job security and income stability
- [ ] Monitor family and health situations
- [ ] Maintain communication with attorney about any concerns

Quarterly Assessment:

- [ ] Analyze plan performance over longer term
- [ ] Review changed circumstances or life events
- [ ] Evaluate need for plan adjustments
- [ ] Plan for predictable changes (job transitions, family events)
- [ ] Build small emergency reserves if possible

Crisis Response Protocol

Immediate Actions (Within 48 Hours):

- [ ] Contact bankruptcy attorney to discuss situation
- [ ] Notify trustee of crisis and potential payment problems
- [ ] Begin gathering documentation of changed circumstances
- [ ] Assess immediate family needs and safety
- [ ] Explore emergency resources and support systems

Short-term Actions (Within 2 Weeks):

- [ ] Complete documentation for modification request
- [ ] File emergency motion if immediate relief needed
- [ ] Communicate with employer about accommodations if applicable

- [ ] Assess all available options and resources
- [ ] Develop realistic timeline for resolution

Long-term Adaptation

Modification Implementation:

- [ ] Comply with all modified plan terms
- [ ] Monitor new payment schedule and budget
- [ ] Communicate regularly with attorney and trustee
- [ ] Address any implementation problems promptly
- [ ] Focus on successful completion of modified plan

Building Resilience:

- [ ] Develop multiple income streams if possible
- [ ] Build emergency fund appropriate to modified budget
- [ ] Improve job skills and marketability
- [ ] Strengthen family and social support networks
- [ ] Learn from modification experience for future planning

The Bottom Line: Modifications as Tools for Success

Plan modifications aren't signs of failure - they're tools for success. Chapter 13's modification system recognizes that life rarely goes according to plan, especially over a 3-5 year period. The key to successful modification is:

Early Recognition: Identify problems before they become crises. The earlier you act, the more options you have.

Honest Assessment: Be realistic about your situation and what changes are necessary for long-term success.

Professional Guidance: Work with experienced bankruptcy professionals who understand modification law and procedures.

Family Collaboration: Involve your family appropriately in understanding and adapting to necessary changes.

Long-term Perspective: Focus on successful plan completion, not perfect adherence to original terms.

Learning and Growth: Use the modification experience to build resilience and better financial management skills.

Remember: The goal of Chapter 13 isn't to punish you with an inflexible payment plan - it's to provide a structured path to financial recovery that can adapt to life's realities. Modifications help ensure you can complete that journey successfully, regardless of what challenges arise along the way.

In the next chapter, we'll explore the final phase of Chapter 13: completing your plan, receiving your discharge, and transitioning to life after bankruptcy with improved financial skills and genuine debt relief.

15

Finishing Chapter 13

The Discharge and Beyond

The Finish Line: You Made It

After 3-5 years of monthly payments, careful budgeting, and financial discipline, you're approaching something remarkable: the successful completion of your Chapter 13 bankruptcy plan. This isn't just a legal milestone - it's a personal achievement that represents perseverance, commitment, and growth through one of life's most challenging experiences.

Think about where you started: overwhelmed by debt, possibly facing foreclosure or repossession, stressed about money, and uncertain about your financial future. Now you're months away from eliminating the remaining portion of your debts while having kept the property that mattered to you most.

But completing a Chapter 13 plan is more than just making your final payment. There are important steps to take, requirements to meet, and strategies to implement as you transition from bankruptcy supervision to independent financial management. Most importantly, you need to prepare for life after Chapter 13 - building on the foundation you've created to establish lasting financial security.

In this chapter, we'll guide you through the final phase of Chapter 13, explain exactly what happens when you complete your plan, help you understand your discharge and its benefits, and provide a roadmap for building the prosperous financial future that your hard work has made possible.

Understanding Chapter 13 Completion

What "Completion" Really Means

More Than Just Final Payment: Completing your Chapter 13 plan involves more than making your last payment to the trustee. You must satisfy several requirements to earn your discharge and successfully close your case.

Complete Plan Performance:

- All required plan payments made in full
- All plan terms and conditions satisfied
- Current on all ongoing obligations (mortgage, car payments, etc.)
- Compliance with court orders throughout the case
- No outstanding violations or unresolved issues

Additional Requirements:

- Completion of financial management course
- Filing of required certificates and reports
- Current on all post-petition taxes
- Current on domestic support obligations (child support, alimony)
- Resolution of any pending issues or disputes

The Final Year: Preparing for Completion

12 Months Before Completion: Your final year in Chapter 13 is crucial for setting yourself up for post-discharge success:

Financial Preparation:

- Ensure all payments are current and will remain so

- Begin building emergency fund for post-discharge life
- Plan for transition from court supervision to independent management
- Research credit rebuilding strategies
- Consider refinancing opportunities for post-discharge

Administrative Preparation:

- Complete financial management course if not already done
- Ensure all required annual reports are filed
- Address any pending issues with trustee or creditors
- Update contact information with court
- Organize financial records for post-discharge reference

Personal Preparation:

- Reflect on lessons learned during the bankruptcy process
- Develop strategies for avoiding future financial problems
- Build confidence in your money management abilities
- Plan for major financial goals after discharge
- Prepare family for transition to independent financial management

The Financial Management Course

Completing Your Second Required Course

Course Requirement: Just as you completed credit counseling before filing Chapter 13, you must complete a financial management course before receiving your discharge. This is often called "debtor education" or the "second course."

Course Details:

- **Duration:** Approximately 2 hours (can be completed in multiple sessions)

- **Format:** Online, telephone, or in-person
- **Cost:** Typically $25-$50 (fee waivers available for qualified individuals)
- **Provider:** Must be approved by the U.S. Trustee Program
- **Timing:** Must be completed after filing but before discharge

Course Content: The financial management course covers practical topics designed to help you succeed after bankruptcy:

Budget Development:

- Creating realistic monthly budgets
- Tracking income and expenses
- Planning for irregular expenses
- Building emergency funds

Credit Management:

- Understanding credit reports and scores
- Rebuilding credit responsibly
- Avoiding predatory lending
- Using credit cards wisely

Money Management Tools:

- Banking and financial services
- Insurance planning
- Investment basics
- Long-term financial planning

Consumer Protection:

- Recognizing and avoiding financial scams
- Understanding your rights as a consumer
- Dealing with financial emergencies

- Making major financial decisions

Certificate Filing

Certificate Requirement: After completing the course, you'll receive a certificate that must be filed with the bankruptcy court. **Your discharge cannot be granted without this certificate.**

Filing Responsibility:

- You or your attorney must file the certificate
- Must be filed before the case can be closed
- Keep copies for your records
- Ensure court receives and processes the filing

Final Plan Requirements

Ensuring Complete Performance

Payment Verification: The trustee will prepare a final accounting showing:

- All payments received during the plan
- Distribution of funds to creditors
- Administrative expenses paid
- Any remaining balances or issues

Creditor Payments: Your trustee's final report will show:

- Priority debts paid in full as required
- Secured debt arrears paid according to plan
- Percentage paid to unsecured creditors
- Any disputed or unclaimed funds

Ongoing Obligation Status: You must be current on all ongoing obligations:

- Mortgage payments (if keeping home)

- Car loan payments (if keeping vehicle)
- Post-petition taxes
- Child support and alimony
- Insurance premiums and property taxes

Resolving Final Issues

Common Final-Year Issues:

Payment Discrepancies:

- Creditor payment disputes
- Trustee accounting questions
- Missing or misdirected payments
- Interest calculation disputes

Ongoing Obligation Problems:

- Falling behind on mortgage during final months
- Car payment issues
- New tax obligations
- Changes in support obligations

Administrative Issues:

- Missing documentation
- Address changes not reported
- Insurance lapses
- Court order violations

Resolution Strategies:

- Address issues immediately when identified
- Work with attorney to resolve complex problems
- Communicate with trustee about discrepancies

- Maintain documentation of all payments and compliance

The Chapter 13 Discharge

What Discharge Means

Legal Effect: Your Chapter 13 discharge is a federal court order that:

- Permanently eliminates your legal obligation to pay discharged debts
- Prohibits creditors from attempting to collect discharged debts
- Provides permanent protection from collection efforts
- Gives you a genuine fresh start

Discharge vs. Chapter 7: Chapter 13 discharge is actually **broader** than Chapter 7 discharge in some important ways:

- Discharges some debts that survive Chapter 7
- Includes certain tax debts that Chapter 7 cannot eliminate
- May discharge some divorce-related property settlement debts
- Covers debts incurred during the bankruptcy case (in some circumstances)

What Gets Discharged in Chapter 13

Typical Discharged Debts:

- Remaining balances on credit cards and personal loans
- Medical bills and collection accounts
- Deficiency balances from surrendered property
- Some older tax debts
- Certain business debts
- Most court judgments
- Remaining portions of cramdown car loans

- Some divorce-related property settlement debts

Enhanced Discharge Benefits: Chapter 13 can discharge some debts that Chapter 7 cannot:

- Debts from willful and malicious injury (some circumstances)
- Debts from property settlements in divorce (not support)
- Some tax debts that don't meet Chapter 7 requirements
- Debts incurred to pay non-dischargeable taxes

What Survives Chapter 13 Discharge

Non-Dischargeable Debts: Even Chapter 13's broader discharge cannot eliminate:

- Student loans (except in rare hardship cases)
- Recent income tax debts
- Child support and alimony obligations
- Criminal fines and restitution
- Some government penalties
- Debts from fraud or intentional wrongdoing
- Most HOA fees and property taxes
- Debts incurred after filing (except in limited circumstances)

Secured Debt Obligations:

- Ongoing mortgage payments (if you kept the home)
- Ongoing car payments (if you kept the vehicle)
- Property taxes and insurance obligations
- Other secured debts where you kept the collateral

The Discharge Order Process

Final Trustee Report: Before discharge, the trustee files a final report with the court showing:

- Complete accounting of all plan payments
- Distribution of funds to all creditors
- Resolution of any disputes or issues
- Recommendation for discharge

Court Review: The bankruptcy judge reviews:

- Trustee's final report and recommendation
- Completion of all plan requirements
- Filing of financial management course certificate
- Current status on ongoing obligations
- Any objections or outstanding issues

Discharge Order: If everything is in order, the court issues the discharge order:

- Eliminates remaining eligible debts
- Provides permanent collection protection
- Allows case to proceed to closure
- Triggers final administrative steps

Notice to Creditors: The court sends notice to all creditors:

- Informing them of the discharge
- Prohibiting future collection efforts on discharged debts
- Establishing permanent protection for the debtor
- Providing deadline for any final claims or issues

Case Closure and Final Steps

Administrative Closure

Final Trustee Actions:

- Distribute any remaining funds to creditors
- File final accounting with the court
- Return any unclaimed funds appropriately
- Close trustee records and accounts

Court Closure:

- Review all final documents and reports
- Ensure all requirements have been met
- Issue final order closing the case
- Update court records to show successful completion

Your Final Actions:

- Obtain copies of discharge order and closure documents
- Update personal records with discharge information
- Notify relevant parties of case completion
- Begin implementing post-discharge financial plans

Important Documents to Preserve

Keep Permanent Records:

- Discharge order (original court document)
- Case closure order
- Final trustee report
- Financial management course certificate
- Copies of all plan payments and receipts
- Property retention documents
- Insurance and tax records from bankruptcy period

Why Documentation Matters:

- Proof of discharge for future creditor challenges
- Evidence of successful completion for credit applications
- Tax records for potential future issues
- Reference for any post-discharge disputes
- Historical record of your financial recovery

Credit Report Impact and Cleanup

Understanding Credit Reporting After Discharge

Chapter 13 Timeline:

- Chapter 13 bankruptcy notation remains on credit report for **7 years** from filing date
- Individual discharged accounts may be reported separately
- Positive payment history during Chapter 13 may help credit score
- Successful completion shows commitment to paying debts

Credit Report Cleanup: After discharge, check your credit reports to ensure:

- Discharged debts show $0 balances
- Accounts correctly marked as "included in bankruptcy" or "discharged"
- No new collection efforts on old debts
- Accurate reporting of successful completion
- No errors or fraudulent accounts

Disputing Errors: Common post-discharge credit report errors:

- Discharged debts still showing balances owed
- Old accounts marked as "past due" after discharge
- Collection agencies reporting on discharged debts
- Failure to update account status to "discharged"

Credit Score Recovery Timeline

Immediate Post-Discharge (Months 1-6):

- Credit score may improve slightly due to reduced debt-to-income ratio
- Begin credit rebuilding activities
- Focus on establishing new positive payment history
- Monitor credit reports for accuracy

Short-term Recovery (Months 6-18):

- Gradual credit score improvement with responsible credit use
- May qualify for secured credit cards and credit-builder loans
- Consider becoming authorized user on family member's account
- Continue building emergency fund and financial stability

Medium-term Recovery (Years 2-3):

- Credit score often reaches 650-700 range with good management
- May qualify for unsecured credit cards at reasonable rates
- Could be eligible for auto loans at competitive rates
- May qualify for FHA mortgage (2 years post-discharge)

Long-term Recovery (Years 3-7):

- Credit score often reaches 700+ with continued responsible management
- Access to conventional mortgages and most credit products
- Interest rates approach market standards
- Chapter 13 notation has diminishing impact over time

Building Your Post-Discharge Financial Life

The Foundation You've Built

Financial Skills Developed: Your Chapter 13 experience has given you valuable skills:

- Budgeting and expense management
- Discipline in making regular payments
- Understanding of credit and debt consequences
- Appreciation for emergency funds and financial planning
- Knowledge of legal rights and protections

Improved Financial Position: Compared to when you filed, you now have:

- Significantly reduced debt burden
- Protected essential property (home, vehicle)
- Improved cash flow from eliminated debt payments
- Better understanding of your financial capabilities
- Foundation for building long-term wealth

Post-Discharge Financial Strategy

Immediate Priorities (Months 1-6):

Emergency Fund Building:

- Start with small but consistent savings
- Target initial goal of $1,000-2,500
- Keep emergency fund separate from checking account
- Use automatic transfers to build discipline

Credit Rebuilding:

- Apply for secured credit card if not already obtained
- Use credit card for small purchases and pay in full monthly
- Consider credit-builder loan from credit union

- Monitor credit score monthly and track improvements

Budget Optimization:

- Adjust budget to reflect elimination of trustee payments
- Allocate former plan payment toward savings and goals
- Maintain expense discipline learned during Chapter 13
- Plan for annual and irregular expenses

Medium-term Goals (Months 6-24):

Enhanced Emergency Fund:

- Build emergency fund to 3-6 months of essential expenses
- Consider multiple savings accounts for different purposes
- Maintain easy access but separate from daily spending accounts

Credit Expansion:

- Apply for unsecured credit card after 12-18 months of good history
- Keep credit utilization below 30% of available limits
- Consider store cards or gas cards for additional credit mix
- Continue perfect payment history on all accounts

Major Purchase Planning:

- Begin saving for vehicle replacement if needed
- Research mortgage options if interested in homeownership changes
- Plan for large purchases without using debt when possible
- Consider timing of major financial decisions

Long-term Wealth Building (Years 2-5+):

Investment and Retirement:

- Maximize employer 401(k) contributions, especially any matching
- Consider IRA contributions for additional retirement savings

- Learn about basic investing principles and options
- Focus on long-term wealth building, not quick returns

Property and Asset Building:

- Consider refinancing mortgage if rates improve
- Evaluate home improvements that add value
- Build assets that appreciate over time
- Maintain and protect property investments

Advanced Financial Planning:

- Consider working with fee-only financial planner
- Develop comprehensive financial plan with specific goals
- Plan for children's education if applicable
- Consider advanced tax planning strategies

Common Post-Discharge Challenges

Avoiding Financial Regression

The Temptation Trap: After discharge, you may be tempted to:

- Relax financial discipline now that court supervision has ended
- Use increased cash flow for lifestyle inflation rather than savings
- Apply for multiple credit cards or loans
- Make large purchases using newly available credit

Staying Disciplined:

- Remember the lessons that led to bankruptcy originally
- Maintain the budgeting habits developed during Chapter 13
- Focus on building wealth rather than accumulating possessions
- Use credit as a tool, not a source of funds

Creditor Contact After Discharge

Discharge Violations: Occasionally, creditors may attempt to collect discharged debts:

- Usually due to poor record-keeping or automated systems
- Clear violations of the discharge order
- Subject to legal penalties and sanctions

Your Response:

- Send written notice of discharge with copy of discharge order
- Keep detailed records of any collection attempts
- Report persistent violations to your attorney
- Know that you have legal rights if discharge is violated

Family and Social Adjustments

Explaining Success:

- Help family understand the transition from court supervision
- Involve older children in age-appropriate financial planning
- Use your experience to teach others about responsible money management
- Take pride in your achievement and commitment

Social Relationships:

- Some people may not understand the commitment you've shown
- Focus on relationships with financially responsible people
- Consider helping others who face financial difficulties
- Remember that successful Chapter 13 completion is an achievement

Giving Back: Helping Others

Sharing Your Experience

Mentoring Opportunities: Your successful Chapter 13 completion makes you valuable to others facing financial difficulties:

- Volunteer with nonprofit credit counseling organizations
- Share experience at financial literacy workshops
- Mentor others going through bankruptcy process
- Provide realistic perspective on bankruptcy recovery

Educational Contributions:

- Write about your experience (blog, social media, articles)
- Speak to community groups about financial recovery
- Help debunk myths and stigma about bankruptcy
- Advocate for fair treatment of people in financial distress

Professional and Community Involvement

Professional Development:

- Consider career advancement opportunities enabled by improved finances
- Invest in education or training that increases earning potential
- Network with other professionals who've overcome financial challenges
- Use financial stability as foundation for career growth

Community Contribution:

- Support local organizations that help people in financial distress
- Volunteer with legal aid organizations
- Contribute to causes that matter to you (when financially appropriate)
- Use your experience to advocate for fair bankruptcy laws

Real Success Stories: Life After Chapter 13

The Homeowner's Victory: Robert and Maria's New Beginning

Background: Robert and Maria, married with two teenagers, Buffalo, NY. Filed Chapter 13 to save their home from foreclosure and address business debt.

Chapter 13 Journey:

- 5-year plan paying $850/month
- Caught up on $22,000 in mortgage arrears
- Protected home and essential business assets
- Discharged $48,000 in unsecured debt

Post-Discharge Success (5 Years Later):

- **Home equity:** Increased from $15,000 to $78,000
- **Emergency fund:** Built $12,000 emergency fund
- **Credit scores:** Both spouses over 720
- **Business growth:** Expanded electrical contracting business
- **Family stability:** Both children graduated high school and attended college
- **Community involvement:** Volunteer with local financial literacy program

Key Lessons:

- Property protection provided foundation for wealth building
- Discipline learned in Chapter 13 continued after discharge
- Family worked together toward financial goals
- Success enabled helping others in similar situations

The Career Transformation: Jennifer's Professional Growth

Background: Jennifer, single mother, Sacramento, CA. Filed Chapter 13 after divorce left her with unmanageable debt and reduced income.

Chapter 13 Experience:

- 3-year plan paying $475/month
- Kept reliable vehicle for work
- Discharged $32,000 in credit card debt
- Maintained stable housing for children

Post-Discharge Achievement:

- **Education:** Completed nursing degree during final year of plan
- **Career advancement:** Promoted to charge nurse within 2 years
- **Income growth:** Increased from $38,000 to $72,000
- **Homeownership:** Purchased home with FHA loan 3 years post-discharge
- **Financial security:** Built 6-month emergency fund
- **Family impact:** Provided college funding for both children

Transformation Elements:

- Used financial stability to invest in education
- Career advancement provided income security
- Homeownership rebuilt family wealth
- Became mentor for other single mothers

The Business Recovery: David's Entrepreneurial Success

Background: David, small business owner, San Diego, CA. Filed Chapter 13 after business downturn created personal and business debt crisis.

Chapter 13 Strategy:

- 5-year plan paying $1,100/month
- Protected business assets and home
- Maintained business operations throughout plan
- Separated personal and business finances

Post-Discharge Business Growth:

- **Business expansion:** Opened second location within 18 months
- **Revenue growth:** Doubled business income over 3 years
- **Employee growth:** Hired 8 additional employees
- **Property investment:** Purchased commercial building for business
- **Personal wealth:** Built substantial investment portfolio
- **Community impact:** Created jobs and supported local economy

Business Lessons:

- Chapter 13 provided breathing room for business recovery
- Improved financial management prevented future crises
- Success enabled job creation and community contribution
- Proper business structure protected personal assets

Your Post-Discharge Action Plan

Immediate Actions (Months 1-3)

Financial Cleanup:

- [ ] Obtain and review all three credit reports for accuracy
- [ ] Dispute any errors or outdated information
- [ ] Organize and file all bankruptcy-related documents
- [ ] Update budget to reflect end of trustee payments

- [ ] Begin building emergency fund with automatic transfers

Credit Rebuilding:

- [ ] Apply for secured credit card if not already obtained
- [ ] Set up automatic payment for full balance monthly
- [ ] Consider becoming authorized user on family member's account
- [ ] Monitor credit score monthly to track improvement
- [ ] Avoid applying for multiple credit accounts simultaneously

Goal Setting:

- [ ] Define short-term financial goals (6-24 months)
- [ ] Identify medium-term objectives (2-5 years)
- [ ] Create long-term wealth building plan (5+ years)
- [ ] Involve family in goal setting and financial planning
- [ ] Document lessons learned from Chapter 13 experience

Short-term Development (Months 3-12)

Financial Strengthening:

- [ ] Build emergency fund to $2,500-5,000
- [ ] Optimize budgeting and expense management
- [ ] Research and plan major purchases (vehicle replacement, etc.)
- [ ] Begin retirement savings if not already contributing
- [ ] Consider additional income sources or career advancement

Credit Enhancement:

- [ ] Request credit limit increases on existing accounts
- [ ] Apply for unsecured credit card after 6-12 months good history
- [ ] Maintain credit utilization below 30% of available limits
- [ ] Continue perfect payment history on all accounts

- [ ] Research mortgage options if interested in homeownership changes

Education and Growth:

- [ ] Continue financial education through books, courses, podcasts
- [ ] Attend financial planning or investment workshops
- [ ] Consider working with fee-only financial planner
- [ ] Develop expertise in areas relevant to your financial goals
- [ ] Share experience with others who could benefit

Long-term Wealth Building (Years 1-5+)

Asset Development:

- [ ] Maximize retirement savings and employer matching
- [ ] Build diversified investment portfolio appropriate to risk tolerance
- [ ] Consider real estate investment if appropriate to situation
- [ ] Protect assets with appropriate insurance coverage
- [ ] Plan for major life goals (home purchase, children's education, etc.)

Legacy Building:

- [ ] Create or update will and estate planning documents
- [ ] Consider life insurance needs for family protection
- [ ] Plan for children's education funding if applicable
- [ ] Develop strategies for intergenerational wealth transfer
- [ ] Continue contributing to community and helping others

Professional and Personal Growth:

- [ ] Invest in career development and education
- [ ] Consider entrepreneurial opportunities if appropriate
- [ ] Build professional network and relationships

- [ ] Maintain work-life balance and family priorities
- [ ] Use financial security as foundation for personal fulfillment

Measuring Your Success

Financial Metrics

Quantitative Measures:

- **Net worth growth:** Track assets minus liabilities over time
- **Credit score improvement:** Monitor monthly progress toward 700+ scores
- **Emergency fund adequacy:** Build to 3-6 months of essential expenses
- **Debt-to-income ratio:** Keep total debt payments below 20% of income
- **Savings rate:** Target saving 10-20% of income for various goals

Qualitative Indicators:

- **Financial confidence:** Comfort making financial decisions
- **Stress reduction:** Decreased anxiety about money matters
- **Family harmony:** Improved relationships due to financial stability
- **Future planning:** Ability to make long-term financial plans
- **Helping others:** Capacity to assist family and community

Lifestyle Improvements

Immediate Benefits:

- Improved sleep and reduced stress
- Better family relationships and communication
- Increased confidence and self-esteem
- Greater focus on non-financial life goals

- Enhanced sense of security and stability

Long-term Achievements:

- Financial independence and security
- Ability to pursue dreams and interests
- Capacity to help children and family members
- Freedom to make career and life choices based on passion, not just money
- Legacy of financial responsibility and wisdom

The Bottom Line: Your Chapter 13 Success

Completing a Chapter 13 bankruptcy plan is a remarkable achievement that demonstrates:

Personal Qualities:

- **Commitment:** You stuck with a 3-5 year plan despite challenges
- **Discipline:** You lived within a court-supervised budget and made every payment
- **Resilience:** You adapted to changes and overcame obstacles
- **Growth:** You learned valuable financial skills and lessons
- **Responsibility:** You met your obligations while protecting what mattered most

Financial Accomplishments:

- **Debt elimination:** Discharged significant amounts of unmanageable debt
- **Property protection:** Kept your home, vehicle, and other essential assets
- **Credit foundation:** Built the basis for future credit rebuilding
- **Financial education:** Gained knowledge and skills for lifelong financial success

- **Stability creation:** Established foundation for long-term financial security

Future Opportunities: Your successful Chapter 13 completion opens doors to:

- Homeownership or refinancing at better rates
- Business opportunities and career advancement
- Investment and wealth building strategies
- Educational opportunities for yourself and your family
- The satisfaction of helping others facing financial difficulties

Remember: Chapter 13 bankruptcy wasn't a setback - it was a strategic tool that allowed you to reorganize your finances, protect what mattered most, and build a foundation for long-term success. The discipline, knowledge, and resilience you developed during your plan will serve you well for the rest of your life.

You didn't just survive Chapter 13 - you thrived through it and emerged stronger, wiser, and better prepared for whatever financial challenges and opportunities the future may bring.

Welcome to your new financial life. You've earned it.

In the next chapter, we'll explore how bankruptcy intersects with divorce - one of the most complex and emotionally challenging combinations of legal proceedings that many people face.

16

Bankruptcy and Divorce

Untangling the Financial Fallout

When Financial Crisis Meets Family Crisis

Divorce and bankruptcy are two of the most stressful and emotionally challenging experiences in life. When they happen together - as they often do - they create a perfect storm of legal complexity, emotional turmoil, and financial devastation that can feel overwhelming to navigate.

The statistics tell a sobering story: divorce is one of the leading causes of personal bankruptcy, and financial stress is one of the leading causes of divorce. When a marriage ends, one household income must suddenly support two households, legal fees accumulate, and the financial foundation that supported a family often crumbles under the strain.

But while the combination of divorce and bankruptcy is challenging, it's not insurmountable. With proper understanding, strategic planning, and professional guidance, you can navigate both processes successfully and emerge with a genuine fresh start. The key is understanding how these two legal processes interact, what options are available to you, and how to coordinate them for the best possible outcome.

In this chapter, we'll explore the complex relationship between bankruptcy and divorce, help you understand your options and timing considerations, and provide strategies for protecting yourself and your family during these difficult transitions.

Why Divorce and Bankruptcy Often Go Together

The Financial Perfect Storm

The Income Problem: When a married couple divorces, their combined household income must suddenly support two separate households. Expenses that were shared - housing, utilities, insurance, vehicles - now must be duplicated or significantly increased.

Real Example: *Jennifer and Mark, married 12 years, Sacramento*

- **During marriage:** Combined income $85,000, single household expenses $68,000
- **After divorce:** Jennifer's income $38,000, expenses $42,000; Mark's income $47,000, expenses $45,000
- **Result:** Both spouses now have expenses exceeding their individual incomes

The Legal Cost Reality: Divorce itself creates significant new debt:

- Attorney fees (often $10,000-$50,000+ for contested divorces)
- Court costs and filing fees
- Expert witness fees (appraisers, accountants, therapists)
- Temporary housing and moving expenses
- Duplicate household setup costs

The Asset Division Impact:

- Liquid assets often depleted by legal fees and temporary support
- Retirement accounts may be divided, reducing security
- Family home may need to be sold, creating housing instability
- Debt division may leave one spouse with unmanageable obligations

Common Divorce-to-Bankruptcy Scenarios

Scenario 1: The Financially Vulnerable Spouse *Sarah, age 42, stay-at-home mother for 15 years*

- Divorce left her with limited work history and lower earning capacity
- Awarded spousal support but ex-husband inconsistent with payments
- Received half of marital debt but only 30% of income-earning capacity
- Filed Chapter 7 bankruptcy 18 months after divorce

Scenario 2: The Breadwinner's Burden *Michael, age 45, primary income earner*

- Ordered to pay substantial alimony and child support
- Left with most marital debt despite asset division
- Income sufficient during marriage became inadequate for two households
- Filed Chapter 13 to reorganize support obligations and debt

Scenario 3: The Joint Financial Collapse *Robert and Lisa, both working professionals*

- Accumulated debt during marriage breakdown (therapy, legal fees, separate housing)
- Bitter divorce consumed life savings and created new debt
- Both spouses filed separate bankruptcies within 2 years of divorce

The Timing Question: Before or After Divorce?

Filing Bankruptcy Before Divorce

Advantages of Pre-Divorce Bankruptcy:

Cost Efficiency:

- One joint bankruptcy case instead of two separate cases
- Shared attorney fees and court costs
- Single trustee and administrative process
- Reduced overall complexity and expense

Simplified Debt Division:

- Joint debts eliminated before property division
- Cleaner divorce proceedings without debt allocation disputes
- Simplified property settlement negotiations
- Reduced ongoing financial entanglements

Strategic Benefits:

- Both spouses can benefit from debt elimination
- Protected assets go into divorce proceedings
- Reduced financial stress during divorce negotiations
- Clear financial foundation for post-divorce planning

Pre-Divorce Bankruptcy Example: *James and Patricia, married 18 years, Buffalo*

- Accumulated $78,000 in joint credit card debt
- Facing foreclosure on family home
- Filed joint Chapter 7 before divorce proceedings
- Eliminated all unsecured debt, saved home through strategic planning
- Divorce negotiations focused on asset division, not debt allocation
- Both emerged with clean financial slates

Requirements for Joint Filing:

- Both spouses must qualify for bankruptcy
- Must agree on exemption choices

- Need cooperation throughout the process
- Must jointly complete credit counseling and financial management courses

Filing Bankruptcy After Divorce

When Post-Divorce Filing Makes Sense:

Relationship Factors:

- High conflict divorce with no cooperation possible
- Different financial circumstances requiring different bankruptcy chapters
- One spouse doesn't qualify for bankruptcy
- Domestic violence or safety concerns

Strategic Reasons:

- Ability to discharge certain divorce-related debts in Chapter 13
- Different exemption strategies for different asset types
- Timing benefits related to residence requirements
- Income changes post-divorce affecting bankruptcy options

Post-Divorce Bankruptcy Challenges:

- Individual responsibility for joint debts
- Limited discharge of divorce-related obligations
- More complex planning with separate legal proceedings
- Higher total costs for separate cases

Joint Debt Liability: The Hidden Trap

The Critical Reality: Divorce decrees don't eliminate joint debt liability. If your name is on a joint credit card or loan, you remain liable to the creditor regardless of what your divorce agreement says.

How Joint Debt Survives Divorce:

- Creditors are not parties to your divorce
- Divorce courts cannot bind creditors to debt allocation agreements
- If your ex-spouse doesn't pay assigned debt, creditors can pursue you
- Your credit remains at risk from your ex-spouse's financial problems

Real-Life Disaster: *Michelle, divorced, Long Island*

- Divorce decree assigned $45,000 credit card debt to ex-husband
- Ex-husband filed bankruptcy 8 months later
- Credit card companies pursued Michelle for full balance
- Had to file her own bankruptcy to eliminate debt she thought was resolved

Protection Strategies:

- File joint bankruptcy before divorce to eliminate joint debts
- Require actual debt payoff, not just assignment, in divorce settlement
- Include indemnification clauses in divorce agreements
- Consider keeping joint debts in your name if you don't trust ex-spouse's financial responsibility

Bankruptcy's Treatment of Divorce-Related Debts

Understanding Domestic Support Obligations

What Qualifies as Domestic Support: These obligations **cannot be discharged** in any form of bankruptcy:

- Current and past-due child support
- Current and past-due spousal support/alimony
- Obligations "in the nature of support" even if called something else
- Attorney fees related to establishing or modifying support

Support vs. Property Settlement: The distinction between support and property settlement is crucial for bankruptcy purposes:

Support Characteristics (Non-Dischargeable):

- Based on income and need analysis
- Continues until specific termination events
- Subject to modification based on changed circumstances
- Designated as support in divorce decree

Property Settlement Characteristics (May Be Dischargeable in Chapter 13):

- One-time or finite payment obligation
- Based on asset division, not ongoing need
- Not modifiable based on changed circumstances
- Labeled as property division in divorce decree

Chapter 7 vs. Chapter 13: Different Rules

Chapter 7 Limitations:

- Cannot discharge any divorce-related debt obligations
- Support obligations survive completely
- Property settlement obligations survive completely
- Very limited relief for divorce-related financial problems

Chapter 13 Advantages:

- Can discharge some property settlement debts (not support)
- Provides structure for paying support arrears over time
- Protects co-signers (including ex-spouses) during plan period
- Allows catch-up on support without additional penalties

Strategic Chapter 13 Use: *David, divorced, Sacramento*

- Owed $25,000 in spousal support arrears

- Owed $35,000 in property settlement to ex-wife
- Chapter 13 plan: Paid support arrears as priority debt over 5 years
- Property settlement treated as dischargeable debt
- Successfully completed plan, eliminating property settlement obligation

Attorney Fee Obligations

Support-Related Attorney Fees: Attorney fees for establishing, modifying, or enforcing support are generally non-dischargeable.

Property-Related Attorney Fees: Attorney fees for property division may be dischargeable in Chapter 13 if properly characterized.

Strategic Considerations:

- How attorney fees are characterized in divorce decree affects bankruptcy treatment
- Timing of bankruptcy filing relative to attorney fee obligations
- Negotiating fee arrangements that consider bankruptcy implications

Coordinating Bankruptcy and Divorce Proceedings

Legal and Procedural Complications

Automatic Stay Effects: When you file bankruptcy, the automatic stay can complicate divorce proceedings:

What the Stay Stops:

- Collection of property settlement obligations
- Some aspects of property division
- Enforcement of money judgments from divorce

What the Stay Doesn't Stop:

- Divorce proceedings themselves

- Determination of child custody and visitation
- Establishment of support obligations
- Some family court proceedings

Coordinating Court Systems:

- Bankruptcy court (federal) vs. family court (state)
- Different judges, rules, and procedures
- Potential conflicts between court orders
- Need for coordination between attorneys

Timing Strategies

Pre-Divorce Bankruptcy Timeline:

- File bankruptcy 3-6 months before divorce
- Complete bankruptcy process before filing for divorce
- Use debt-free status to simplify divorce negotiations
- Focus divorce on asset division and support, not debt allocation

Concurrent Proceedings:

- File bankruptcy early in divorce process
- Coordinate attorneys and court appearances
- Use automatic stay strategically in divorce negotiations
- Resolve both proceedings simultaneously

Post-Divorce Bankruptcy Planning:

- Wait for divorce to be final
- Assess individual financial situation
- File bankruptcy based on post-divorce circumstances
- Use Chapter 13 to address divorce-related obligations

Professional Coordination

Legal Team Requirements:

- Experienced bankruptcy attorney
- Family law attorney familiar with bankruptcy implications
- Coordination between legal teams
- Clear communication about strategy and timing

Financial Professional Support:

- Accountants for tax implications
- Financial planners for post-divorce/bankruptcy planning
- Appraisers for asset valuation
- Business valuators if self-employment involved

Special Considerations for Different Family Situations

High-Asset Divorces

Complex Asset Protection:

- Multiple properties and investment accounts
- Business ownership and professional practices
- Retirement accounts and pension benefits
- Intellectual property and royalty income

Bankruptcy Strategy for High-Asset Cases:

- Chapter 13 often preferable to protect non-exempt assets
- Strategic timing relative to asset transfers
- Coordination with estate planning considerations
- Tax implications of debt discharge and asset division

Business Owner Divorces

Business Valuation Challenges:

- Impact of divorce on business operations
- Debt guarantees and business liability
- Customer and vendor relationship disruption
- Cash flow problems during divorce proceedings

Bankruptcy Options for Business Owners:

- Chapter 13 to reorganize business and personal debt
- Chapter 7 for failed businesses with personal guarantees
- Coordination with business bankruptcy if necessary
- Protection of essential business assets

Real Business Owner Example: *Patricia, restaurant owner, San Diego*

- Divorce disrupted business operations and cash flow
- Personal guarantees on business debt became unmanageable
- Filed Chapter 13 to reorganize both business and personal obligations
- Maintained business operations while addressing divorce settlement
- Successfully completed plan and rebuilt both business and personal life

Domestic Violence Situations

Safety Considerations:

- Bankruptcy filing creates public records
- Address confidentiality concerns
- Court appearance safety planning
- Protection from financial abuse continuation

Strategic Approaches:

- Individual bankruptcy filing for safety
- Use of Chapter 13 protections for stability
- Coordination with domestic violence legal services
- Building financial independence through bankruptcy relief

Military Family Considerations

Military-Specific Issues:

- Deployment effects on court proceedings
- Military pension division
- Geographic complications with multiple states
- Security clearance implications

Servicemembers Civil Relief Act (SCRA):

- Protection from default judgments during deployment
- Ability to stay proceedings during military service
- Coordination with bankruptcy automatic stay
- Special protections for military families

Protecting Yourself During Divorce and Bankruptcy

Financial Self-Protection Strategies

Document Everything:

- All marital assets and debts
- Income and expense records
- Evidence of separate property
- Financial misconduct by spouse

- Hidden assets or income

Separate Your Finances:

- Open individual bank accounts
- Establish individual credit
- Remove spouse from joint accounts when possible
- Monitor credit reports for unauthorized activity

Protect Your Credit:

- Close joint credit accounts
- Remove spouse as authorized user
- Monitor joint accounts for abuse
- Document all debt obligations and payments

Legal Protection Strategies

Bankruptcy Timing:

- Consider filing before separation to eliminate joint debts
- Don't delay if financial situation is deteriorating
- Coordinate with divorce attorney on optimal timing
- Consider both spouses' financial situations

Divorce Negotiation:

- Understand bankruptcy implications of proposed settlements
- Negotiate actual debt payoff, not just assignment
- Include indemnification clauses for joint debts
- Consider future bankruptcy possibilities in settlement terms

Asset Protection:

- Understand exemption laws in your state
- Plan asset purchases and sales strategically

- Consider retirement account protection
- Coordinate with estate planning documents

Real-Life Case Studies: Lessons from Success and Failure

Success Story: The Strategic Joint Filing

Background: *Michael and Lisa, married 16 years, Buffalo, NY*

- Two children, ages 12 and 15
- Combined income $95,000, accumulated debt $85,000
- Marriage breakdown due to communication issues, not financial abuse
- Both committed to children's welfare despite marital problems

Strategic Approach:

- Recognized marriage was ending but maintained cooperation for financial and family benefits
- Filed joint Chapter 7 bankruptcy before separation
- Eliminated all credit card and medical debt
- Protected family home and vehicles through exemptions

Divorce Settlement:

- Asset division focused on protected property, not debt allocation
- No fights over who would pay which creditors
- Legal fees reduced due to simplified financial picture
- Both spouses emerged debt-free for fresh starts

Outcomes:

- Both spouses maintained good relationships with children
- No ongoing financial entanglements beyond support obligations

- Both able to rebuild financially within 2-3 years
- Children maintained stability throughout process

Key Lessons:

- Cooperation during crisis benefits entire family
- Strategic timing can eliminate debt for both spouses
- Simplified divorce proceedings when debt is eliminated
- Children's welfare protected through parents' financial stability

Cautionary Tale: The Debt Assignment Disaster

Background: *Jennifer, age 38, Long Island,* NY

- Stay-at-home mother for 12 years
- Divorce assigned $67,000 in credit card debt to ex-husband
- Ex-husband agreed to pay debt in exchange for larger asset share

The Unraveling:

- Ex-husband made payments for 6 months, then stopped
- Lost job and filed Chapter 7 bankruptcy
- Credit card companies pursued Jennifer for full debt amount
- Discovered ex-husband had continued using cards after separation

Financial Devastation:

- Jennifer's credit destroyed by ex-husband's default
- Forced to work multiple jobs to pay debt she thought was resolved
- Could not qualify for mortgage or car loans
- Had to file Chapter 7 bankruptcy 18 months after divorce

Recovery Process:

- Chapter 7 eliminated the assigned debt
- Took 3 years to rebuild credit from bankruptcy

- Eventually purchased home with FHA loan
- Children experienced instability due to multiple moves

Key Lessons:

- Divorce agreements don't protect you from creditors
- Joint debt remains joint until actually paid off
- Trust but verify ex-spouse's financial responsibility
- Consider worst-case scenarios in divorce planning

Success Story: The Chapter 13 Support Solution

Background: *David, age 45, Sacramento, CA*

- Divorce left him with substantial support obligations
- Behind on support due to job loss during divorce proceedings
- Owed $32,000 in support arrears plus ongoing monthly obligations

Chapter 13 Strategy:

- Filed Chapter 13 to address support arrears systematically
- Plan paid support arrears as priority debt over 5 years
- Caught up on support while maintaining current obligations
- Discharged other debt to free income for support payments

Family Benefits:

- Ex-wife received consistent support payments through trustee
- Children's needs met without ongoing conflict
- Reduced litigation and legal fees
- Improved relationship with ex-wife due to reliable payments

Long-term Success:

- Successfully completed 5-year plan
- Maintained good relationship with children

- Rebuilt credit and financial stability
- Eventually helped children with college expenses

Key Lessons:

- Chapter 13 can structure support payments for success
- Consistent payments improve family relationships
- Reduced conflict benefits children's welfare
- Financial responsibility leads to long-term family stability

Tax Implications of Divorce and Bankruptcy

Debt Discharge and Taxable Income

General Rule: Forgiven debt is usually taxable income, but bankruptcy discharge is generally an exception.

Divorce-Related Debt:

- Property settlement debt discharge may have tax implications
- Support obligation discharge (rare) could be taxable
- Timing of discharge relative to divorce may affect tax treatment

Coordination Requirements:

- Work with tax professional familiar with both divorce and bankruptcy
- Plan timing to minimize tax consequences
- Consider impact on both spouses' tax situations
- Understand implications for future tax returns

Alimony and Support Tax Treatment

Current Tax Law:

- Alimony is no longer deductible for payor or taxable for recipient

(divorces after 2018)

- Child support is neither deductible nor taxable
- Property settlement payments are generally not taxable events

Bankruptcy Impact:

- Discharge of support obligations (if it occurs) may create taxable income
- Property settlement discharges may affect basis calculations
- Coordination with divorce settlement tax planning

State-Specific Considerations

New York Divorce and Bankruptcy

New York Specifics:

- Equitable distribution state (not community property)
- Strong creditor protections in some contexts
- Generous homestead exemptions in certain counties
- Complex business valuation rules

Strategic Considerations:

- Timing relative to residence requirements
- Choice between federal and state exemptions
- Coordination with New York family court procedures
- Understanding of local trustee and judge practices

California Divorce and Bankruptcy

California Specifics:

- Community property state with different asset division rules
- Two exemption systems with different benefits

- Complex business and professional practice valuation
- High cost of living affecting support calculations

Strategic Planning:

- Understanding community vs. separate property implications
- Choosing optimal exemption system for post-divorce situation
- Coordination with California family court procedures
- Managing high-asset cases effectively

Your Divorce and Bankruptcy Action Plan

Immediate Assessment (When Crisis Becomes Apparent)

Financial Evaluation:

- [ ] List all marital assets and debts
- [ ] Identify separate vs. joint obligations
- [ ] Assess individual income and expense capacity
- [ ] Evaluate immediate financial survival needs
- [ ] Document spouse's financial behavior and reliability

Legal Consultation:

- [ ] Meet with experienced bankruptcy attorney
- [ ] Consult with family law attorney familiar with bankruptcy
- [ ] Understand coordination requirements and timing options
- [ ] Assess costs and benefits of different approaches
- [ ] Develop integrated legal strategy

Safety and Security:

- [ ] Ensure access to emergency funds

- [ ] Protect important documents and records
- [ ] Consider safety issues if domestic violence present
- [ ] Secure individual credit and banking relationships
- [ ] Plan for temporary housing and support needs

Strategic Planning Phase

Timing Analysis:

- [ ] Evaluate benefits of pre-divorce vs. post-divorce bankruptcy
- [ ] Consider cooperation level with spouse
- [ ] Assess urgency of financial relief needs
- [ ] Coordinate with divorce proceeding timeline
- [ ] Plan for optimal asset protection strategies

Professional Team Assembly:

- [ ] Retain experienced bankruptcy attorney
- [ ] Engage family law attorney with bankruptcy knowledge
- [ ] Consider financial planner for post-crisis planning
- [ ] Engage accountant for tax planning
- [ ] Coordinate communication between professionals

Family Considerations:

- [ ] Plan for children's stability throughout process
- [ ] Consider impact on children's education and activities
- [ ] Develop co-parenting strategies that support financial recovery
- [ ] Plan for family counseling or support services
- [ ] Maintain focus on long-term family welfare

Implementation and Recovery

During Legal Proceedings:

- [ ] Maintain compliance with all court orders
- [ ] Communicate openly with legal team
- [ ] Focus on cooperation where possible for family benefit
- [ ] Document all financial transactions and agreements
- [ ] Plan for post-proceeding financial management

Post-Resolution Planning:

- [ ] Implement credit rebuilding strategies
- [ ] Build emergency fund for future stability
- [ ] Develop sustainable budgeting and spending habits
- [ ] Plan for major life goals (housing, education, retirement)
- [ ] Consider helping others facing similar challenges

The Bottom Line: Crisis as Opportunity

While the combination of divorce and bankruptcy represents one of life's most challenging periods, it also provides an opportunity for genuine renewal and fresh starts. The key principles for success are:

Strategic Thinking:

- Understand how divorce and bankruptcy interact legally and financially
- Plan timing and coordination for optimal outcomes
- Consider both immediate relief and long-term consequences
- Work with experienced professionals who understand both areas

Family Focus:

- Prioritize children's welfare and stability throughout the process
- Seek cooperation where possible, even during difficult times
- Use financial relief to reduce conflict and improve family

relationships

- Build foundation for healthy post-divorce family dynamics

Financial Responsibility:

- Take control of your individual financial situation
- Don't rely on ex-spouse for financial security
- Build skills and resources for independent financial management
- Use crisis as motivation for better financial habits

Personal Growth:

- Learn from the experience to avoid future problems
- Develop resilience and problem-solving skills
- Build support networks and professional relationships
- Help others who face similar challenges

Long-term Perspective:

- Focus on successful completion of both processes
- Build foundation for long-term financial and personal stability
- Create opportunities for career and personal growth
- Maintain optimism about the future despite current difficulties

Remember: Millions of people have successfully navigated both divorce and bankruptcy and gone on to build prosperous, fulfilling lives. While the journey is challenging, it's also an opportunity to eliminate financial burdens, protect what matters most, and build a foundation for a better future - for yourself and your family.

The crisis will end. The skills, knowledge, and resilience you develop during this period will serve you well for the rest of your life.

In the next chapter, we'll explore another complex intersection: bankruptcy and student loans - understanding your options when educational debt becomes unmanageable and exploring the rare but possible paths to student loan relief through bankruptcy.

17

Bankruptcy and Student Loans

The Toughest Debt to Erase

The Student Loan Crisis: America's $1.7 Trillion Problem

Student loans represent one of the most frustrating aspects of the American bankruptcy system. While bankruptcy can eliminate credit card debt from an expensive vacation or medical bills from a health crisis, the debt you incurred to get an education - something that should improve your financial prospects - is notoriously difficult to discharge.

This seems fundamentally unfair to many people, and frankly, it is. Student loans have become a form of modern indentured servitude for millions of Americans, following them through job loss, disability, retirement, and even death in some cases. Unlike virtually every other form of debt, student loans seem designed to be permanent obligations.

But while student loan discharge in bankruptcy is difficult, it's not impossible. Recent changes in federal policy have made discharge somewhat more accessible, and there are strategies both within and outside of bankruptcy that can provide relief. More importantly, bankruptcy can often provide significant indirect relief by eliminating other debts and freeing up income to manage student loans more effectively.

In this chapter, we'll explore the complex relationship between bankruptcy and student loans, examine the rare but real possibilities for discharge, and provide practical strategies for managing student loan debt even when discharge isn't possible.

The Legal Framework: Why Student Loans Are Different

Historical Context: How We Got Here

Pre-1976: Student Loans Were Dischargeable Originally, student loans could be discharged in bankruptcy just like any other debt. However, concerns about abuse led Congress to begin restricting discharge.

The Progressive Restrictions:

- **1976:** 5-year waiting period before discharge
- **1990:** Waiting period extended to 7 years
- **1998:** Private student loans became non-dischargeable
- **2005:** All student loans (federal and private) became presumptively non-dischargeable

The Current Standard: Today, both federal and private student loans can only be discharged by proving "undue hardship" - a deliberately difficult standard that very few borrowers can meet.

What Counts as a "Student Loan"

Protected Student Loans:

- Federal student loans (Stafford, PLUS, Perkins, consolidation loans)
- Private student loans from banks and other lenders
- Loans guaranteed by government agencies
- Loans made under any program funded in whole or part by

government or nonprofit institution

What Might NOT Be Protected:

- Private loans not used for qualified educational expenses
- Loans that exceed the cost of education
- Loans made directly to borrower, not through school's financial aid office
- Credit cards or personal loans used for education (if not structured as student loans)
- Bar study loans and some professional exam preparation loans

The Importance of Loan Characterization: Whether a loan qualifies for special protection can determine whether it survives bankruptcy. This analysis requires careful examination of loan documents and purposes.

The Undue Hardship Standard

The Brunner Test: The Three-Part Challenge

Most federal courts use the **Brunner test** to determine undue hardship. You must prove **all three** of these elements:

1. Minimal Standard of Living Test: You cannot maintain a minimal standard of living for yourself and your dependents if forced to repay the student loans.

What Courts Consider:

- Current income vs. reasonable living expenses
- Ability to meet basic needs (food, shelter, transportation, medical care)
- Impact on dependents and family obligations
- Comparison to poverty guidelines and local cost of living

2. Persistence Test: Your current financial hardship is likely to persist for the significant portion of the student loan repayment period.

What Courts Examine:

- Age and health status
- Education level and job skills
- Employment prospects in your field
- Disability or chronic health conditions
- Local job market conditions
- Career advancement potential

3. Good Faith Test: You have made good faith efforts to repay the student loans.

Evidence of Good Faith:

- Participation in forbearance or deferment programs
- Attempts to use income-driven repayment plans
- Consistent payment history when financially able
- Efforts to increase income or reduce expenses
- Seeking employment counseling or job training

Alternative Tests: Some Courts Use Different Standards

Totality of Circumstances Test: Some courts use a more flexible analysis considering:

- Current financial situation
- Future financial prospects
- Borrower's education and employability
- Good faith efforts to repay
- Policy implications of discharge

This approach may be more borrower-friendly but is used in fewer courts.

Recent Changes: The Path to Relief Gets Easier

Department of Justice Policy Changes (2022-2023)

Streamlined Process for Federal Loans: The Department of Justice and Department of Education have implemented new guidelines making it easier to prove undue hardship for federal student loans.

Key Improvements:

- **Standardized attestation form** for documenting hardship
- **Clearer guidance** on what constitutes undue hardship
- **Presumptive approval** for certain circumstances
- **Reduced litigation** for qualifying cases

Who Benefits Most:

- Borrowers over age 50 with loans over 20 years old
- Disabled borrowers unable to work
- Borrowers with income below poverty guidelines for extended periods
- Those facing exceptional circumstances like serious illness

The Attestation Process

How It Works: Instead of requiring extensive litigation, borrowers can submit a detailed attestation form documenting their financial hardship and inability to repay.

Required Information:

- Detailed financial statement
- Employment history and prospects
- Medical conditions affecting earning capacity
- Family circumstances and obligations
- Previous repayment efforts

Government Review: The Department of Education reviews the attestation and may agree to discharge without requiring a full adversary proceeding in bankruptcy court.

Strategies for Student Loan Discharge

When to Consider Adversary Proceedings

Strong Discharge Candidates:

- **Older borrowers** (50+) with long-term payment struggles
- **Disabled individuals** unable to work in their trained field
- **Borrowers with serious health conditions** affecting earning capacity
- **Those with extended unemployment** or underemployment despite education
- **People whose education provided no economic benefit**

Weaker Discharge Cases:

- Recent graduates with short payment history
- Borrowers with strong earning potential in their field
- Those who haven't attempted income-driven repayment plans
- People with good health and employment prospects

The Adversary Proceeding Process

Step 1: File Bankruptcy You must first file either Chapter 7 or Chapter 13 bankruptcy.

Step 2: File Adversary Proceeding This is a separate lawsuit within your bankruptcy case specifically challenging the student loan debt.

Step 3: Discovery and Evidence Both sides gather evidence about:

- Your financial situation and prospects
- Your education and employment history

- Your good faith efforts to repay
- The value received from your education

Step 4: Trial or Settlement

- Cases may settle if government agrees discharge is appropriate
- If no settlement, case goes to trial before bankruptcy judge
- Burden of proof is on you to demonstrate undue hardship

Step 5: Decision Judge decides whether to:

- Grant full discharge of student loans
- Grant partial discharge
- Deny discharge completely

Partial Discharge Options

What Partial Discharge Can Accomplish:

- Reduce loan balance to affordable amount
- Eliminate interest or fees
- Modify payment terms
- Discharge some loans while keeping others

When Partial Discharge Makes Sense:

- You can afford some payment but not full obligation
- Interest has substantially increased original debt
- Some loans provide less value than others
- Settlement opportunity exists

Alternative Relief: Income-Driven Repayment Plans

Federal Loan Forgiveness Programs

Income-Driven Repayment (IDR) Plans:

Income-Based Repayment (IBR):

- Payment based on income and family size
- Forgiveness after 20-25 years of payments
- Interest may be subsidized during hardship

Pay As You Earn (PAYE):

- Generally 10% of discretionary income
- Forgiveness after 20 years
- Only for newer borrowers

Revised Pay As You Earn (REPAYE):

- Available to all borrowers regardless of when borrowed
- Forgiveness after 20-25 years depending on loan type
- Interest benefits during low-income periods

Income-Contingent Repayment (ICR):

- 20% of discretionary income or 12-year standard payment
- Forgiveness after 25 years
- Available for PLUS loans to parents

Public Service Loan Forgiveness (PSLF)

Program Requirements:

- Work for government or qualifying nonprofit organization
- Make 120 qualifying payments (10 years)
- Be enrolled in income-driven repayment plan
- Have federal Direct Loans

Qualifying Employment:

- Federal, state, local government jobs
- 501(c)(3) nonprofit organizations
- Other nonprofits providing qualifying public services
- AmeriCorps, Peace Corps, and similar programs

Recent Improvements:

- Limited PSLF waiver allowing credit for non-qualifying payments
- Improved processing and customer service
- Clearer guidance on qualifying employment

Tax Implications of Forgiveness

Current Law (Through 2025): Forgiven student loan debt under IDR plans is **not taxable income** due to recent legislative changes.

Future Uncertainty:

- Tax-free treatment currently expires after 2025
- May revert to taxable income for future forgiveness
- Important to plan for potential tax liability

Bankruptcy's Indirect Benefits for Student Loan Borrowers

Freeing Up Income for Student Loan Management

The Cash Flow Strategy: Even when student loans can't be discharged, bankruptcy can dramatically improve your ability to manage them by eliminating other debts.

Real Example: *Sarah, nurse, Buffalo,* NY

- Student loans: $85,000
- Credit card debt: $32,000
- Medical bills: $18,000

- Monthly minimums before bankruptcy: $1,480
- After Chapter 7 (student loans only): $650
- **Result:** $830/month freed up to pay student loans aggressively or build emergency fund

Strategic Approaches:

- Use Chapter 7 to eliminate other debts, focus income on student loans
- Use Chapter 13 to reorganize all debts while maintaining student loan payments
- Build emergency fund to avoid future borrowing
- Increase student loan payments with freed-up income

Chapter 13 and Student Loan Management

Payment Suspension During Chapter 13: While your Chapter 13 plan is active, you may be able to suspend student loan payments if they're not included in your plan.

Benefits:

- Three to five years of payment relief
- Time to improve income and job prospects
- Focus on completing Chapter 13 plan successfully
- Build savings for post-plan student loan management

Considerations:

- Interest may continue accruing during plan
- Loans may be in default status
- Need post-plan strategy for student loan resumption
- Coordinate with loan servicer about plan period

Private Student Loan Strategies

Challenging Private Loan Characterization

Why It Matters: Private loans that don't meet the technical definition of "student loans" under bankruptcy law may be dischargeable as regular unsecured debt.

Factors That May Help:

- Loan funds used for living expenses beyond education costs
- Loans exceeding reasonable education expenses
- Loans made directly to borrower without school involvement
- Loans not certified by educational institution
- Credit cards or personal loans used for education

Investigation Required:

- Review original loan documents
- Examine use of loan proceeds
- Analyze relationship between lender and school
- Consider timing and purpose of borrowing

Private Loan Discharge Successes

Real Case Example: *Michael, law school graduate*

- Borrowed $45,000 from private lender for "living expenses"
- Loan exceeded school's certified cost of attendance
- Court found loan was personal loan, not protected educational debt
- Successfully discharged in Chapter 7

Key Factors in Success:

- Loan amount exceeded reasonable educational expenses
- No school certification or involvement in loan process
- Funds used for general living expenses, not tuition

- Lender couldn't prove educational purpose

Special Circumstances and Exceptions

Closed School Discharge

When Available:

- School closes while you're enrolled
- You withdraw within 180 days before closure
- Unable to complete program due to closure

Benefits:

- Complete discharge of federal loans for that program
- Possible refund of payments already made
- Restoration of federal aid eligibility
- No tax consequences

False Certification Discharge

Grounds for Discharge:

- School falsely certified your eligibility
- School signed your name on loan documents without authorization
- School failed to refund loans as required

Examples:

- Identity theft by school officials
- Forged signatures on loan documents
- Failure to obtain required licenses or approvals

Unpaid Refund Discharge

When It Applies:

- You withdrew from school
- School failed to pay required refund to loan program
- You're entitled to partial discharge

Common Scenarios:

- Early withdrawal from programs
- School keeps tuition despite withdrawal
- Federal regulations require refunds that weren't made

Practical Strategies for Managing Student Loan Debt

Before Considering Bankruptcy

Exhaust Federal Relief Options:

- Apply for income-driven repayment plans
- Request forbearance or deferment for temporary hardship
- Investigate Public Service Loan Forgiveness eligibility
- Consider loan consolidation for better terms
- Explore state-based loan forgiveness programs

Document Your Hardship:

- Keep detailed records of income and expenses
- Document health conditions affecting earning capacity
- Maintain records of job search efforts
- Track participation in relief programs
- Get professional evaluations for disabilities

During Bankruptcy Planning

Analyze All Debt:

- Identify which debts can be discharged
- Calculate impact of eliminating other debts
- Determine best bankruptcy chapter for overall situation
- Consider timing relative to student loan status

Consider Professional Help:

- Consult with attorney experienced in student loan discharge
- Get evaluation of undue hardship case strength
- Understand costs and likelihood of success
- Explore settlement possibilities

After Bankruptcy

Student Loan Rehabilitation:

- Work with servicer to rehabilitate defaulted loans
- Use improved income position to make consistent payments
- Consider loan forgiveness program eligibility
- Build emergency fund to avoid future default

Long-term Planning:

- Focus on career advancement to increase income
- Consider additional education for better job prospects
- Plan for potential tax liability from future forgiveness
- Help others understand student loan options

Real-Life Case Studies

Success Story: The Disabled Professional

Background: *Jennifer, age 52, former financial advisor*

- MBA from respected university, student loans $120,000
- Developed multiple sclerosis, unable to continue high-stress career
- Attempted various jobs but health prevented consistent work
- Exhausted savings and family support over 8 years

Bankruptcy Strategy:

- Filed Chapter 7 to eliminate credit card debt
- Filed adversary proceeding for student loan discharge
- Documented medical condition and employment attempts
- Showed good faith through previous payment efforts

Evidence Presented:

- Medical records showing progressive disability
- Employment history showing inability to maintain work
- Financial records showing persistent poverty
- Evidence of previous payment efforts and forbearance use

Outcome:

- Court granted full discharge of student loans
- Eliminated all other debt through Chapter 7
- Qualified for disability benefits during process
- Rebuilt life with volunteer work and part-time consulting

Key Factors in Success:

- Documented disability preventing work in trained field
- Age and health made future improvement unlikely
- Extensive previous efforts to repay loans
- Clear evidence of good faith throughout process

Partial Success: The Older Borrower

Background: *Robert, age 58, social worker*

- Graduate degree in social work, student loans $85,000
- Worked in public service but never qualified for PSLF
- Health issues limited earning capacity in recent years
- Divorced, supporting elderly parents

Adversary Proceeding:

- Argued age and health made full repayment impossible
- Documented limited income potential in remaining work years
- Showed good faith through consistent payment efforts
- Requested partial discharge based on circumstances

Settlement Negotiation:

- Department of Education agreed to settle case
- Reduced loan balance to $25,000
- Eliminated all accrued interest and fees
- Established affordable payment plan for remaining balance

Final Resolution:

- Manageable remaining debt of $25,000
- Monthly payment reduced from $850 to $180
- Able to maintain basic living standard
- Completed remaining payments within 3 years

Challenge Case: The Law School Graduate

Background: *David, age 35, law school graduate*

- Law degree from mid-tier school, student loans $180,000
- Unable to pass bar exam after multiple attempts
- Working in document review and contract positions

- Income insufficient for standard repayment

Discharge Attempt:

- Filed adversary proceeding arguing education provided no benefit
- Claimed inability to work in legal profession
- Documented low income despite advanced degree
- Argued law school misrepresented job prospects

Court Decision:

- Court denied discharge despite sympathetic circumstances
- Found borrower still had earning potential with law degree
- Noted availability of income-driven repayment plans
- Determined good faith not established due to recent graduation

Alternative Resolution:

- Enrolled in income-driven repayment plan
- Payment reduced to $120/month based on income
- Pursuing alternative careers using legal education
- Building experience for potential future bar exam success

Lessons Learned:

- Recent graduation makes discharge more difficult
- Courts reluctant to discharge professional school debt for young borrowers
- Income-driven plans may provide better relief than discharge
- Career development may improve situation over time

State-Specific Considerations

New York Student Loan Protections

State Programs:

- New York State loan forgiveness programs for certain professions
- Enhanced consumer protections for private loan borrowers
- State-funded loan repayment assistance programs

Bankruptcy Considerations:

- Choice between federal and state exemptions may affect strategy
- Strong homestead exemption may protect property during proceeding
- Local bankruptcy court experience with student loan cases

California Student Loan Landscape

State Initiatives:

- California student loan forgiveness programs
- Enhanced consumer protection laws
- State attorney general enforcement against predatory lenders

Bankruptcy Factors:

- Two exemption systems provide strategic options
- High cost of living supports undue hardship arguments
- Active bankruptcy courts with student loan experience

Your Student Loan and Bankruptcy Action Plan

Assessment Phase

Evaluate Your Situation:

- [ ] List all student loans (federal and private)
- [ ] Document current income and employment prospects
- [ ] Assess health conditions affecting earning capacity

- [ ] Calculate total debt and monthly payment obligations
- [ ] Review previous payment history and good faith efforts

Explore Non-Bankruptcy Options:

- [ ] Apply for income-driven repayment plans
- [ ] Investigate loan forgiveness program eligibility
- [ ] Research employer-based repayment assistance
- [ ] Consider loan rehabilitation for defaulted loans
- [ ] Evaluate closed school or false certification claims

Bankruptcy Evaluation

Discharge Prospects Analysis:

- [ ] Consult with attorney experienced in student loan discharge
- [ ] Evaluate strength of undue hardship case
- [ ] Understand costs and timeline for adversary proceeding
- [ ] Consider likelihood of success vs. alternative strategies
- [ ] Assess partial discharge or settlement possibilities

Overall Debt Strategy:

- [ ] Analyze benefit of eliminating other debts through bankruptcy
- [ ] Calculate impact on ability to manage student loans
- [ ] Consider Chapter 7 vs. Chapter 13 for overall situation
- [ ] Plan timing relative to student loan status and income

Implementation Strategy

If Pursuing Discharge:

- [ ] File appropriate bankruptcy chapter
- [ ] Gather comprehensive documentation for adversary proceeding

- [ ] Prepare detailed financial and medical evidence
- [ ] Work with experienced attorney throughout process
- [ ] Consider settlement opportunities if they arise

If Focusing on Other Debt Relief:

- [ ] Use bankruptcy to eliminate dischargeable debts
- [ ] Free up income for student loan management
- [ ] Build emergency fund to avoid future borrowing
- [ ] Develop long-term student loan repayment strategy
- [ ] Plan for career advancement and income growth

Long-term Management

Post-Bankruptcy Planning:

- [ ] Rehabilitate student loans if in default
- [ ] Enroll in appropriate repayment programs
- [ ] Build emergency fund for financial stability
- [ ] Focus on career development and income growth
- [ ] Plan for potential loan forgiveness programs

Ongoing Monitoring:

- [ ] Stay informed about changing student loan laws
- [ ] Monitor eligibility for forgiveness programs
- [ ] Track progress toward loan forgiveness timelines
- [ ] Maintain good payment history for future opportunities
- [ ] Help others understand student loan options

The Future of Student Loans and Bankruptcy

Potential Legal Changes

Congressional Proposals:

- Bills to restore student loan dischargeability
- Proposals for expanded forgiveness programs
- Enhanced bankruptcy relief for student borrowers
- Consumer protection improvements

Judicial Trends:

- Some courts becoming more borrower-friendly
- Increased recognition of student loan crisis
- Better implementation of existing discharge standards
- More partial discharge and settlement agreements

Advocacy and Policy Development

What You Can Do:

- Contact representatives about student loan reform
- Share your story with policymakers and media
- Support organizations advocating for student loan reform
- Help others understand their rights and options
- Vote for candidates who support student loan relief

The Bottom Line: Hope Despite the Challenges

Student loans represent the most difficult debt to discharge in bankruptcy, but they're not impossible to address. The key principles for success are:

Realistic Assessment:

- Understand that discharge is difficult but not impossible
- Evaluate your situation honestly and objectively

- Consider all options, not just bankruptcy discharge
- Get professional evaluation of your prospects

Strategic Thinking:

- Use bankruptcy to eliminate other debts even if student loans survive
- Focus on improving your overall financial situation
- Plan for long-term student loan management
- Consider indirect benefits of bankruptcy relief

Persistence and Documentation:

- Maintain detailed records of hardship and payment efforts
- Stay informed about changing laws and programs
- Don't give up on seeking relief through available programs
- Help others understand their options

Professional Guidance:

- Work with attorneys experienced in student loan discharge
- Get evaluation from multiple professionals if necessary
- Understand costs and likelihood of success before proceeding
- Consider all alternatives before committing to expensive litigation

Long-term Perspective:

- Focus on building overall financial stability
- Use bankruptcy relief to improve your position for student loan management
- Plan for career advancement and income growth
- Stay informed about evolving relief programs and options

Remember: While student loans are the most challenging debt in bankruptcy, millions of people are successfully managing them through income-driven plans, forgiveness programs, and strategic financial planning. Bankruptcy may not eliminate your student loans, but it can eliminate other debts and provide the financial breathing room you need to develop a sustainable long-term strategy.

The student loan crisis is real, but so are the growing number of relief options. Stay informed, stay persistent, and don't lose hope. Your educational investment should enhance your life, not destroy it.

In the next chapter, we'll explore another complex area where bankruptcy law intersects with other obligations: tax debt and how bankruptcy can provide relief from overwhelming obligations to the IRS and state tax agencies.

18

Bankruptcy and Tax Debt

What You Can and Can't Discharge

Tax Debt: The Government's Special Collection Powers

Few things strike fear into people's hearts like a letter from the IRS or state tax agency. Unlike other creditors who must sue you to collect debts, tax agencies have extraordinary collection powers. They can seize your wages, empty your bank accounts, place liens on your property, and even take your home - all without going to court first.

This overwhelming collection power makes tax debt particularly scary, but it also makes bankruptcy potentially very valuable for people struggling with tax obligations. While tax debts have special protections in bankruptcy that other debts don't enjoy, bankruptcy can still provide significant relief in many situations.

The key is understanding which tax debts can be eliminated, which ones survive bankruptcy, and how to use bankruptcy strategically to manage tax obligations you can't discharge. Sometimes bankruptcy can eliminate tax debt completely. Other times, it provides breathing room and structure for paying taxes without the IRS's aggressive collection tactics.

In this chapter, we'll demystify the complex rules governing tax debt in bankruptcy, help you understand your options, and provide strategies for dealing with tax obligations both within and outside the bankruptcy system.

Understanding Tax Debt in Bankruptcy

Why Tax Debts Get Special Treatment

Government as Creditor: Tax debts are treated differently in bankruptcy because:

- Taxes fund essential government services
- Everyone should pay their fair share
- Tax collection supports the public good
- Government needs reliable revenue sources

Policy Rationale: Congress decided that allowing easy discharge of tax debts would:

- Encourage tax avoidance and non-compliance
- Undermine the tax system's integrity
- Create unfair advantages for those who file bankruptcy
- Reduce government revenue needed for public services

The Balance: Bankruptcy law tries to balance:

- Individual relief from overwhelming debt
- Government's need to collect taxes
- Fairness between taxpayers who pay and those who don't
- Protection of the tax system's integrity

Types of Tax Debts

Income Taxes:

- Federal income taxes
- State income taxes
- Local income taxes (where applicable)

Employment Taxes:

- Employee withholdings (Social Security, Medicare, income tax)
- Employer's share of payroll taxes
- Unemployment insurance taxes

Other Taxes:

- Sales taxes (for businesses)
- Property taxes
- Excise taxes
- Penalties and interest on tax debts

Each type has different rules for discharge in bankruptcy.

Income Tax Discharge Rules: The Five-Part Test

The General Rule: Recent Taxes Survive

Basic Principle: Recent income tax debts cannot be discharged in bankruptcy. However, older tax debts that meet specific criteria can be eliminated just like credit card debt.

The Five Requirements for Income Tax Discharge

All five conditions must be met for income tax discharge:

1. The Three-Year Rule

Requirement: The tax return was due at least **3 years** before your bankruptcy filing date (including extensions).

How to Calculate:

- Start with the original return due date (usually April 15)
- Add any extensions (typically 6 months for individuals)
- Count forward 3 years to determine discharge eligibility

Example:

- 2020 tax return due April 15, 2021 (with extension October 15, 2021)
- Earliest discharge date: October 15, 2024
- If you file bankruptcy on November 1, 2024, the 2020 taxes may be dischargeable

2. The Two-Year Rule

Requirement: You must have filed the tax return at least **2 years** before your bankruptcy filing date.

Important Notes:

- The return must be actually filed, not just due
- Late-filed returns start the 2-year clock from actual filing date
- Substitute returns filed by the IRS don't count
- Amended returns may restart the clock

Example:

- 2019 taxes due April 15, 2020
- You filed the return on September 1, 2022 (2+ years late)
- Earliest discharge date: September 1, 2024 (2 years from actual filing)

3. The 240-Day Assessment Rule

Requirement: The tax must have been **assessed** by the IRS at least **240 days** before your bankruptcy filing (or not assessed at all).

What "Assessment" Means:

- IRS formally records the tax debt in their system
- Usually happens when return is filed or audit is completed
- Assessment date can be found on IRS transcripts

Extensions: The 240-day period can be extended by:

- Previous bankruptcy filings
- Offers in compromise
- Collection due process hearings

4. No Fraud or Willful Evasion

Requirement: You must not have committed tax fraud or willfully attempted to evade paying taxes.

What Constitutes Fraud:

- Filing false tax returns
- Claiming fraudulent deductions
- Hiding income or assets
- Using false Social Security numbers
- Maintaining false books and records

Willful Evasion Examples:

- Deliberately failing to file returns
- Hiding assets to avoid collection
- Using nominee entities to conceal ownership
- Cashing paychecks to avoid wage garnishment

5. Legitimate Return Filed

Requirement: You must have filed a legitimate tax return for the tax year in question.

What Counts:

- Returns filed by the taxpayer
- Late returns that are complete and honest
- Amended returns correcting errors

What Doesn't Count:

- Substitute for returns (SFRs) filed by the IRS
- Returns filed solely to meet bankruptcy requirements
- Fraudulent returns

Practical Application: Tax Discharge Analysis

Example Analysis: *Jennifer, small business owner, filing bankruptcy in 2025*

2020 Taxes:

- Due date: April 15, 2021
- Filed date: April 10, 2021
- Assessment date: May 1, 2021
- No fraud involved
- **Analysis:** Meets all five tests ✓ **DISCHARGEABLE**

2021 Taxes:

- Due date: April 15, 2022
- Filed date: October 1, 2023 (late filing)
- Assessment date: November 1, 2023
- No fraud involved
- **Analysis:** Fails 2-year rule (filed October 2023) ✗ **NOT DISCHARGEABLE**

2022 Taxes:

- Due date: April 15, 2023
- Never filed

- **Analysis:** Fails multiple tests ✗ **NOT DISCHARGEABLE**

Employment and Payroll Taxes: Always Survive

Trust Fund Taxes: The Personal Liability Trap

What Are Trust Fund Taxes: When businesses withhold taxes from employee paychecks, those funds are held "in trust" for the government. This includes:

- Federal income tax withholdings
- Social Security and Medicare withholdings
- State income tax withholdings

Personal Liability: Certain individuals can be held personally liable for unpaid trust fund taxes:

- Business owners
- Corporate officers
- Payroll managers
- Anyone with authority over payroll decisions

Why They're Never Dischargeable:

- The money belongs to employees and the government, not the business
- Personal liability is designed to ensure these taxes get paid
- Policy strongly favors protecting employee withholdings

Employer's Share of Payroll Taxes

What These Include:

- Employer's share of Social Security and Medicare taxes
- Federal and state unemployment taxes
- Other employer-specific tax obligations

Discharge Rules:

- Generally not dischargeable in bankruptcy
- Treated as priority debts that must be paid in full
- May be subject to different rules than trust fund taxes

Real Business Owner Example

Background: *David, restaurant owner, Sacramento*

- Restaurant failed during pandemic
- Owed $45,000 in employment taxes
- $25,000 trust fund taxes (employee withholdings)
- $20,000 employer's share

Bankruptcy Result:

- Trust fund taxes: **NOT DISCHARGEABLE** (personal liability)
- Employer's share: **NOT DISCHARGEABLE** (priority debt)
- **Total remaining after bankruptcy:** $45,000

Chapter 13 Strategy:

- Filed Chapter 13 to pay employment taxes over 5 years
- Monthly payment: $750 for employment taxes
- Discharged other business debts
- Maintained personal residence and family stability

Chapter 7 vs. Chapter 13: Different Benefits for Tax Debt

Chapter 7: Clean Discharge for Qualifying Taxes

Benefits:

- Complete elimination of dischargeable income taxes

- No payment plan required
- Fast resolution (3-4 months)
- Clean slate for qualifying tax years

Limitations:

- Cannot help with non-dischargeable taxes
- No structure for paying remaining tax obligations
- May lose property if significant tax liens exist
- Limited relief for employment taxes

Chapter 13: Structure and Time for All Tax Debts

Unique Chapter 13 Powers:

Priority Debt Treatment:

- Pay non-dischargeable taxes over 3-5 years
- No additional penalties or interest (in most cases)
- Protection from IRS collection actions
- Structured payment plan with court oversight

Interest and Penalty Relief:

- Interest stops accruing on most tax debts during plan
- Penalties may be eliminated or reduced
- Focus on paying principal balance
- Significant savings compared to IRS payment plans

Discharge Benefits:

- Enhanced discharge of some tax debts at plan completion
- May discharge taxes that survive Chapter 7
- Discharge of tax penalties in many cases

Strategic Comparison Example

Robert's Tax Debt Situation:

- 2019 taxes: $15,000 (dischargeable in Chapter 7)
- 2021 taxes: $25,000 (not dischargeable)
- 2022 taxes: $18,000 (not dischargeable)
- Employment taxes: $30,000 (not dischargeable)

Chapter 7 Result:

- Discharges: $15,000 (2019 taxes only)
- Remaining debt: $73,000
- IRS can resume collection immediately after discharge

Chapter 13 Alternative:

- Discharges: $15,000 (2019 taxes)
- Pays remaining $73,000 over 5 years ($1,217/month)
- No additional interest or penalties
- IRS collection activities stopped for 5 years
- Possible additional discharge at plan completion

Tax Liens: The Permanent Attachment

How Tax Liens Work

What Is a Tax Lien: A legal claim against all property you own or acquire, securing payment of tax debt.

When Liens Attach:

- IRS or state assesses tax debt
- Sends demand for payment
- You don't pay within specified time

- Lien automatically attaches to all property

What Liens Cover:

- Real estate (home, land, rental property)
- Personal property (cars, boats, equipment)
- Financial accounts
- Future acquired property
- Business assets and inventory

Liens in Bankruptcy

Critical Rule: Bankruptcy can eliminate your personal obligation to pay taxes, but tax liens may survive and remain attached to property.

The Practical Effect:

- You no longer owe the tax debt personally
- The lien remains attached to property you owned when bankruptcy was filed
- IRS can still enforce the lien against that specific property
- Cannot pursue you personally or attach new property acquired after bankruptcy

Lien Avoidance and Strategic Planning

When Liens Can Be Avoided:

- Lien impairs exemptions in certain circumstances
- Procedural errors in lien filing
- Timing issues with lien attachment

Strategic Options:

- Challenge lien validity or priority
- Negotiate lien subordination for refinancing

- Plan property sales to address lien obligations
- Use Chapter 13 to pay down liens over time

Real Lien Example: *Maria, homeowner, Buffalo*

- Home value: $180,000
- Mortgage: $120,000
- Tax lien: $35,000
- Home equity: $60,000

Chapter 7 Result:

- Tax debt discharged (met all requirements)
- Tax lien remains on home
- Must pay $35,000 to sell or refinance home
- Lien doesn't attach to new property

Chapter 13 Alternative:

- Pay tax debt through plan over 5 years
- Lien removed after plan completion
- Full equity available for future use

State Tax Considerations

State Income Taxes

General Rules: State income taxes follow similar rules to federal taxes:

- Must meet the same five-part test for discharge
- Subject to state-specific timing requirements
- May have different assessment and collection procedures

State Variations:

- Different statute of limitations periods

- Varying penalty and interest policies
- Different lien and collection procedures
- State-specific exemptions and protections

New York State Tax Issues

New York Specifics:

- Aggressive collection procedures
- Quick lien filing practices
- High penalties and interest rates
- Limited settlement opportunities

Bankruptcy Strategies:

- Coordinate federal and state tax analysis
- Consider timing of bankruptcy filing
- Evaluate exemption strategies for tax liens
- Plan for post-bankruptcy state tax compliance

California Tax Considerations

California Characteristics:

- Franchise Tax Board has strong collection powers
- High state income tax rates create large debts
- Complex business tax issues
- Active audit and collection programs

Strategic Planning:

- Analyze federal and state taxes separately
- Consider California's exemption options
- Plan for ongoing tax compliance

- Coordinate with federal tax strategies

Practical Strategies for Tax Debt Management

Pre-Bankruptcy Planning

Tax Debt Analysis:

- Obtain IRS and state tax transcripts
- Identify which taxes qualify for discharge
- Calculate total dischargeable vs. non-dischargeable debt
- Assess lien status and property implications

Timing Considerations:

- Plan filing date to maximize dischargeable taxes
- Consider impact of pending audits or assessments
- Coordinate with other debt relief strategies
- Account for seasonal income variations

Documentation Gathering:

- Tax returns for all years in question
- IRS transcripts showing assessment dates
- State tax records and correspondence
- Lien documentation and property records

Chapter 13 Tax Strategies

Plan Design:

- Structure plan to pay priority taxes over 3-5 years
- Minimize interest and penalties through plan protection
- Coordinate tax payments with other plan obligations

- Plan for discharge of eligible tax debt at completion

Ongoing Compliance:

- Stay current on post-petition tax obligations
- File all required returns during plan period
- Make estimated tax payments if self-employed
- Coordinate with trustee on tax issues

Post-Bankruptcy Tax Management

Compliance Strategies:

- Establish systems for ongoing tax compliance
- Build emergency fund for future tax obligations
- Consider quarterly estimated payments
- Work with tax professional for complex situations

Lien Resolution:

- Address remaining tax liens strategically
- Negotiate lien subordination when beneficial
- Plan property transactions around lien obligations
- Consider lien settlement opportunities

Special Circumstances and Advanced Strategies

Offer in Compromise During Bankruptcy

Coordination Issues:

- Bankruptcy and OIC proceedings can conflict
- Timing considerations for both processes
- Asset disclosure requirements in both proceedings

- Impact on discharge timing and eligibility

Strategic Approaches:

- Generally complete bankruptcy before pursuing OIC
- Use bankruptcy to eliminate other debts first
- Focus OIC on non-dischargeable taxes
- Coordinate with experienced professionals

Business Tax Debt and Personal Guarantees

Trust Fund Tax Liability:

- Personal liability for employee withholdings
- Cannot be discharged in any form of bankruptcy
- May require Chapter 13 for structured payment
- Consider impact on business operations and family

Sales Tax and Other Business Taxes:

- May be dischargeable if income tax rules are met
- Often subject to personal guarantees
- Consider business vs. personal bankruptcy strategies
- Coordinate with business wind-down or restructuring

International Tax Issues

Foreign Income and Assets:

- FBAR and other reporting requirements
- Potential penalties for non-compliance
- Coordination with international tax treaties
- Impact on expatriation or immigration status

Complex Strategies:

- Require specialized professional guidance
- May involve multiple jurisdictions
- Coordination with immigration and estate planning
- Significant penalties for errors

Real-Life Case Studies

Success Story: The Contractor's Tax Debt Elimination

Background: *Robert, self-employed contractor, San Diego*

- Built successful contracting business over 15 years
- Fell behind on taxes during economic downturn
- Accumulated large tax debt while struggling to rebuild

Tax Debt Analysis:

- 2018 taxes: $25,000 (dischargeable - met all tests)
- 2019 taxes: $18,000 (dischargeable - met all tests)
- 2020 taxes: $22,000 (dischargeable - met all tests)
- 2021 taxes: $15,000 (not dischargeable - too recent)
- 2022 taxes: $12,000 (not dischargeable - too recent)

Chapter 7 Strategy:

- Filed Chapter 7 in late 2024
- Discharged $65,000 in older tax debt
- Remaining $27,000 in recent taxes
- Eliminated $45,000 in other debt (credit cards, equipment loans)

Post-Bankruptcy Management:

- Arranged payment plan with IRS for remaining $27,000
- Used savings from eliminated debt to make tax payments

- Rebuilt business with debt-free foundation
- Established quarterly estimated payment system

Long-term Success:

- Completed IRS payment plan in 2 years
- Business thrived without debt burden
- Built emergency fund for tax compliance
- Helped other contractors understand tax obligations

Complex Case: The Failed Restaurant Owner

Background: *Patricia, restaurant owner, Buffalo*

- Operated family restaurant for 8 years
- Failed during pandemic, accumulated large employment tax debt
- Personal guarantees on business debts and leases

Employment Tax Crisis:

- Trust fund taxes: $65,000 (employee withholdings)
- Employer's share: $28,000
- Total employment tax debt: $93,000
- Personal liability for entire amount

Bankruptcy Strategy:

- Filed Chapter 13 to address employment tax debt
- 5-year plan paying $1,550/month for all priority debts
- Discharged credit card debt and personal guarantees
- Maintained family home throughout process

Plan Structure:

- Employment taxes: $93,000 over 60 months
- Other priority debts: $8,000 (recent income taxes)

- Administrative costs: $250/month
- Unsecured creditors: $200/month (minimal payment)

Successful Completion:

- Completed 5-year plan without modification
- Eliminated personal guarantee liability
- Paid all employment taxes without additional penalties
- Family maintained stability throughout process

Lessons Learned:

- Chapter 13 provided structure for unmanageable employment tax debt
- Protected family assets while addressing business obligations
- Prevented IRS collection actions that would have devastated family
- Demonstrated that business failure doesn't mean personal financial ruin

Challenge Case: The Audit and Assessment Timing

Background: *Michael, sales professional, Long Island*

- Audited by IRS for multiple years
- Assessments made during bankruptcy planning process
- Complex timing issues affecting discharge eligibility

Audit Complications:

- 2019 audit completed January 2024, additional $35,000 assessed
- 2020 audit pending during bankruptcy planning
- 2021 return filed late, assessment timing unclear

Timing Analysis:

- 2019 taxes: Original assessment July 2020, additional assessment January 2024

- Need 240 days from latest assessment for discharge eligibility
- Bankruptcy filing delayed to September 2024 to meet timing requirements

Strategic Approach:

- Delayed bankruptcy filing to maximize dischargeable taxes
- Cooperated with ongoing audit to control assessment timing
- Amended returns where beneficial to restart timing periods
- Coordinated with tax attorney on audit strategy

Complex Resolution:

- Filed Chapter 7 in September 2024
- Discharged 2019 taxes (met timing requirements)
- 2020 taxes partially dischargeable after audit completion
- Used saved time and money to address remaining tax obligations

Key Insights:

- Timing is crucial for tax debt discharge
- Professional coordination essential for complex cases
- Patience with timing can result in significant additional discharge
- Audit cooperation may support discharge timing strategies

Your Tax Debt and Bankruptcy Action Plan

Initial Assessment Phase

Tax Debt Inventory:

- [ ] Obtain IRS tax transcripts for all years with debt
- [ ] Get state tax records and transcripts
- [ ] Identify employment tax obligations if applicable

- [ ] Document any existing tax liens
- [ ] Calculate total tax debt by year and type

Discharge Analysis:

- [ ] Apply five-part test to each year of income tax debt
- [ ] Identify dischargeable vs. non-dischargeable taxes
- [ ] Calculate potential savings from tax discharge
- [ ] Consider timing adjustments to maximize discharge
- [ ] Evaluate lien implications for property

Strategic Planning Phase

Chapter Choice Analysis:

- [ ] Compare Chapter 7 vs. Chapter 13 benefits for tax debt
- [ ] Consider impact on other debts and overall financial situation
- [ ] Evaluate property protection needs
- [ ] Assess ability to make Chapter 13 plan payments
- [ ] Consider time preferences (quick vs. structured relief)

Professional Consultation:

- [ ] Meet with bankruptcy attorney experienced in tax debt
- [ ] Consult with tax professional about compliance and planning
- [ ] Understand costs and timeline for different approaches
- [ ] Coordinate strategy between legal and tax professionals
- [ ] Get second opinions for complex situations

Implementation Phase

Pre-Filing Preparation:

- [ ] Complete credit counseling requirement

- [ ] Gather all required documentation
- [ ] Address any pending tax compliance issues
- [ ] Plan timing to maximize tax discharge benefits
- [ ] Prepare for immediate post-filing obligations

During Bankruptcy:

- [ ] Stay current on post-petition tax obligations
- [ ] File all required returns during case
- [ ] Respond to trustee requests promptly
- [ ] Make estimated payments if self-employed
- [ ] Maintain communication with tax agencies as needed

Post-Bankruptcy Management

Tax Compliance:

- [ ] Establish systems for ongoing tax compliance
- [ ] Set up quarterly estimated payment schedule if needed
- [ ] Build emergency fund for future tax obligations
- [ ] Work with tax professional for complex situations
- [ ] Monitor for lien release or satisfaction

Long-term Planning:

- [ ] Rebuild credit and financial stability
- [ ] Plan for major financial decisions with tax implications
- [ ] Maintain emergency fund for tax compliance
- [ ] Consider professional development to increase income
- [ ] Help others understand tax debt options

Advanced Considerations

Tax Court vs. Bankruptcy Court

Jurisdiction Issues:

- Tax Court handles disputes about tax liability
- Bankruptcy Court handles discharge and collection issues
- Coordination required for pending Tax Court cases
- Timing considerations for both proceedings

Strategic Coordination:

- Resolve liability disputes before bankruptcy if possible
- Consider impact of bankruptcy filing on Tax Court proceedings
- Coordinate with professionals familiar with both courts
- Plan timing to optimize results in both forums

Innocent Spouse Relief

When It Applies:

- Joint tax returns with spouse's undisclosed income or deductions
- Separation or divorce situations
- One spouse unaware of other's tax violations

Coordination with Bankruptcy:

- May eliminate personal liability for certain tax debts
- Can be pursued during or after bankruptcy
- May affect discharge analysis and strategy
- Requires coordination with family law issues

Estate and Gift Tax Issues

High-Net-Worth Considerations:

- Estate tax debt and personal liability
- Gift tax obligations and penalties
- Generation-skipping transfer tax issues
- Coordination with estate planning strategies

Complex Planning:

- Requires specialized professional guidance
- May involve multiple jurisdictions and courts
- Significant penalties for errors
- Impact on family wealth transfer strategies

The Bottom Line: Tax Debt Strategy and Relief

Tax debt in bankruptcy is complex, but understanding the rules and working with experienced professionals can provide significant relief. Key principles for success:

Knowledge Is Power:

- Understand which taxes can be discharged and when
- Know the difference between personal liability and lien obligations
- Recognize the benefits of Chapter 13 for non-dischargeable taxes
- Stay informed about changing tax and bankruptcy laws

Timing Matters:

- Plan bankruptcy filing to maximize tax discharge
- Consider impact of pending audits and assessments
- Coordinate with other debt relief strategies
- Account for seasonal business and income variations

Professional Guidance Is Essential:

- Work with attorneys experienced in tax debt bankruptcy

- Coordinate with tax professionals for compliance and planning
- Get specialized help for complex business or international issues
- Don't try to navigate complex tax rules alone

Compliance Is Critical:

- Stay current on post-bankruptcy tax obligations
- Establish systems for ongoing tax compliance
- Build emergency funds for future tax obligations
- Learn from the experience to avoid future problems

Strategic Thinking:

- Consider both immediate relief and long-term implications
- Balance tax debt relief with other financial goals
- Plan for property implications of tax liens
- Use bankruptcy relief to build foundation for future success

Remember: Tax debt may seem insurmountable, but bankruptcy provides powerful tools for both eliminating old tax debt and managing current obligations. The key is understanding your options, working with experienced professionals, and developing a comprehensive strategy that addresses both your tax obligations and your overall financial recovery.

The IRS and state tax agencies are formidable creditors, but bankruptcy law provides meaningful protection and relief options. With proper planning and execution, you can address even overwhelming tax debt and build a foundation for long-term financial stability and tax compliance.

In the next chapter, we'll explore how bankruptcy can stop foreclosures and repossessions - providing immediate relief from aggressive creditor actions and tools for protecting your most essential property.

19

Stopping Foreclosures and Repossessions

Using the Automatic Stay to Save Your Home, Car, and Peace of Mind

When the Sheriff's Sale Is Next Week

Imagine opening your mail to find a notice that your home will be sold at foreclosure auction in 30 days. Or coming home to find a repossession notice on your car windshield. These scenarios represent some of the most terrifying moments in anyone's financial life - the imminent loss of property that's essential to your survival and your family's stability.

The panic is understandable. Foreclosure and repossession represent more than just financial loss - they threaten your security, your children's stability, your ability to work, and your sense of control over your life. When you're facing these collection actions, you need immediate, powerful relief.

This is where bankruptcy's **automatic stay** becomes one of the most valuable legal protections available to consumers. The moment you file bankruptcy, all collection activity stops - including foreclosure sales and vehicle repossessions. This immediate relief gives you breathing room to evaluate your options and develop a strategy for protecting what matters most.

But the automatic stay is just the beginning. Bankruptcy provides sophisticated tools for addressing secured debt problems, catching up on missed payments, and sometimes even reducing what you owe. In this chapter, we'll explore how bankruptcy can stop foreclosures and repossessions, what options are available for keeping your property, and how to use these tools strategically to protect your family's essential assets.

Understanding the Automatic Stay

The Most Powerful Legal Protection for Consumers

What the Automatic Stay Is: The automatic stay is a federal court order that goes into effect **immediately** when you file bankruptcy. It stops virtually all collection activity by creditors, including:

- Foreclosure sales and proceedings
- Vehicle repossessions
- Wage garnishments
- Bank account seizures
- Lawsuit filings and proceedings
- Collection calls and letters
- Utility shutoffs (in most cases)

Why It's So Powerful:

- Takes effect **immediately** upon filing, even at 11:59 PM
- Applies to **all creditors**, including the IRS and other government agencies
- Violations can result in **significant penalties** for creditors
- Provides **breathing room** to develop strategy and negotiate solutions

Real-Life Example: *Jennifer, Sacramento, CA*

- Foreclosure sale scheduled for Friday at 10:00 AM
- Filed bankruptcy Thursday at 4:00 PM
- Sheriff's sale automatically canceled
- Gained time to evaluate options and develop plan

How the Automatic Stay Works in Practice

Immediate Effects:

- **Foreclosure proceedings halt** completely
- **Repossession activities stop** immediately
- **Collection calls must end** (creditors may contact your attorney only)
- **Garnishments are released** back to your paycheck
- **Lawsuits are suspended** until bankruptcy is resolved

What Creditors Must Do:

- **Stop all collection activity** immediately upon notice
- **Return garnished wages** that haven't been dispersed
- **Halt foreclosure sales** even if scheduled for the next day
- **Notify their attorneys** and collection agencies to cease activity

Creditor Violations: If creditors violate the automatic stay, they can face:

- **Monetary sanctions** including actual damages
- **Punitive damages** for willful violations
- **Attorney fees** for the debtor
- **Contempt of court** charges

Limitations of the Automatic Stay

What the Stay Doesn't Stop:

- **Criminal proceedings** and fines
- **Certain tax proceedings** (some exceptions apply)
- **Child support and alimony** establishment or modification
- **Some eviction proceedings** (limited exceptions)
- **Certain regulatory actions** by government agencies

Duration Limitations:

- **First bankruptcy:** Stay remains in effect for entire case
- **Second bankruptcy within 1 year:** Stay may expire after 30 days
- **Third bankruptcy within 1 year:** No automatic stay (but can request one)

Foreclosure: Understanding the Process and Intervention Points

The Foreclosure Timeline

Understanding foreclosure timing helps you plan intervention strategies:

Phase 1: Default and Notice (30-90 days behind)

- **Late payment notices** and phone calls
- **Default notices** from lender
- **Acceleration demands** (full balance due immediately)
- **Foreclosure warning letters**

Phase 2: Formal Foreclosure Proceedings (90-180 days behind)

- **Notice of Default** or **Lis Pendens** filed
- **Legal proceedings** initiated in court (judicial states)
- **Notice of Sale** published and posted

- **Redemption period** begins (in some states)

Phase 3: Sale and Aftermath (180+ days behind)

- **Foreclosure auction** or sheriff's sale
- **Deed transfer** to new owner
- **Eviction proceedings** if necessary
- **Deficiency judgment** pursuit (in some states)

State Variations: Judicial vs. Non-Judicial Foreclosure

Judicial Foreclosure States (including New York):

- **Court supervision** required for foreclosure
- **Longer timeline** (often 12-18 months)
- **More opportunities** for intervention and negotiation
- **Greater procedural protections** for homeowners

Non-Judicial Foreclosure States (including California):

- **Faster process** (often 4-6 months)
- **Less court oversight** of foreclosure process
- **Fewer procedural protections** but still significant rights
- **More urgent need** for quick intervention

Mixed Systems: Some states allow both judicial and non-judicial foreclosure, depending on the mortgage terms and lender choice.

How Bankruptcy Stops Foreclosure

Immediate Relief: The automatic stay **immediately stops** all foreclosure proceedings, regardless of how far advanced they are:

- **Sale scheduled for tomorrow:** Canceled immediately
- **Sheriff's sale in progress:** Must be halted

- **Deed already prepared:** Transfer cannot occur
- **Eviction proceedings:** Usually stopped (some exceptions)

Critical Timing: Bankruptcy must be filed **before** the foreclosure sale is completed. Once the property is sold and deed is transferred, it's generally too late to save the home through bankruptcy.

Post-Sale Considerations:

- **Redemption rights:** Some states allow redemption even after sale
- **Procedural challenges:** Bankruptcy may allow challenges to improper sales
- **Deficiency claims:** Bankruptcy can eliminate personal liability for deficiency

Chapter 7 vs. Chapter 13: Different Tools for Homeowners

Chapter 7: Temporary Relief and Strategic Options

What Chapter 7 Can Do:

- **Stop foreclosure immediately** through automatic stay
- **Eliminate personal liability** for mortgage debt (if surrendering home)
- **Buy time** to negotiate with lender or find alternative solutions
- **Eliminate other debts** to improve ability to maintain mortgage payments

Chapter 7 Limitations for Homeowners:

- **No mechanism** to catch up on missed payments over time
- **Temporary relief only** unless you can quickly cure default
- **Must stay current** on ongoing payments to keep home
- **Limited long-term solutions** for mortgage arrears

When Chapter 7 Works for Homeowners:

- You're **current on mortgage payments** but need to eliminate other debts
- You want to **surrender the home** and eliminate deficiency liability
- You can **quickly cure** the mortgage default with available funds
- You need **temporary relief** while arranging other solutions

Chapter 13: The Homeowner's Tool

Chapter 13's Unique Powers for Homeowners:

Cure and Maintain

- **Catch up on missed payments** over 3-5 years through your plan
- **Resume regular payments** outside the plan going forward
- **Stop interest and fees** on arrears in most cases
- **Maintain homeownership** throughout the process

Lien Stripping

- **Eliminate second mortgages** if home is underwater
- **Convert unsecured liens** to dischargeable debt
- **Increase available equity** for homeowner

Modification Support

- **Provide structure** for loan modification negotiations
- **Demonstrate payment capacity** to lenders
- **Coordinate bankruptcy and modification** processes

Chapter 13 Requirements for Homeowners:

- **Regular income** sufficient to support plan payments
- **Ability to resume** regular mortgage payments going forward

- **Commitment** to 3-5 years of plan payments
- **Feasible budget** that includes housing costs

Strategic Choice Framework

Choose Chapter 7 if:

- You want to **surrender the home** and eliminate deficiency
- You're **current on mortgage** but need other debt relief
- You **lack regular income** for Chapter 13 plan
- You can **quickly cure default** with available resources

Choose Chapter 13 if:

- You're **behind on mortgage** and want to keep the home
- You have **regular income** to support catch-up payments
- You want to **strip second mortgages** or other liens
- You need **long-term structure** for managing mortgage obligations

Real Foreclosure Prevention Examples

Success Story: The Chapter 13 Foreclosure Save

Background: *Robert and Maria, Buffalo,* NY

- Married couple, two teenage children
- Combined income: $75,000/year
- Home: $220,000 value, $165,000 mortgage
- Behind on mortgage: $18,000 (12 months of payments)
- Foreclosure sale scheduled in 6 weeks

The Crisis:

- Robert reduced hours during economic downturn

- Used credit cards to maintain lifestyle
- Fell behind on mortgage when credit cards maxed out
- Received foreclosure notice while recovering from job loss

Chapter 13 Solution:

- **Filed bankruptcy** 3 weeks before foreclosure sale
- **Plan payment:** $850/month for 5 years
- **Mortgage arrearage:** $300/month for 5 years ($18,000 ÷ 60)
- **Other debt:** $35,000 credit cards discharged
- **Ongoing mortgage:** $1,385/month continued outside plan

Successful Outcome:

- **Stopped foreclosure** and kept family home
- **Children remained** in same school district
- **Completed plan** successfully after 5 years
- **Home equity increased** to $95,000 during plan period
- **Family financial stability** restored

Key Lessons:

- Early intervention prevented loss of family home
- Chapter 13 provided affordable structure for catch-up payments
- Eliminating other debt made mortgage affordable
- Family stability preserved during financial recovery

Strategic Surrender: The Chapter 7 Fresh Start

Background: *Jennifer, Long Island, NY*

- Single mother, nurse, income $65,000
- Home: $380,000 value, $420,000 mortgage (underwater)
- Behind on mortgage: $24,000 (18 months)

- Credit card debt: $45,000

Strategic Analysis:

- **Home underwater** by $40,000
- **Mortgage payment** $3,200/month (60% of income)
- **Cannot afford** current mortgage even without other debt
- **Better options available** for housing family

Chapter 7 Strategy:

- **Filed Chapter 7** to eliminate all unsecured debt
- **Surrendered home** to eliminate mortgage liability
- **Eliminated deficiency** exposure ($40,000)
- **Discharged credit cards** and other unsecured debt

Positive Outcome:

- **Rented appropriate housing** for $1,800/month
- **Eliminated all debt** except student loans
- **Improved school district** for children
- **Built emergency fund** with payment savings
- **Purchased appropriate home** 3 years later with FHA loan

Strategic Benefits:

- Recognized that keeping unaffordable home wasn't beneficial
- Used bankruptcy to eliminate all liability cleanly
- Relocated to better situation for family's future
- Built foundation for appropriate future homeownership

Vehicle Repossession: Protection and Recovery

Understanding Vehicle Repossession

How Repossession Works:

- **Self-help repossession:** Lender can take vehicle without court order
- **No advance notice required** in most states
- **Peaceful repossession only:** Cannot "breach the peace"
- **Sale and deficiency:** Vehicle sold, deficiency claimed if insufficient proceeds

Repossession Timeline:

- **Default:** Missing payments or violating loan terms
- **Acceleration:** Lender demands full balance
- **Repossession:** Vehicle taken (often without warning)
- **Sale:** Vehicle sold at auction (usually for less than retail value)
- **Deficiency:** Borrower liable for remaining balance after sale

How Bankruptcy Stops Repossession

Immediate Protection:

- **Automatic stay** stops all repossession activity immediately
- **Vehicle must be returned** if repossessed but not yet sold
- **No further repossession attempts** while case is pending
- **Time to evaluate options** and develop strategy

Post-Repossession Recovery: If your vehicle was recently repossessed but not yet sold:

- **File bankruptcy immediately** to stop sale
- **Request return** of vehicle under automatic stay
- **Negotiate with lender** for return and reinstatement
- **Include in Chapter 13 plan** to catch up on payments

Critical Timing:

- **Act quickly** after repossession before vehicle is sold
- **File bankruptcy immediately** if repossession is threatened
- **Document condition** and mileage if vehicle is returned

Chapter 13 Vehicle Protection Strategies

Catching Up on Car Payments:

- **Include arrears** in Chapter 13 plan
- **Spread missed payments** over 3-5 years
- **Resume regular payments** outside the plan
- **Stop additional fees and charges** on arrears

Cramdown Benefits: For vehicles owned more than 910 days (about 2.5 years):

- **Reduce loan balance** to current vehicle value
- **Treat excess as unsecured debt** (may be discharged)
- **Reduce interest rate** to current market rates
- **Save thousands of dollars** over loan term

Real Cramdown Example: *Michael, Sacramento, CA*

- **2019 pickup truck** essential for construction work
- **Loan balance:** $28,000
- **Current value:** $18,000
- **Owned for 3+ years** (qualifies for cramdown)

Cramdown Result:

- **Secured debt:** $18,000 at market interest rate
- **Unsecured debt:** $10,000 (included with other unsecured debt)
- **Monthly payment:** Reduced from $485 to $310
- **Total savings:** Over $12,000 including interest

Advanced Strategies for Property Protection

Second Mortgage and HELOC Stripping

When Lien Stripping Is Available:

- **Home value** less than first mortgage balance
- **Second mortgage/HELOC** completely underwater
- **Chapter 13 case** (not available in Chapter 7)
- **Successful plan completion** required

How Lien Stripping Works:

- **Second mortgage** treated as unsecured debt in plan
- **Payments** made through plan like other unsecured debt
- **Lien permanently removed** after plan completion
- **Full equity** restored to homeowner

Lien Stripping Example: *Carlos and Elena, Los Angeles*

- **Home value:** $450,000
- **First mortgage:** $485,000
- **Second mortgage:** $75,000
- **Home underwater** by $35,000 on first mortgage

Lien Strip Result:

- **Second mortgage** treated as unsecured debt
- **Paid 25%** to unsecured creditors through plan
- **$56,250 saved** on second mortgage
- **Lien permanently removed** after plan completion

Property Tax and HOA Issues

Property Tax Arrears:

- **Treated as priority debt** in Chapter 13
- **Must be paid in full** through plan
- **Protection from tax sale** during bankruptcy
- **Structured payment** over plan period

HOA Fees and Assessments:

- **Pre-petition arrears** may be dischargeable
- **Post-petition fees** must be paid to retain property
- **Assessment disputes** can be addressed in bankruptcy
- **Lien priority issues** may be resolved

Manufactured Housing and Unique Properties

Mobile Home and Manufactured Housing:

- **Different lien laws** may apply
- **Personal property vs. real estate** classification issues
- **Park rental vs. owned land** complications
- **Specialized exemption considerations**

Unique Property Types:

- **Cooperative apartments:** Special rules and considerations
- **Condominiums:** HOA issues and assessment priorities
- **Life estates:** Complex ownership and lien issues
- **Trust property:** Beneficial interest protection strategies

Emergency Filing Strategies

Last-Minute Foreclosure Prevention

When You Have Days or Hours:

- **Gather essential documents** quickly
- **File emergency petition** with basic information
- **Add remaining schedules** within 14 days
- **Focus on stopping sale first**, complete paperwork later

Emergency Filing Checklist:

- [ ] Voluntary petition (Form 101)
- [ ] Creditor matrix with foreclosure lender
- [ ] Filing fee or fee waiver application
- [ ] Credit counseling certificate (if available)
- [ ] Essential contact information

Professional Help for Emergencies:

- **Call bankruptcy attorney immediately** if foreclosure imminent
- **Emergency filings possible** even on weekends/holidays
- **Electronic filing** can be done 24/7 in most districts
- **Paralegal services** may be available for basic emergency filings

Post-Filing Emergency Actions

Immediate Steps After Emergency Filing:

- [ ] **Notify foreclosure attorney** of bankruptcy filing immediately
- [ ] **Provide case number** and filing confirmation
- [ ] **Document all communication** with lender and attorneys
- [ ] **Complete remaining paperwork** within court deadlines

Follow-Up Requirements:

- **Complete all schedules** within 14 days
- **File missing documents** to avoid dismissal

- **Attend 341 meeting** as scheduled
- **Maintain ongoing obligations** (insurance, property taxes)

Common Mistakes and How to Avoid Them

Timing Mistakes

Filing Too Late:

- **After foreclosure sale:** Generally cannot recover property
- **After vehicle sale:** Cannot get vehicle back
- **Missing court deadlines:** May result in dismissal and loss of protection

Filing Too Early:

- **Before understanding options:** May choose wrong chapter
- **Without proper planning:** May not achieve goals
- **Rushing without counsel:** May miss opportunities or make errors

Strategic Errors

Wrong Chapter Choice:

- **Chapter 7 when Chapter 13 needed:** Cannot catch up on arrears
- **Chapter 13 when Chapter 7 sufficient:** Unnecessary complexity and cost
- **Not considering cramdown opportunities:** Missing significant savings

Inadequate Planning:

- **Unrealistic budgets:** Cannot maintain plan payments
- **Ignoring ongoing obligations:** Property taxes, insurance, maintenance
- **Not addressing root causes:** May face same problems again

Documentation Problems

Insufficient Records:

- **Missing payment history:** Difficult to calculate arrears accurately
- **Inadequate property values:** May affect exemption planning
- **Poor communication records:** Cannot prove lender violations

Better Documentation Practices:

- **Keep detailed payment records** for all secured debts
- **Document all lender communication** including phone calls
- **Maintain property insurance** and tax payment records
- **Photograph property condition** if disputes arise

Working with Lenders During Bankruptcy

Communication Strategies

Automatic Stay Compliance:

- **All communication** must go through your attorney if represented
- **Lenders cannot contact you directly** about dischargeable debts
- **Ongoing obligations** (like insurance requirements) may still require communication
- **Violations should be documented** and reported

Loan Modification Coordination:

- **Bankruptcy doesn't prevent** modification applications
- **Court approval required** for modification during Chapter 13
- **Timing coordination** between bankruptcy and modification processes
- **Professional guidance essential** for complex situations

Reaffirmation and Ride-Through

Reaffirmation Agreements (Chapter 7):

- **Legal commitment** to continue paying debt despite discharge
- **Court approval required** in most cases
- **Cannot be revoked** once approved
- **Not recommended** unless beneficial terms

Ride-Through Strategy:

- **Continue payments** without reaffirming debt
- **Keep property** as long as payments current
- **Retain discharge protection** if payments become unaffordable
- **Preferred strategy** for many vehicle loans

State-Specific Considerations

New York Foreclosure Process

Judicial Foreclosure State:

- **Court supervision** required for all foreclosures
- **Longer timeline** provides more intervention opportunities
- **Settlement conferences** required in many cases
- **Strong procedural protections** for homeowners

New York Specific Strategies:

- **Coordinate with foreclosure defense** attorneys
- **Use settlement conference process** for negotiation
- **Consider New York's homestead exemption** benefits
- **Plan timing** around court schedules and procedures

California Foreclosure Considerations

Non-Judicial Foreclosure:

- **Faster timeline** requires quicker response
- **Limited court oversight** of process
- **Notice requirements** provide specific timing windows
- **Right to reinstate** available until sale

California Bankruptcy Strategy:

- **Act quickly** due to faster foreclosure timeline
- **Coordinate with** California's foreclosure prevention programs
- **Choose optimal exemption system** for property protection
- **Consider lien stripping** opportunities in underwater markets

Your Property Protection Action Plan

Immediate Crisis Response (Days or Hours)

If Foreclosure Sale Is Imminent:

- [ ] **Contact bankruptcy attorney immediately** (emergency consultation)
- [ ] **Gather essential documents** (mortgage statements, foreclosure notices)
- [ ] **Prepare for emergency filing** if beneficial
- [ ] **Document foreclosure timeline** and communications
- [ ] **Notify family members** of potential emergency filing

If Vehicle Repossession Is Threatened:

- [ ] **Secure vehicle** in private garage if possible
- [ ] **Contact lender** to negotiate temporary arrangement

- [ ] **Gather loan documents** and payment history
- [ ] **Evaluate bankruptcy options** for long-term solution
- [ ] **Document vehicle condition** and location

Strategic Planning Phase (Weeks)

Property Evaluation:

- [ ] **Assess current property values** and equity positions
- [ ] **Calculate total arrears** and ongoing payment obligations
- [ ] **Evaluate affordability** of keeping vs. surrendering property
- [ ] **Consider alternatives** (refinancing, modification, downsizing)
- [ ] **Analyze exemption protection** for all property

Chapter Choice Analysis:

- [ ] **Compare Chapter 7 vs. Chapter 13** benefits for your situation
- [ ] **Evaluate cramdown opportunities** for vehicles
- [ ] **Consider lien stripping potential** for underwater properties
- [ ] **Assess income stability** for Chapter 13 plan feasibility
- [ ] **Plan timing** to maximize protection and benefits

Implementation and Success

During Bankruptcy:

- [ ] **Maintain ongoing obligations** (insurance, property taxes, regular payments)
- [ ] **Communicate through attorney** with secured creditors
- [ ] **Complete all court requirements** promptly and accurately
- [ ] **Monitor compliance** with automatic stay by creditors
- [ ] **Plan for post-bankruptcy** property management

Long-term Property Management:

- [ ] **Build emergency fund** for property maintenance and taxes
- [ ] **Maintain adequate insurance** coverage
- [ ] **Stay current** on all ongoing obligations
- [ ] **Plan for refinancing** opportunities as credit improves
- [ ] **Consider property improvements** that add value and equity

The Bottom Line: Property Protection Through Bankruptcy

Bankruptcy's property protection tools are among the most powerful consumer rights in American law. The automatic stay provides immediate relief from foreclosure and repossession, while Chapters 7 and 13 offer different strategies for addressing secured debt problems. Key principles for success:

Act Quickly:

- **Time is critical** when facing foreclosure or repossession
- **Emergency filings possible** even when time is very short
- **Professional help essential** for crisis situations
- **Document everything** throughout the process

Choose the Right Strategy:

- **Chapter 7** for quick relief and strategic surrenders
- **Chapter 13** for catching up and keeping property
- **Consider cramdown** and lien stripping opportunities
- **Plan for long-term affordability** and maintenance

Understand Your Rights:

- **Automatic stay** provides immediate powerful protection
- **Creditor violations** can result in damages and sanctions

- **Property exemptions** protect essential assets
- **Professional guidance** optimizes outcomes

Plan for Success:

- **Realistic budgeting** for ongoing property obligations
- **Emergency fund building** for future stability
- **Credit rebuilding** for future refinancing opportunities
- **Long-term property planning** for wealth building

Remember: Foreclosure and repossession represent threats, not certainties. Bankruptcy provides powerful tools for protecting your home, vehicle, and other essential property. The key is understanding your options, acting quickly when necessary, and working with experienced professionals who can help you navigate the process successfully.

Your home and vehicle aren't just property - they're the foundation of your family's stability and your ability to earn a living. Bankruptcy's property protection tools can help you preserve that foundation while addressing your overall debt situation and building a more secure financial future.

In the next chapter, we'll explore one of the most serious topics in bankruptcy law: bankruptcy fraud and the critical mistakes to avoid that could derail your case or even result in criminal charges.

20

Bankruptcy Fraud and Mistakes to Avoid

How to Stay Safe and Honest

The High Stakes of Honesty

Bankruptcy is one of the most honest legal processes in America. Unlike many areas of law where advocacy and selective disclosure are the norm, bankruptcy requires **complete transparency** about your financial life. You must disclose every asset, every debt, every source of income, and every financial transaction. In exchange for this radical honesty, the law provides powerful relief from overwhelming debt.

This transparency requirement isn't just a legal technicality - it's the foundation that makes bankruptcy relief possible. The system works because it's based on trust, verified by documentation, and protected by serious consequences for those who abuse it. Understanding this framework is crucial not just for ethical reasons, but for practical ones: mistakes in disclosure can delay your case, cost you your discharge, or even result in criminal prosecution.

The overwhelming majority of people who file bankruptcy are honest, hardworking individuals facing genuine financial crises. They provide complete and accurate information, receive their discharge, and go on to rebuild successful financial lives. But a small percentage make mistakes - sometimes innocent, sometimes intentional - that can derail their cases and create serious legal problems.

In this chapter, we'll explore what constitutes bankruptcy fraud, identify common mistakes that can look like fraud even when they're not, and provide a roadmap for maintaining the transparency and honesty that ensure your bankruptcy case succeeds.

Understanding Bankruptcy Fraud

What Bankruptcy Fraud Actually Is

Legal Definition: Bankruptcy fraud occurs when someone **knowingly and fraudulently** makes false statements or omissions in bankruptcy proceedings, or attempts to manipulate the system for improper gain.

Key Elements:

- **Knowledge:** You knew the information was false or misleading
- **Intent:** You intended to deceive the court, trustee, or creditors
- **Materiality:** The false information could affect the outcome of your case
- **Action:** You took concrete steps to conceal or misrepresent facts

Important Distinction: Honest mistakes are not fraud. Bankruptcy fraud requires intentional deception, not simple errors or omissions.

Common Types of Bankruptcy Fraud

Concealment of Assets:

- Hiding property, money, or other valuable assets
- Transferring assets to friends or family to keep them from creditors
- Failing to disclose bank accounts, investments, or valuable property

- Using nominee entities or straw parties to conceal ownership

False Statements:

- Lying about income, expenses, or debts
- Providing false documentation or forged records
- Making false statements under oath at the 341 meeting
- Concealing sources of income or financial transactions

Fraudulent Transfers:

- Selling property for less than fair market value to friends or family
- Giving away valuable assets before filing bankruptcy
- Creating artificial debts to preferred creditors
- Backdating transactions to avoid scrutiny

Multiple Filings:

- Filing bankruptcy in multiple states using false information
- Using false names or Social Security numbers
- Filing repeatedly to abuse the automatic stay
- Concealing previous bankruptcy filings

Petition Mill Schemes:

- Mass-produced fraudulent bankruptcy petitions
- False documentation factories
- Identity theft in bankruptcy filings
- Professional fraud schemes targeting vulnerable consumers

The Consequences of Bankruptcy Fraud

Criminal Penalties:

- **Federal felony charges** with up to 5 years in prison
- **Fines up to $250,000** for individuals

- **Criminal record** affecting employment and other opportunities
- **Restitution payments** to victims

Civil Consequences:

- **Denial of discharge** for all debts (not just fraudulent ones)
- **Dismissal of bankruptcy case** without debt relief
- **Asset forfeiture** and recovery by trustee
- **Civil damages** and attorney fees

Professional Consequences:

- **Loss of professional licenses** (lawyers, accountants, real estate agents)
- **Employment consequences** for positions requiring security clearances
- **Immigration impacts** for non-citizens
- **Credit consequences** beyond normal bankruptcy impact

Long-term Effects:

- **Permanent federal court records** of fraud findings
- **Difficulty with future bankruptcy filings**
- **Enhanced scrutiny** in any future legal proceedings
- **Reputation damage** in professional and personal contexts

Common Innocent Mistakes That Look Like Fraud

Asset Disclosure Errors

The Problem: Many people don't understand what constitutes an "asset" that must be disclosed, leading to inadvertent omissions that can appear fraudulent.

Common Misunderstandings:

"It's Not Worth Anything":

- **Broken electronics or old furniture:** Must be disclosed even if minimal value
- **Collections or hobby items:** May have unexpected value
- **Damaged vehicles:** Even non-running cars have value
- **Old tools or equipment:** May be worth more than expected

"It's Not Really Mine":

- **Gifts from family:** If in your name, it's your asset
- **Items you're holding for others:** May create legal ownership rights
- **Joint ownership with family:** Your interest must be disclosed
- **Business equipment:** Personal vs. business ownership confusion

"I Forgot About It":

- **Old bank accounts:** Even dormant accounts must be disclosed
- **Retirement accounts:** All accounts regardless of balance
- **Insurance policies:** Life insurance with cash value
- **Pending lawsuits:** Potential legal claims are assets

Safe Practice: Disclose everything you own or might own, regardless of value or condition. Let the trustee determine what's significant.

Income Reporting Mistakes

The Problem: Bankruptcy requires disclosure of **all income from all sources**, but many people don't understand what constitutes "income."

Commonly Overlooked Income:

Irregular Income:

- **Side gig earnings:** Uber, DoorDash, freelance work
- **Cash payments:** Babysitting, lawn care, handyman work
- **Seasonal work:** Holiday retail, tax preparation, seasonal labor

- **Hobby income:** Crafts, online sales, garage sales

Family Support:

- **Regular financial help:** From parents, siblings, adult children
- **Housing assistance:** Free or below-market rent from family
- **Utility payments:** Family members paying your bills
- **Expense assistance:** Others paying for your necessities

Investment and Other Income:

- **Rental income:** Even from casual arrangements
- **Interest and dividends:** From investments or savings
- **Pension or retirement benefits:** All sources and amounts
- **Government benefits:** Unemployment, disability, assistance programs

Business Income:

- **Cash business income:** All receipts regardless of record-keeping
- **Bartering or trade:** Value of goods or services received
- **Partnership distributions:** Even irregular payments
- **1099 income:** All sources even if taxes not yet filed

Transfer and Payment Mistakes

The Problem: Normal financial transactions can look suspicious if they occur close to bankruptcy filing or involve family members.

Innocent Transactions That Create Problems:

Family Financial Help:

- **Paying back family loans:** Can look like preference payments
- **Giving money to adult children:** May appear to be asset concealment
- **Helping with family emergencies:** Normal generosity that looks

suspicious

- **Holiday or birthday gifts:** Timing can create appearance problems

Normal Business Transactions:

- **Paying essential business expenses:** May be scrutinized if business failing
- **Equipment sales:** May look like below-market transfers
- **Customer refunds:** Normal business practice that appears unusual
- **Vendor payments:** Timing may suggest preference

Reasonable Financial Planning:

- **Increasing exempted assets:** Using non-exempt cash to pay down mortgage
- **Purchasing necessary items:** Replacing broken appliances before filing
- **Insurance purchases:** Buying adequate coverage before filing
- **Necessary professional services:** Paying for medical care, legal advice

Protection Strategy: Document the legitimate purpose of all significant financial transactions. Keep records showing the business or personal necessity for all transfers and payments.

Pre-Filing Mistakes That Create Problems

Credit Card and Cash Advance Issues

The Dangerous Zone: Using credit cards or taking cash advances shortly before filing bankruptcy can create presumptions of fraud, even if your intent was innocent.

High-Risk Activities:

Luxury Purchases (90 days before filing):

- **Individual purchases over $725** for luxury goods or services

- **Vacation expenses, jewelry, expensive electronics**
- **Non-essential home improvements or furnishings**
- **Entertainment expenses and recreational activities**

Cash Advances (70 days before filing):

- **Individual cash advances over $1,000**
- **ATM withdrawals from credit cards**
- **Balance transfers used to obtain cash**
- **Credit card convenience checks**

Why These Create Problems:

- **Legal presumption:** These debts are presumed non-dischargeable
- **Burden shifts to you:** You must prove legitimate need and intent to repay
- **Creditor challenges:** Banks will object to discharge of these debts
- **Pattern evidence:** Multiple transactions suggest abuse

Safe Practices:

- **Stop using all credit cards** when you start considering bankruptcy
- **Use cash only** for essential purchases
- **Avoid large purchases** unless absolutely necessary
- **Document necessities** with receipts and explanations

Asset Transfer Problems

The Look-Back Period: Bankruptcy trustees examine **all transfers** made within 2 years before filing (sometimes longer for fraud cases).

Transfers That Create Scrutiny:

Below-Market Sales:

- **Selling car to family member** for less than market value

- **Business equipment sales** to friends or competitors
- **Real estate transfers** at below-market prices
- **Valuable collectibles** sold cheaply to family

Gifts to Family and Friends:

- **Holiday and birthday gifts** above normal patterns
- **Financial help** to adult children or relatives
- **Payment of others' debts** or expenses
- **Property transfers** for no consideration

Business Entity Transfers:

- **Moving assets** between business entities
- **Changing ownership structures** before filing
- **Liquidating business assets** to related parties
- **Creating new entities** to hold assets

Timing Considerations:

- **Transfers within 1 year:** Heavy scrutiny and potential recovery
- **Transfers within 2 years:** Requires documentation and justification
- **Transfers to insiders:** Longer look-back period (up to 1 year)
- **Fraudulent transfers:** No time limit for recovery

Employment and Business Issues

Employment Changes:

- **Job changes** that affect income calculations
- **Starting new employment** after deciding to file but before filing
- **Bonus or commission timing** relative to filing date
- **Severance package** negotiations and timing

Business Decisions:

- **Winding down business operations** before filing
- **Customer notification** and transition planning
- **Equipment and inventory** disposition
- **Employee termination** and final payments

Documentation and Record-Keeping

What Records to Keep

Essential Documentation:

Income Records:

- **Pay stubs** for past 6 months from all jobs
- **Tax returns** for past 2-3 years
- **Bank statements** showing all deposits
- **1099 forms** and other income documentation
- **Cash income records** even if informal

Asset Documentation:

- **Real estate deeds** and mortgage information
- **Vehicle titles** and loan documentation
- **Bank account statements** for all accounts
- **Investment account statements**
- **Insurance policies** with cash value information

Debt Documentation:

- **Credit card statements** for all accounts
- **Loan agreements** and payment records
- **Medical bills** and collection notices
- **Court judgments** and legal documents

- **Tax debt** notices and correspondence

Transaction Records:

- **Large purchase receipts** and explanations
- **Transfer documentation** with business purposes
- **Gift records** with dates and recipients
- **Loan agreements** with family members

Organizing Your Records

Create a Systematic Approach:

Physical Organization:

- **File folders** for each category of documents
- **Chronological order** within each category
- **Copies** of all original documents
- **Backup storage** in secure location

Digital Backup:

- **Scan important documents** to digital format
- **Cloud storage** for backup security
- **Password protection** for sensitive information
- **Multiple access points** in case of emergency

Professional Assistance:

- **Accountant review** of business records
- **Attorney guidance** on sensitive transactions
- **Document preparation services** if needed
- **Professional organization** for complex cases

The 341 Meeting: Honesty Under Oath

Understanding the Meeting of Creditors

What It Really Is: The 341 meeting is a **sworn examination** where you testify under oath about your financial affairs. Despite its name, creditors rarely attend - it's primarily between you and the trustee.

The Oath's Significance:

- **Federal perjury laws** apply to all testimony
- **Transcripts may be created** for complex cases
- **Inconsistent statements** can create fraud allegations
- **Preparation is essential** but honesty is paramount

Common 341 Meeting Questions

Standard Questions:

Identity and Petition Review:

- "Please state your name and current address."
- "Did you sign the petition and schedules?"
- "Did you read them before signing?"
- "Are they true and correct?"

Asset and Income Verification:

- "Do you own any real estate?"
- "Have you listed all your assets?"
- "Is your income accurately stated?"
- "Do you expect any tax refunds?"

Transaction Inquiries:

- "Have you transferred any property in the past year?"
- "Have you made any large payments to creditors?"
- "Do you have any pending lawsuits?"

- "Are there any changes since filing?"

Preparation Strategies:

- **Review your petition** thoroughly before the meeting
- **Understand every entry** and be able to explain it
- **Bring requested documents** organized and accessible
- **Answer only what's asked** clearly and concisely
- **Ask for clarification** if you don't understand a question

Handling Difficult Questions

When You Don't Know:

- **"I don't recall"** is acceptable for details you genuinely can't remember
- **"I'd need to check my records"** for specific dates or amounts
- **Never guess** or provide information you're not certain about
- **Offer to provide follow-up** documentation if needed

When You Made Mistakes:

- **Acknowledge errors** honestly and directly
- **Explain the mistake** without making excuses
- **Provide correct information** if you have it
- **Offer to amend schedules** if necessary

When Questions Are Unclear:

- **Ask for clarification** rather than guessing at meaning
- **Rephrase questions** to confirm your understanding
- **Take time to think** before answering complex questions
- **Request breaks** if you become confused or overwhelmed

Working with Professionals Ethically

Attorney-Client Relationships

Your Responsibilities:

- **Complete honesty** with your attorney about all financial matters
- **Timely disclosure** of new information or changes
- **Full cooperation** with document requests and deadlines
- **Clear communication** about your goals and concerns

What to Expect from Your Attorney:

- **Competent representation** within bankruptcy law
- **Honest assessment** of your options and prospects
- **Confidential treatment** of all information you provide
- **Professional conduct** in all court proceedings

Red Flags in Attorney Relationships:

- **Attorneys who suggest** hiding assets or income
- **Pressure to sign** documents you haven't reviewed
- **Promises of results** that seem too good to be true
- **Requests for cash payments** without proper documentation

Document Preparation Services

Legitimate Services:

- **Form completion** based on information you provide
- **Filing assistance** with court procedures
- **Administrative support** for self-represented debtors
- **Document organization** and preparation

Warning Signs:

- **Legal advice** from non-attorneys

- **Suggestions about** what to disclose or hide
- **Guarantees about outcomes** or discharge
- **Pressure to sign** documents without review

Professional Ethics and Your Case

Maintaining Ethical Standards:

- **Never ask professionals** to help you hide information
- **Don't rely on others** to make disclosure decisions for you
- **Report unethical behavior** by professionals to appropriate authorities
- **Understand** that you're ultimately responsible for your petition's accuracy

Correcting Mistakes and Voluntary Disclosure

When You Discover Errors

Immediate Steps:

- **Contact your attorney** immediately about any discovered errors
- **Document the mistake** and the correct information
- **Assess the significance** of the error with professional help
- **Plan correction strategy** appropriate to the situation

Types of Corrections:

Minor Clerical Errors:

- **Amended schedules** can correct most simple mistakes
- **Supplemental documentation** may be sufficient
- **Trustee notification** of corrections shows good faith

Significant Omissions:

- **Reopening cases** may be necessary for major omissions
- **Full disclosure** with explanation of oversight
- **Professional guidance** essential for complex corrections

Material Changes:

- **New asset discovery** requires immediate disclosure
- **Income changes** during case must be reported
- **Family status changes** may affect exemptions or eligibility

Voluntary Disclosure Benefits

Why Honesty Pays:

- **Credibility with court** and trustee
- **Reduced suspicion** of intentional fraud
- **Mitigation of consequences** for honest mistakes
- **Protection of discharge** and case completion

How to Disclose Properly:

- **Work with attorney** to prepare disclosure
- **Provide complete information** about discovered issues
- **Explain circumstances** that led to initial error
- **Demonstrate good faith** through prompt correction

Red Flags That Attract Scrutiny

Financial Red Flags

Patterns That Create Suspicion:

Unusual Financial Activity:

- **Large cash transactions** without clear source

- **Multiple bank account transfers** close to filing
- **Sudden asset liquidation** before bankruptcy
- **Complex business transactions** involving family

Income and Expense Inconsistencies:

- **Lifestyle exceeding reported income**
- **Unexplained cash flow** or asset acquisition
- **Business income inconsistencies** with tax returns
- **Living expense estimates** that seem unrealistic

Transfer Timing Issues:

- **Multiple transfers** to family members
- **Asset sales** at below-market prices
- **Business entity changes** before filing
- **Real estate transactions** with relatives

Behavioral Red Flags

Actions That Create Problems:

Non-Cooperation:

- **Failure to provide** requested documentation
- **Evasive answers** at 341 meeting
- **Missing deadlines** for court requirements
- **Hostile attitude** toward trustee or process

Inconsistent Information:

- **Conflicting statements** in different documents
- **Changes in testimony** between meetings
- **Documentation contradicts** verbal statements
- **Multiple versions** of the same transaction

Obvious Concealment:

- **Reluctance to discuss** certain assets or transactions
- **Vague answers** to specific questions
- **Missing documentation** for significant items
- **Complex explanations** for simple transactions

Building a Fraud-Proof Case

Documentation Strategy

Comprehensive Record-Keeping:

- **Document every asset** regardless of value
- **Explain unusual transactions** with written records
- **Keep receipts** for significant purchases
- **Maintain business records** that support reported income

Professional Valuation:

- **Real estate appraisals** for valuable property
- **Vehicle valuations** from reliable sources
- **Business valuations** for ownership interests
- **Professional assessment** of collections or specialty items

Transaction Explanation:

- **Written explanations** for family transfers
- **Business purpose documentation** for entity transactions
- **Necessity justification** for large purchases
- **Timing explanations** for suspicious activity

Communication Strategy

With Your Attorney:

- **Complete disclosure** of all financial information
- **Regular updates** on any changes or discoveries
- **Questions about** uncertain or complex situations
- **Clear understanding** of all advice and recommendations

With the Trustee:

- **Prompt responses** to all requests
- **Complete documentation** for all questions
- **Professional demeanor** at all meetings
- **Honest answers** to all inquiries

With Creditors:

- **No direct communication** about dischargeable debts
- **All communication through attorney** when represented
- **Compliance** with automatic stay requirements
- **Professional handling** of ongoing obligations

Real-Life Fraud Prevention Examples

Success Story: The Honest Mistake Recovery

Background: *David, small business owner, Sacramento*

- Filed Chapter 7 to address business and personal debt
- Forgot to list a small investment account worth $3,500
- Discovered error 2 months after filing

The Discovery:

- **Found old statement** while organizing records
- **Immediately contacted attorney** about the omission

- **Researched account status** and current value
- **Prepared explanation** for the oversight

Correction Process:

- **Filed amended Schedule B** listing the account
- **Provided explanation** of inadvertent omission
- **Demonstrated good faith** through prompt disclosure
- **Cooperated fully** with trustee's additional questions

Successful Outcome:

- **Account was exempt** under wildcard exemption
- **No fraud allegations** due to prompt disclosure
- **Case proceeded normally** to discharge
- **Trustee commended** honesty and prompt correction

Key Lessons:

- Prompt voluntary disclosure prevents fraud allegations
- Honest mistakes are correctable if handled properly
- Good faith cooperation protects case integrity
- Professional guidance essential for correction process

Cautionary Tale: The Transfer Trap

Background: *Jennifer, divorced, Long Island*

- Sold car to her brother for $5,000 cash
- Car was worth approximately $12,000
- Sale occurred 4 months before filing bankruptcy
- Needed quick cash for legal fees and moving expenses

The Problem:

- **Below-market sale** to family member created suspicion

- **Cash transaction** without proper documentation
- **Timing** close to bankruptcy filing was problematic
- **Inadequate explanation** for below-market price

Trustee Investigation:

- **Questioned transaction** at 341 meeting
- **Requested documentation** of car's value and condition
- **Investigated family relationship** and payment method
- **Considered recovery action** for benefit of estate

Resolution Process:

- **Detailed explanation** of car's mechanical problems
- **Repair estimates** showing needed $4,000 in work
- **Documentation** of urgent need for cash
- **Family member testimony** about transaction circumstances

Final Outcome:

- **Trustee accepted explanation** after full investigation
- **No fraud charges** but significant stress and delay
- **Additional attorney fees** for defending transaction
- **Case completed successfully** but with complications

Lessons Learned:

- Document all transactions with family members thoroughly
- Below-market sales require clear business justification
- Timing of transactions matters significantly
- Professional advice essential for complex family transactions

Your Fraud Prevention Action Plan

Pre-Filing Phase

Complete Disclosure Preparation:

- [ ] **List every asset** you own or have interest in, regardless of value
- [ ] **Document all income sources** including irregular and cash income
- [ ] **Gather records** for all significant financial transactions in past 2 years
- [ ] **Explain unusual transactions** with written documentation
- [ ] **Review with attorney** any questionable or complex situations

Transaction Review:

- [ ] **Stop using credit cards** immediately when considering bankruptcy
- [ ] **Avoid large purchases** unless absolutely necessary for health/safety
- [ ] **Document necessity** for any significant expenses
- [ ] **Don't transfer assets** to family or friends without attorney guidance
- [ ] **Maintain detailed records** of all financial activities

During the Case

Ongoing Compliance:

- [ ] **Report changes** in income, assets, or circumstances immediately
- [ ] **Maintain complete records** of all financial activities during case
- [ ] **Respond promptly** to all trustee requests and court deadlines
- [ ] **Attend all required meetings** and hearings
- [ ] **Stay current** on post-petition obligations

Communication Excellence:

- [ ] **Answer truthfully** and completely at all meetings
- [ ] **Ask for clarification** if you don't understand questions
- [ ] **Admit mistakes** honestly and offer to correct them
- [ ] **Provide additional documentation** when requested
- [ ] **Maintain professional demeanor** throughout process

Post-Filing Vigilance

Continued Honesty:

- [ ] **Report discovered assets** or income immediately
- [ ] **Correct any errors** as soon as discovered
- [ ] **Maintain transparency** throughout entire case
- [ ] **Complete all educational requirements** honestly
- [ ] **Comply with discharge injunction** after case completion

Professional Relationship Maintenance:

- [ ] **Stay in contact** with attorney throughout case
- [ ] **Report any issues** or concerns immediately
- [ ] **Follow professional advice** on complex situations
- [ ] **Document any changes** in circumstances
- [ ] **Prepare for discharge** and post-bankruptcy obligations

The Bottom Line: Integrity as Your Foundation

Bankruptcy fraud is serious, but it's also rare among honest people who approach the process with integrity and transparency. The key principles for staying safe and honest are:

Complete Disclosure:

- List every asset, debt, and source of income
- Explain unusual transactions clearly and honestly

- Don't hide anything, regardless of how minor it seems
- When in doubt, disclose and let the trustee decide significance

Professional Guidance:

- Work with experienced, ethical professionals
- Follow legal advice about disclosure and compliance
- Get help with complex situations rather than guessing
- Don't try to navigate complicated issues alone

Prompt Correction:

- Fix mistakes immediately when discovered
- Voluntarily disclose errors rather than hoping they won't be found
- Explain circumstances honestly without making excuses
- Demonstrate good faith through transparent cooperation

Long-term Perspective:

- Focus on successful case completion, not gaming the system
- Build foundation for honest financial management going forward
- Use bankruptcy as fresh start opportunity, not endpoint
- Help others understand the importance of honesty in the process

Remember: The vast majority of bankruptcy cases proceed smoothly with honest debtors receiving the relief they need and deserve. By maintaining complete honesty, working with ethical professionals, and focusing on legitimate debt relief rather than system manipulation, you protect both your case and your future.

Your bankruptcy discharge is worth far more than any asset you might be tempted to hide or any advantage you might gain through deception. Protect that discharge - and your integrity - through complete transparency and honest cooperation with the process.

The fresh start that bankruptcy provides is built on a foundation of honesty. Make sure that foundation is solid, and your new financial life will be built on firm ground.

In the next chapter, we'll explore how to find and work with the right bankruptcy attorney - ensuring you have experienced, ethical representation to guide you through this complex process successfully.

21

Finding the Right Attorney

Getting Help You Can Trust

Bankruptcy is one of the most important legal decisions you'll ever make. It's a complex process filled with paperwork, strict deadlines, and intricate rules that can make or break your financial fresh start. While the law allows you to file without an attorney, the reality is that having qualified legal representation dramatically increases your chances of success and helps you avoid costly mistakes that could haunt you for years.

Think of bankruptcy like performing surgery on your financial life. Sure, you could try to do it yourself with a YouTube tutorial, but would you really want to? The stakes are too high, and the consequences of errors too severe.

In this comprehensive chapter, we'll guide you through every aspect of finding, evaluating, and working with a bankruptcy attorney. We'll also show you how to access free or low-cost legal help if private counsel isn't within your budget, with special focus on resources available in New York and California.

The Real Question: Do You Actually Need a Bankruptcy Attorney?

Legally speaking? No. Federal law allows you to file "pro se," which means representing yourself without an attorney. Thousands of people do this every year.

Practically speaking? In most cases, absolutely yes. Here's why the legal right to self-representation doesn't mean it's a good idea.

When You Definitely Need Professional Help

You should strongly consider hiring an attorney if any of these apply to your situation:

Asset Protection Concerns

- You own a home with equity
- You have valuable personal property (cars, jewelry, collectibles)
- You own business assets or equipment
- You have retirement accounts or investment portfolios

Complex Debt Situations

- You're behind on mortgage or car payments
- You have tax debts to the IRS or state
- You're dealing with student loans
- You have business debts or personal guarantees
- You owe money to family members or friends

Challenging Circumstances

- You're filing Chapter 13 (repayment plans are notoriously complex)
- You've filed bankruptcy before
- You had a previous case dismissed
- You're going through a divorce simultaneously
- You have recent large purchases or cash advances
- You transferred assets to family members recently

Income and Expense Complications

- Your income varies significantly (self-employed, commissioned sales, seasonal work)
- You have multiple income sources
- Your expenses are unusual or difficult to categorize
- You're dealing with garnishments or lawsuits

What a Good Attorney Actually Does for You

Even in seemingly straightforward Chapter 7 cases, a qualified bankruptcy attorney provides invaluable services:

Accuracy and Completeness Your bankruptcy petition contains dozens of forms and hundreds of questions. One wrong answer or omission can delay your case, cost you property, or even result in criminal charges for bankruptcy fraud. An attorney ensures everything is complete and accurate.

Strategic Exemption Planning Every state has different rules about what property you can keep in bankruptcy. An experienced attorney knows how to maximize your exemptions and may suggest legal steps to better protect your assets before filing.

Creditor Protection Once you file, creditors must stop calling and collecting. But they don't always follow the rules. Your attorney becomes your shield against creditor harassment and violations of the automatic stay.

Court Navigation Bankruptcy courts have their own procedures, local rules, and unwritten customs. Your attorney knows what the trustees and judges expect and how to present your case in the best light.

Problem Prevention Experienced attorneys spot potential issues before they become disasters. They can identify problems with your case and fix them before filing, rather than scrambling to address trustee objections later.

What Makes a Truly Excellent Bankruptcy Attorney?

Not all attorneys are created equal. Here's what separates the excellent from the adequate:

Essential Qualifications

State Licensing and Local Knowledge Your attorney must be licensed in your state and familiar with local court procedures. Bankruptcy law is federal, but each district has its own customs and preferences. An attorney who practices regularly in your local bankruptcy court is invaluable.

Bankruptcy Specialization You want an attorney who focuses primarily on bankruptcy law, not a general practitioner who handles bankruptcies occasionally. Bankruptcy law changes frequently, and specialists stay current with new developments.

Experience with Your Type of Case If you're filing Chapter 7, ensure your attorney handles many Chapter 7 cases. If you need Chapter 13, find someone experienced with repayment plans. If you have a business, find an attorney who handles business bankruptcies.

Personal Qualities That Matter

Clear Communication Your attorney should explain things in plain English, return calls promptly, and keep you informed throughout the process. Bankruptcy is stressful enough without wondering what's happening with your case.

Patience and Empathy Financial distress is emotionally difficult. The right attorney understands this and treats you with respect and compassion, not judgment.

Transparency About Fees Your attorney should provide clear, written fee agreements with no hidden costs. They should explain exactly what services are included and what might cost extra.

Accessibility You should be able to reach your attorney or their staff with reasonable ease. Avoid attorneys who are consistently unavailable or delegate everything to untrained staff.

Questions to Ask Potential Attorneys

During your initial consultation, ask these critical questions:

About Their Experience

- How many bankruptcy cases have you handled in the past year?

- What percentage of your practice is bankruptcy law?
- Do you handle both Chapter 7 and Chapter 13 cases?
- Have you handled cases similar to mine?
- How often do you appear in this particular bankruptcy court?

About Their Process

- Will you personally prepare my bankruptcy forms?
- Who will I primarily work with during my case?
- Will you personally represent me at the 341 meeting of creditors?
- How do you communicate with clients during the case?
- What's your typical timeline for a case like mine?

About Fees and Costs

- What are your total fees for my type of case?
- What services are included in that fee?
- What might cost extra?
- Do you offer payment plans?
- What are the court filing fees and other costs I'll need to pay?

About Your Specific Situation

- Based on what I've told you, do you see any potential problems with my case?
- Which chapter of bankruptcy do you recommend for me and why?
- What property will I be able to keep?
- How will bankruptcy affect my specific situation (job, spouse, etc.)?

Understanding Bankruptcy Attorney Fees

Legal fees can seem expensive when you're already struggling financially, but understanding the typical costs helps you budget and avoid overpaying.

Chapter 7 Fee Structure

Typical Fee Ranges (varies by region)

- Simple cases: $1,200 - $1,800
- Complex cases: $1,800 - $3,000
- High-asset cases: $2,500 - $5,000+

Payment Requirements Chapter 7 attorney fees typically must be paid in full before filing. This is because once you file bankruptcy, the debt to your attorney becomes dischargeable, creating a conflict of interest.

What's Usually Included

- Initial consultation
- Preparation of all bankruptcy forms
- Communication with creditors
- Representation at 341 meeting of creditors
- Handling routine trustee requests
- Post-discharge follow-up

What Often Costs Extra

- Adversary proceedings (lawsuits within bankruptcy)
- Appealing trustee decisions
- Extensive asset protection planning
- Dealing with complex business issues
- Reopening closed cases

Chapter 13 Fee Structure

Typical Fee Ranges

- Standard cases: $3,000 - $4,500
- Complex cases: $4,500 - $6,500

- Business or high-income cases: $6,000+

Payment Flexibility Chapter 13 attorneys can receive partial payment upfront and the remainder through your repayment plan. Typical arrangements include $1,500-$2,000 down and the balance paid monthly through your plan.

Additional Considerations Chapter 13 cases last 3-5 years, so your attorney relationship is long-term. Factor in their availability for plan modifications, payment adjustments, and ongoing issues.

Court Costs and Additional Expenses

Beyond attorney fees, you'll pay:

- Chapter 7 filing fee: $338
- Chapter 13 filing fee: $313
- Credit counseling courses: $20-50
- Debt education course: $20-50
- Document preparation fees: $50-200
- Potential appraisal or valuation costs: $200-500

Getting the Most Value

Free Consultations Most bankruptcy attorneys offer free initial consultations. Use these to:

- Understand your options
- Compare different attorneys
- Get multiple opinions on complex situations
- Negotiate fees and payment terms

Payment Plans Many attorneys offer payment plans even for Chapter 7 cases. Don't let upfront costs prevent you from getting proper representation.

Value vs. Price The cheapest attorney isn't always the best value. Consider:

- Experience and specialization

- Quality of service and communication
- Reputation and track record
- What's included in the fee
- Long-term relationship for Chapter 13 cases

Where to Find Qualified Bankruptcy Attorneys

Professional Associations and Directories

State Bar Associations Your state bar association maintains directories of licensed attorneys and can verify credentials and disciplinary history.

- **New York:** www.nysba.org - Use their attorney search tool and filter by bankruptcy/debtor-creditor law
- **California:** www.calbar.ca.gov - Their attorney search includes practice areas and disciplinary records

National Association of Consumer Bankruptcy Attorneys (NACBA)

- Website: www.nacba.org
- Specialized directory of attorneys who focus on consumer bankruptcy
- Members must meet experience requirements and continuing education standards
- Provides attorney ratings and reviews

American Bankruptcy Institute (ABI)

- Website: www.abi.org
- Professional organization for bankruptcy professionals
- Directory includes attorneys, judges, and trustees
- Offers attorney certification programs

Personal Referrals and Recommendations

Other Attorneys If you know any attorneys (even in different practice areas), ask for referrals. Lawyers often know who handles good bankruptcy work in their area.

Financial Professionals CPAs, financial planners, and credit counselors often work with bankruptcy attorneys and can provide referrals based on client experiences.

Previous Clients If you know someone who's been through bankruptcy, ask about their attorney experience. Personal testimonials are valuable.

Online Resources and Reviews

Google Reviews and Yelp Read client reviews, but remember that very happy and very unhappy clients are most likely to leave reviews. Look for patterns in feedback rather than individual complaints.

Legal Rating Services

- Martindale-Hubbell: Peer review ratings
- Avvo: Combines peer reviews, client reviews, and background information
- Super Lawyers: Selective listing based on peer nominations and research

Better Business Bureau Check for complaints and resolution patterns, though few attorneys participate actively in BBB ratings.

Free and Low-Cost Legal Help Options

If you can't afford private counsel, several options provide quality bankruptcy assistance at reduced cost or free.

Legal Aid Organizations

Legal aid societies provide free legal services to qualifying low-income individuals. They often have bankruptcy specialists who are as experienced as private attorneys.

Law School Clinics

Many law schools operate clinics where senior students, supervised by experienced attorneys, provide free or low-cost legal services. These clinics often handle bankruptcy cases and can provide excellent representation.

Pro Bono Programs

Many bankruptcy attorneys participate in pro bono (free) programs through bar associations or legal aid organizations. You may qualify for free representation from a private attorney.

Self-Help Resources

Some courts and legal aid organizations provide:

- Self-help centers with trained staff
- Form preparation assistance
- Educational workshops
- Online resources and tutorials

Comprehensive Resources for New York Residents

Major Legal Aid Organizations

Legal Services NYC

- Website: www.legalservicesnyc.org
- Phone: 917-661-4500
- Services: Chapter 7 filings, creditor defense, foreclosure prevention
- Coverage: All five boroughs of New York City
- Eligibility: Income-based guidelines

New York Legal Assistance Group (NYLAG)

- Website: www.nylag.org
- Phone: 212-613-5000

- Services: Pro bono bankruptcy clinics, debt counseling
- Special programs: Veterans legal clinic, senior citizen assistance
- Coverage: New York City and surrounding areas

Empire Justice Center

- Website: www.empirejustice.org
- Phone: Multiple offices across New York
- Services: Consumer law, bankruptcy, foreclosure defense
- Coverage: Rochester, Albany, Central New York, Western New York

Legal Aid Society of Mid-New York

- Website: www.lasmny.org
- Phone: 315-703-6700
- Coverage: Central New York including Syracuse, Utica, Watertown
- Services: Full bankruptcy representation for qualifying clients

Regional and Specialized Services

Nassau/Suffolk Law Services Committee

- Website: www.nslawservices.org
- Coverage: Long Island
- Services: Bankruptcy, foreclosure, consumer debt

Legal Services of the Hudson Valley

- Website: www.lshv.org
- Coverage: Westchester, Putnam, Dutchess, Orange, Rockland, Sullivan, and Ulster Counties
- Services: Bankruptcy and debt counseling

Neighborhood Legal Services (Buffalo)

- Website: www.nls.org

- Coverage: Western New York
- Services: Consumer bankruptcy and debt relief

Statewide Resources

LawHelpNY

- Website: www.lawhelpny.org
- Comprehensive directory of free legal services
- Search by location and legal issue
- Includes self-help resources and forms

New York State Bar Association Pro Bono Program

- Website: www.nysba.org
- Connects low-income individuals with volunteer attorneys
- Bankruptcy-specific referral programs

Comprehensive Resources for California Residents

Major Legal Aid Organizations

Legal Aid Foundation of Los Angeles (LAFLA)

- Website: www.lafla.org
- Phone: 800-399-4529
- Services: Consumer debt counseling, bankruptcy assistance, foreclosure prevention
- Coverage: Los Angeles County
- Special programs: Immigration-related debt issues

Bay Area Legal Aid

- Website: www.baylegal.org
- Phone: 510-250-5270

- Services: Free bankruptcy help for low-income residents
- Coverage: Northern California including San Francisco, Oakland, San Jose
- Eligibility: Strict income guidelines

Legal Services of Northern California

- Website: www.lsnc.net
- Phone: 916-551-2150
- Coverage: 23 Northern California counties
- Services: Full bankruptcy representation and counseling

Inland Counties Legal Services

- Website: www.inlandlegal.org
- Coverage: Riverside and San Bernardino Counties
- Services: Bankruptcy, foreclosure defense, consumer protection

Regional Specialists

Public Law Center (Orange County)

- Website: www.publiclawcenter.org
- Phone: 714-541-1010
- Services: Free bankruptcy clinics, self-help workshops
- Special programs: Senior legal services

Legal Aid Society of San Diego

- Website: www.lassd.org
- Phone: 877-734-3258
- Services: Bankruptcy, debt counseling, consumer protection
- Special programs: Military family assistance

Central California Legal Services

- Website: www.centralcallegal.org
- Coverage: Fresno, Kings, Madera, Merced, Tulare Counties
- Services: Full bankruptcy representation

Kern County Legal Services

- Website: No website available
- Phone: 661-325-3627
- Coverage: Kern County (Bakersfield area)
- Services: Limited bankruptcy assistance

Statewide Resources

LawHelpCA

- Website: www.lawhelpca.org
- Comprehensive search tool for finding legal aid
- Filter by county and legal issue
- Includes bankruptcy-specific resources

State Bar of California Pro Bono Program

- Website: www.calbar.ca.gov
- Connects qualifying individuals with volunteer attorneys
- Includes bankruptcy specialist referrals

California Courts Self-Help Center

- Website: www.courts.ca.gov/selfhelp
- Forms, instructions, and educational materials
- Video tutorials for common procedures

Red Flags: Avoiding Scams and Predatory Services

The bankruptcy and debt relief industry attracts both legitimate professionals and predatory scam artists. Knowing the warning signs can save you money and protect your case.

Common Scams to Avoid

"Debt Relief" Companies These companies promise to eliminate your debt without bankruptcy, often through bogus "legal loopholes" or debt settlement programs that leave you worse off.

Warning signs:

- Promise to eliminate all debt without bankruptcy
- Charge upfront fees before providing any services
- Claim they can "fix" your credit immediately
- Use high-pressure sales tactics
- Guarantee specific results

Bankruptcy Mills These are high-volume operations that process bankruptcy cases like an assembly line, with little individual attention to your specific situation.

Warning signs:

- Extremely low fees that seem too good to be true
- Pressure to sign up immediately
- No meaningful consultation or case evaluation
- Paralegal or non-attorney staff handle most interactions
- Cookie-cutter approach to all cases

Unlicensed "Legal" Services Some companies masquerade as law firms but have no licensed attorneys involved in your case.

Warning signs:

- No licensed attorney identified
- Staff cannot answer basic legal questions

- Documents prepared by non-attorneys
- No representation at court hearings
- Evasive answers about attorney involvement

Specific Red Flags in Attorney Selection

Fee-Related Warning Signs

- Demands full payment before any consultation
- Fees significantly higher or lower than market rates
- No written fee agreement
- Unclear about what services are included
- Adds unexpected charges throughout the process

Service-Related Warning Signs

- Cannot provide references or examples of similar cases
- Promises guaranteed outcomes
- Discourages you from asking questions
- Rushes you through the process
- Unavailable for reasonable client communication

Credential Warning Signs

- Cannot provide bar license number
- Evasive about experience level
- No malpractice insurance
- Disciplinary actions or complaints
- Not familiar with local bankruptcy court procedures

How to Verify Attorney Credentials

State Bar License Verification Always verify that your attorney is licensed and in good standing:

- New York: www.nysba.org (attorney search)
- California: www.calbar.ca.gov (attorney search)
- Other states: Contact your state bar association

Check Disciplinary History State bar websites typically show disciplinary actions, suspensions, or other issues with attorneys.

Malpractice Insurance Ask whether your attorney carries malpractice insurance. While not required in all states, it provides protection if they make mistakes.

Court Experience Ask for examples of recent cases in your local bankruptcy court. Experienced attorneys should be able to discuss local procedures and trustees.

Working Effectively with Your Bankruptcy Attorney

Once you've selected an attorney, your relationship with them significantly impacts your case's success. Here's how to make the most of that relationship.

Preparing for Your Initial Consultation

Gather Essential Documents

- Recent pay stubs or income documentation
- Tax returns (last 2 years)
- Bank statements (last 6 months)
- Credit card and loan statements
- Mortgage or rent information
- List of all assets and their approximate values
- List of all debts and monthly payments

Prepare Your Questions Write down your questions in advance. Consider asking about:

- Which chapter of bankruptcy you should file
- What property you can keep
- How bankruptcy will affect your specific situation
- Timeline for your case
- Potential complications or issues
- Alternatives to bankruptcy

Be Completely Honest Bankruptcy requires full financial disclosure. Hiding assets, income, or debts can result in criminal charges. Your attorney needs complete information to represent you effectively.

During Your Case

Respond Promptly Bankruptcy cases have strict deadlines. Respond quickly to requests for information or documents from your attorney.

Stay Organized Keep all bankruptcy-related documents in one place. Your attorney may need additional information throughout the process.

Communicate Changes Notify your attorney immediately of any changes in your financial situation, including:

- New income or job changes
- Additional debts or creditor actions
- Changes in living situation
- New assets or property
- Legal actions or lawsuits

Attend Required Meetings You must attend the 341 meeting of creditors and any other required court appearances. Prepare by reviewing your bankruptcy forms with your attorney.

Complete Required Courses You must complete credit counseling before filing and a debt education course before discharge. Don't wait until the last minute.

Setting Realistic Expectations

Timeline Expectations

- Chapter 7: Typically 4-6 months from filing to discharge
- Chapter 13: 3-5 years depending on your repayment plan
- Complex cases may take longer due to trustee investigations or creditor objections

Communication Expectations Discuss how often you'll hear from your attorney and through what methods (phone, email, mail). Most routine cases require minimal ongoing communication after filing.

Outcome Expectations While most bankruptcy cases proceed smoothly, no attorney can guarantee specific results. Understanding potential complications helps you prepare mentally and financially.

Real-World Case Examples

Case Study 1: Sarah's Chapter 7 Success Story

Background: Sarah, a single mother in Sacramento, lost her job and accumulated $45,000 in credit card debt while caring for her elderly mother.

Attorney Selection Process: Sarah initially considered filing pro se to save money but consulted with three attorneys during free consultations. She chose an attorney who:

- Specialized in consumer bankruptcy
- Explained her options clearly
- Offered a reasonable payment plan
- Had excellent reviews from other single mothers

The Process: Her attorney identified that Sarah could keep her modest home using California's homestead exemption and her car using the motor vehicle exemption. The case proceeded smoothly with no creditor objections.

Outcome: Sarah received a full discharge after 4 months and kept her home and car. She now has a stable financial foundation to rebuild her credit.

Key Lessons:

- Free consultations helped Sarah compare options
- Specialized expertise saved her valuable property
- Investment in legal help provided long-term benefits

Case Study 2: Marcus's Chapter 13 Success

Background: Marcus, a contractor in Queens, New York, faced foreclosure on his home and had $85,000 in various debts, including tax debts that wouldn't be discharged in Chapter 7.

Attorney Selection: Marcus chose an attorney who:

- Had extensive Chapter 13 experience
- Understood construction industry income fluctuations
- Offered partial fee payments through the repayment plan
- Had successfully handled tax debt issues

The Process: His attorney crafted a 5-year repayment plan that:

- Stopped the foreclosure
- Reduced unsecured debt payments to 15% of balances
- Set up manageable tax payments
- Allowed for income fluctuations common in construction

Outcome: Marcus completed his plan successfully and kept his home. His remaining unsecured debts were discharged, and his credit score began improving during the plan period.

Key Lessons:

- Chapter 13 expertise was crucial for complex repayment planning
- Industry-specific knowledge helped address income variability
- Long-term attorney relationship provided ongoing support

Case Study 3: Learning from Mistakes

Background: Janet in Los Angeles initially tried to save money by using a "bankruptcy preparation service" that charged $500 to prepare her forms.

The Problem: The service made several critical errors:

- Failed to claim important exemptions
- Listed incorrect asset values
- Missed filing deadlines
- Provided no legal advice or representation

The Consequence: Janet lost her car to the trustee and faced potential fraud allegations due to incomplete disclosures.

The Solution: Janet hired a qualified bankruptcy attorney who:

- Helped her amend her bankruptcy forms
- Negotiated with the trustee to resolve issues
- Represented her at additional hearings
- Ultimately saved her case from dismissal

Total Cost: Janet ended up paying $500 for useless forms plus $3,500 to fix the problems - far more than hiring a good attorney initially would have cost.

Key Lessons:

- False economy led to much higher total costs
- Proper legal representation prevents costly mistakes
- Attempting to cut corners in legal matters often backfires

Making Your Final Decision

Choosing the right bankruptcy attorney is one of the most important decisions in your financial recovery. Here's how to make that choice confidently.

Evaluation Criteria Checklist

Essential Qualifications (Must-haves)

- [ ] Licensed in your state
- [ ] Focuses primarily on bankruptcy law
- [ ] Experience with your type of case (Chapter 7 or 13)
- [ ] Familiar with your local bankruptcy court
- [ ] Clear fee structure and written agreement
- [ ] Professional liability insurance
- [ ] Good standing with state bar

Preferred Qualifications (Nice-to-haves)

- [ ] NACBA membership or other professional certifications
- [ ] Positive client reviews and testimonials
- [ ] Reasonable availability and communication
- [ ] Experience with your specific debt types
- [ ] Payment plan options
- [ ] Additional services (credit counseling, post-bankruptcy advice)

Warning Signs (Deal-breakers)

- [ ] Unrealistic promises or guarantees
- [ ] Pressure to sign up immediately
- [ ] Significantly higher or lower fees than market rates
- [ ] Poor communication or unavailability
- [ ] Unwillingness to answer questions

- [ ] No clear attorney involvement in your case

Questions for Final Consideration

Before making your decision, honestly answer these questions:

1. **Do I feel comfortable with this attorney?** Trust your instincts about whether you can work effectively with them over several months.
2. **Do I understand the fee structure?** Make sure you know exactly what you'll pay and when.
3. **Am I confident in their expertise?** They should demonstrate knowledge of bankruptcy law and local procedures.
4. **Will they be accessible when I need them?** Consider their communication style and availability.
5. **Do their references check out?** If possible, speak with previous clients or check online reviews.

The Bottom Line on Attorney Selection

The right bankruptcy attorney is more than just someone who fills out forms - they're your advocate, guide, and safeguard during one of the most important legal processes of your life. They should:

- Protect your rights and property
- Navigate complex legal procedures
- Communicate clearly and regularly
- Provide honest advice about your options
- Handle your case with professionalism and competence

Remember, you're not just buying a service - you're investing in your financial future. The difference between a good attorney and a poor one can literally be thousands of dollars in saved assets and years of improved credit recovery.

Action Steps for Finding Your Attorney

Step 1: Initial Research (Week 1)

- Identify 5-7 potential attorneys using the resources in this chapter
- Check their credentials and disciplinary history
- Review their websites and initial information
- Prepare your financial documents for consultations

Step 2: Consultations (Week 2)

- Schedule free consultations with your top 3-4 choices
- Prepare questions specific to your situation
- Take notes during each consultation
- Ask for references or testimonials

Step 3: Decision Making (Week 3)

- Compare attorneys based on expertise, communication, and fees
- Check references if provided
- Make your selection and sign the engagement agreement
- Begin gathering documents for your case

Step 4: Case Preparation (Week 4+)

- Work with your chosen attorney to prepare your case
- Complete required credit counseling
- Gather all necessary financial documents
- Prepare for filing and the 341 meeting

Looking Ahead

Finding the right attorney is a crucial step in your bankruptcy process, but it's not the end of your journey. In our next chapter, we'll explore alternatives to bankruptcy that might be appropriate for your situation. While bankruptcy can be a powerful tool for financial recovery, it's not always the best solution for every person or every debt situation.

Remember, the goal isn't just to get through bankruptcy - it's to build a foundation for long-term financial stability and success. The right attorney will not only handle your current case professionally but also provide guidance for your financial future.

Your choice of legal representation can make the difference between a smooth bankruptcy process that protects your assets and sets you up for success, or a difficult experience that costs you more money and creates unnecessary stress. Take the time to make this decision carefully - your financial future depends on it.

In the next chapter will walk you through the most practical alternatives to bankruptcy, help you determine which option best fits your unique circumstances, and, most importantly, equip you to recognize and steer clear of predatory companies that target individuals facing financial hardship.

22

Beyond Bankruptcy

Finding the Right Path to Financial Freedom

Bankruptcy isn't your only way out of debt. While it can be incredibly powerful for the right situation, many people find that alternative strategies offer a faster, less expensive, or less disruptive route back to financial stability.

This chapter will walk you through the most effective alternatives to bankruptcy, help you understand which option might work best for your specific situation, and most importantly, show you how to spot and avoid the predatory companies that prey on people in financial distress.

When Bankruptcy Might Be Overkill

Before diving into alternatives, let's identify when bankruptcy might not be your best choice. Consider other options if you find yourself in any of these situations:

Your debt load is manageable. If you owe less than $10,000 total, bankruptcy's impact on your credit and public record might outweigh its benefits. The time and cost of filing could exceed what you'd save.

You're facing a temporary setback. Lost your job but expect to find work soon? Dealing with medical bills from a one-time emergency? Short-term hardships often resolve themselves without needing the nuclear option of bankruptcy.

Most of your debt won't disappear anyway. Student loans, recent tax debt, child support, and most government obligations survive bankruptcy. If these make up the bulk of what you owe, bankruptcy won't provide the relief you're seeking.

You can cover minimums but want breathing room. If you're making payments but barely staying afloat, debt restructuring might give you the space you need without the long-term credit consequences.

Money is coming your way. Expecting a tax refund, inheritance, legal settlement, or work bonus? It might make sense to wait and pay off debts in full rather than file bankruptcy.

The key question to ask yourself: "Can I realistically pay off my debts within three to five years?" If the answer is yes, alternatives to bankruptcy deserve serious consideration.

Credit Counseling and Debt Management Plans: The Organized Approach

What Actually Happens

A Debt Management Plan (DMP) through a nonprofit credit counseling agency works like this: instead of juggling multiple credit card payments with different due dates and interest rates, you make one payment to the counseling agency each month. They distribute your payment to all your creditors according to a pre-negotiated plan.

Here's what makes it powerful: legitimate nonprofit agencies have established relationships with major credit card companies. They can often secure interest rate reductions that individual consumers can't get on their own - sometimes dropping rates from 24% down to 6% or even 0%.

The Real Benefits

Lower interest means faster payoff. Sarah from Portland had $8,000 in credit card debt at 22% interest. Making minimum payments, she would have paid over $20,000 total and taken 30+ years to pay off. Through a DMP with 8% average interest, she paid it off in 4 years for about $10,000 total.

Late fees and penalties stop. Once you're enrolled and making payments on time, creditors typically freeze penalty fees. This alone can save hundreds of dollars per year.

No public record. Unlike bankruptcy, DMPs don't appear in court records or legal databases. While your credit report will show you're in a payment plan, there's no permanent public filing.

Credit score recovery. Many people see their credit scores start improving within 12-18 months as they establish a consistent payment history and reduce their balances.

The Limitations You Need to Know

You pay every penny. DMPs don't reduce your principal balance - you'll pay back everything you borrowed, just with better terms. If your debt is truly unmanageable, this might not provide enough relief.

One missed payment can ruin everything. If you fall behind on your DMP payment, creditors can pull out of the plan and restore your original interest rates and fees. You're back where you started, often in a worse position.

Not all creditors participate. While major credit card companies usually work with DMPs, smaller creditors, collection agencies, and non-credit card debts (like medical bills or personal loans) may not participate.

Finding Legitimate Help

Use only nonprofit, accredited agencies. Start your search at:

- **www.nfcc.org** (National Foundation for Credit Counseling)
- **www.consumer.ftc.gov** (Federal Trade Commission consumer information)

Red flags to avoid:

- Companies that charge large upfront fees

- Anyone promising to "eliminate" your debt
- High-pressure sales tactics or same-day enrollment demands
- Companies that won't provide written information about their program

Best for: People with steady income, primarily credit card debt under $25,000, and the discipline to stick with a 3-5 year payment plan.

Debt Settlement: High Risk, High Reward

How It Really Works

Debt settlement means convincing your creditors to accept less than the full amount you owe - typically 30-60% of the original balance. This can happen in two ways: you negotiate directly with creditors yourself, or you hire a company to negotiate on your behalf.

The process usually requires you to stop paying your creditors and instead save money in a separate account until you have enough to make lump-sum settlement offers. This strategy deliberately damages your credit in the short term to create leverage for negotiations.

When It Works Well

Lisa's success story: Lisa owed $18,000 across four credit cards after a divorce left her with reduced income. She stopped making payments and saved $400 monthly for 10 months. With $4,000 in her settlement fund, she called each creditor and offered to settle. Three of the four accepted offers between 25-40% of the balance. She paid $6,200 total to resolve $18,000 in debt.

The key factors in Lisa's success:

- She had access to a lump sum for negotiations
- She handled negotiations herself (no company fees)
- She understood the credit damage was temporary
- She had primarily unsecured debt

The Serious Risks

Credit damage is immediate and severe. Stopping payments will quickly drop your credit score by 100+ points. Settled accounts remain on your credit report for seven years marked as "settled for less than full balance."

No guarantee creditors will negotiate. Many creditors, especially smaller ones, refuse to settle and will simply sue you for the full amount plus interest and fees.

Tax consequences. Forgiven debt over $600 is typically taxable income. If you settle $10,000 in debt for $4,000, you might owe taxes on the $6,000 difference.

Predatory companies dominate this industry. Most debt settlement companies charge 20-25% of your total debt in fees, often collected before they've settled anything. Many provide little value beyond what you could accomplish yourself.

Avoiding Settlement Scams

Never work with any company that:

- Charges fees before settling your debts
- Promises specific settlement amounts or timelines
- Advises you to stop communicating with your creditors
- Claims they can "eliminate" debt without credit damage
- Pressures you to sign up immediately

Best for: People with significant unsecured debt ($15,000+), access to lump-sum settlement funds, and willingness to accept major credit damage for 2-3 years.

Debt Consolidation Loans: Simplification Strategy

The Basic Concept

Debt consolidation means taking out one new loan to pay off multiple existing debts. Instead of managing several payments with different interest rates and due dates, you have one payment to one lender.

This works best when you can qualify for a consolidation loan with a lower interest rate than your current average rate, and when the simplified payment structure helps you stay organized and on track.

Types of Consolidation

Personal loans from banks, credit unions, or online lenders are the most common. These are typically unsecured loans with fixed interest rates and 3-7 year repayment terms.

Balance transfer credit cards offer promotional 0% interest rates for 12-21 months, but usually require excellent credit and charge 3-5% transfer fees.

Home equity loans or lines of credit offer lower interest rates but put your house at risk if you can't make payments.

Real-World Example

Marcus had:

- Credit card A: $4,000 at 24% interest, $120 minimum payment
- Credit card B: $3,500 at 19% interest, $95 minimum payment
- Personal loan: $2,500 at 16% interest, $85 minimum payment
- **Total:** $10,000 debt, $300 monthly payments

After consolidation:

- Personal loan: $10,000 at 12% interest, $225 monthly payment
- **Savings:** $75 per month, $1,800 total interest over the loan term

The Catch

Consolidation doesn't reduce your total debt - it just reorganizes it. If you don't address the spending habits that created the debt, you might find yourself with both the consolidation loan and new credit card balances.

Best for: People with good credit (650+ score), multiple high-interest debts, and the discipline to avoid running up new balances after consolidation.

Direct Negotiation: The DIY Approach

Taking Control of Your Situation

You don't need to hire a company to negotiate with your creditors. If you're behind on payments or struggling to keep up, contacting your creditors directly can often produce surprising results.

Most major creditors have hardship departments specifically designed to help customers avoid default. They'd rather work with you than send your account to collections or write it off as a loss.

What to Ask For

Temporary payment reduction: Lower your monthly payment for 3-6 months while you recover from a temporary setback.

Interest rate reduction: Permanent or temporary reduction in your interest rate, especially if you've been a good customer or can demonstrate financial hardship.

Settlement offer: If you're significantly behind and have access to a lump sum, offer to settle the account for less than the full balance.

Payment plan: Spread past-due amounts over several months while keeping your account current going forward.

How to Negotiate Effectively

Be honest about your situation. Explain what caused your financial difficulties and what steps you're taking to improve your situation.

Have specific numbers ready. Know exactly how much you can afford to pay monthly, or how much you can offer as a lump-sum settlement.

Get everything in writing. Never make payments based on verbal agreements. Request written confirmation of any new payment terms before sending money.

Document everything. Keep records of all phone calls, including dates, times, representative names, and what was discussed.

Success Story

Maria's approach: When Maria lost her job, she immediately called her three credit card companies before missing any payments. She explained her situation and asked for temporary payment reductions. Two companies reduced her minimum payments by 50% for six months. The third company offered a 0% interest rate for four months. These modifications gave her breathing room to find new employment without destroying her credit.

Best for: People who are current on payments but struggling, or those who are recently behind but want to avoid collections.

The "Do Nothing" Strategy: When You're Judgment Proof

Understanding Your Legal Position

Sometimes the best strategy is no strategy at all. If you have no income beyond protected benefits (like Social Security or disability), no assets worth seizing, and no prospect of your situation improving, you might be effectively "judgment proof."

This means that even if creditors sue you and win judgments, they can't collect anything from you because you have nothing they can legally take.

What "Judgment Proof" Means

Protected income: Social Security, disability benefits, unemployment insurance, and certain pensions cannot be garnished for most consumer debts.

Minimal assets: If you don't own a home, have significant savings, or own valuable personal property, there's nothing for creditors to seize.

State protections: Every state protects certain assets from creditors, such as basic household goods, work tools, and modest vehicles.

The Statute of Limitations Factor

Consumer debts have a "statute of limitations" - a time limit for when creditors can sue you. In most states, this is 3-6 years from your last payment. After this period expires, creditors can still try to collect, but they can't successfully sue you if you raise the statute of limitations as a defense.

Risks to Consider

Judgments can last a long time. Even if you're judgment proof now, court judgments can often be renewed for 10-20 years. If your financial situation improves, creditors might be able to collect later.

Credit damage continues. Not paying debts will severely damage your credit for seven years, making it difficult to rent apartments, get utilities connected, or qualify for loans.

Harassment may continue. Collection calls and letters will likely persist until the statute of limitations expires.

When This Makes Sense

Robert's situation: Robert is 68, disabled, and lives solely on Social Security. He has $12,000 in credit card debt from medical expenses but owns no assets and has no other income. Filing bankruptcy would cost $1,500+ in fees and attorney costs - money he doesn't have. His debt will likely become uncollectible before his financial situation improves.

Best for: People with no income except protected benefits, no assets, and no realistic prospect of their situation changing within the statute of limitations period.

Choosing Your Path: A Decision Framework

The right choice depends on your specific situation. Use this framework to evaluate your options:

Step 1: Calculate Your Debt-to-Income Ratio

Add up all your monthly debt payments (minimums) and divide by your monthly income.

- **Under 20%:** You might just need better budgeting or a small consolidation loan
- **20-40%:** Consider debt management plans or consolidation
- **Over 40%:** Look seriously at debt settlement or bankruptcy

Step 2: Assess Your Income Stability

- **Stable income:** DMPs and consolidation loans become viable
- **Irregular income:** Settlement or bankruptcy might be better options
- **No income:** "Do nothing" or bankruptcy if you have assets to protect

Step 3: Evaluate Your Credit Needs

- **Need good credit soon:** Avoid settlement and bankruptcy if possible
- **Don't need credit for 2-3 years:** Settlement becomes more attractive
- **Credit already damaged:** Bankruptcy might provide the fastest recovery

Step 4: Consider Your Debt Types

- **Mostly credit cards:** All options are viable
- **Mix of secured/unsecured debt:** Bankruptcy might be necessary
- **Mostly non-dischargeable debt:** Focus on payment plans and forgiveness programs

Red Flags: Protecting Yourself from Scams

The debt relief industry attracts predatory companies that prey on desperate consumers. Protect yourself by recognizing these warning signs:

Upfront Fee Scams

Legitimate nonprofit credit counseling agencies charge minimal setup fees ($25-50). Debt settlement companies cannot legally charge fees until they actually settle your debts. Any company demanding large upfront payments should be avoided.

Unrealistic Promises

No company can guarantee specific results. Be wary of anyone who promises to:

- "Eliminate your debt without bankruptcy"
- "Remove negative items from your credit report"
- "Stop all collection calls immediately"
- "Reduce your debt by 70% guaranteed"

Pressure Tactics

Legitimate companies will give you time to research and consider your options. Run from anyone who:

- Demands immediate payment or enrollment
- Won't provide written information about their services
- Discourages you from getting second opinions
- Makes you feel rushed or pressured

Attorney Advertising Tricks

Some companies use names like "Law Offices of..." or claim attorney involvement to appear more legitimate. Ask specific questions:

- Will an actual attorney handle your case?
- What is the attorney's role in the process?
- Can you speak directly with the attorney?

Making Your Decision

Remember that there's no universal "right" answer. The best debt relief strategy is the one that:

- You can realistically complete
- Provides meaningful relief from your current situation
- Aligns with your credit and financial goals
- Costs less than the benefit it provides

Take time to research your options thoroughly. Consider speaking with a nonprofit credit counselor even if you're leaning toward other alternatives - they can provide objective analysis of your situation at minimal cost.

Most importantly, be wary of any solution that seems too good to be true. Real debt relief requires time, discipline, and often some sacrifice. But with the right approach for your situation, you can regain control of your finances and build a more secure future.

In the next chapter, we'll explore the specific resources available to residents of New York and California, including court information, legal aid clinics, and state-specific programs that can help you implement whichever debt relief strategy you choose.

23

Essential Resources

Your Lifeline for New York and California Residents

Facing financial crisis can feel isolating and overwhelming. The good news? You're not alone, and you don't have to figure everything out by yourself. Both New York and California have built extensive networks of free and low-cost resources specifically designed to help people in your situation.

This chapter serves as your comprehensive guide to finding real help when you need it most. Whether you're considering bankruptcy, exploring alternatives, or dealing with immediate crises like foreclosure or eviction, these resources can provide the support, guidance, and advocacy you need to navigate your way to financial stability.

Understanding the Support System

Before diving into specific resources, it's important to understand how the help system works. Different organizations serve different needs:

Legal aid organizations provide free legal advice and representation to low-income individuals. They can help with bankruptcy filings, defend against debt collection lawsuits, and protect you from illegal creditor actions.

Nonprofit credit counseling agencies offer financial education, budgeting help, and debt management programs. They're also required providers for the bankruptcy credit counseling and debtor education courses.

Housing assistance programs specifically focus on preventing foreclosure and eviction, helping you stay in your home during financial difficulties.

Court self-help centers provide forms, instructions, and guidance for people representing themselves in legal proceedings.

The key is knowing which resource to contact for your specific situation - and this chapter will help you make those connections quickly and efficiently.

Bankruptcy Courts: Your Starting Point for Official Information

Understanding your local bankruptcy court system is crucial whether you're filing with an attorney or representing yourself. Each court has its own local rules, forms, and procedures that supplement the federal bankruptcy code.

New York Bankruptcy Courts

New York's four federal bankruptcy districts each serve different geographic areas and maintain their own websites with essential resources:

Southern District of New York (SDNY)

- **Covers:** Manhattan, Bronx, Westchester, Rockland, Putnam, Dutchess, Orange, and Sullivan counties
- **Main courthouse:** 300 Quarropas Street, White Plains, NY 10601
- **Website:** www.nysb.uscourts.gov
- **Key features:** Excellent self-help section, detailed local forms, pro se clinic information

Eastern District of New York (EDNY)

- **Covers:** Brooklyn, Queens, Staten Island, Nassau, and Suffolk counties
- **Main courthouse:** 271-C Cadman Plaza East, Brooklyn, NY 11201

- **Website:** www.nyeb.uscourts.gov
- **Key features:** Strong pro se support, multilingual resources, detailed filing guides

Northern District of New York (NDNY)

- **Covers:** Albany, Syracuse, Utica, Binghamton, and surrounding counties
- **Courthouses:** Albany, Syracuse, Utica
- **Website:** www.nynb.uscourts.gov
- **Key features:** Rural-friendly resources, simplified forms for common situations

Western District of New York (WDNY)

- **Covers:** Buffalo, Rochester, Elmira, and surrounding counties
- **Main courthouse:** 300 Pearl Street, Buffalo, NY 14202
- **Website:** www.nywb.uscourts.gov
- **Key features:** Comprehensive local rules, detailed 341 meeting information

California Bankruptcy Courts

California's four districts serve the nation's most populous state with extensive online resources and support systems:

Northern District of California (NDCA)

- **Covers:** San Francisco Bay Area, Oakland, San Jose, Sacramento Valley
- **Main courthouse:** 450 Golden Gate Avenue, San Francisco, CA 94102
- **Website:** www.canb.uscourts.gov
- **Key features:** Excellent video tutorials, comprehensive self-help center, multiple language options

Central District of California (CDCA)

- **Covers:** Los Angeles, Orange, Riverside, San Bernardino, Ventura, Santa Barbara, and Imperial counties
- **Main courthouse:** 255 East Temple Street, Los Angeles, CA 90012
- **Website:** www.cacb.uscourts.gov
- **Key features:** Most comprehensive self-help resources in the nation, detailed video guides, extensive FAQ sections

Eastern District of California (EDCA)

- **Covers:** Sacramento, Fresno, Modesto, Stockton, and surrounding areas
- **Courthouses:** Sacramento, Fresno, Modesto
- **Website:** www.caeb.uscourts.gov
- **Key features:** Strong agricultural debtor resources, simplified small business guides

Southern District of California (SDCA)

- **Covers:** San Diego and Imperial counties
- **Main courthouse:** 325 West F Street, San Diego, CA 92101
- **Website:** www.casb.uscourts.gov
- **Key features:** Bilingual resources, comprehensive border-region guidance

What You'll Find on Court Websites

Every bankruptcy court website provides essential resources:

Official forms and local modifications specific to your district's requirements **Filing fee information** including fee waiver applications for low-income filers **Local rules and procedures** that supplement federal bankruptcy law **341 meeting calendars** showing when and where creditor meetings are held **PACER access** for looking up case information (requires account setup) **Pro se resources** including guides, checklists, and sometimes video tutorials**Contact information** for the clerk's office and self-help centers

Pro tip: Even if you're hiring an attorney, reviewing your court's website helps you understand the process and ask better questions during consultations.

Legal Aid: Your Advocate When You Can't Afford an Attorney

Legal aid organizations provide free legal services to low-income individuals facing consumer debt problems. These aren't just referral services - they offer actual representation and advocacy.

New York Legal Aid Services

Legal Services NYC (LSNYC)

- **Website:** www.legalservicesnyc.org
- **Phone:** (917) 661-4500
- **Services:** Chapter 7 bankruptcy filings, debt collection defense, benefits advocacy, housing law
- **Coverage:** All five NYC boroughs
- **Income requirements:** Generally 125% of federal poverty level
- **Special programs:** Foreclosure prevention, disability advocacy, consumer protection

What makes LSNYC special: They handle complete Chapter 7 cases from start to finish, not just advice. Their consumer law unit specifically focuses on debt collection abuse and credit reporting errors.

New York Legal Assistance Group (NYLAG)

- **Website:** www.nylag.org
- **Phone:** (212) 613-5000
- **Services:** Bankruptcy clinic, debt defense, housing preservation
- **Coverage:** NYC, with some statewide programs
- **Unique features:** Virtual legal clinics, multilingual services, specialized elder law unit

NYLAG's approach: They run regular legal clinics where you can get same-day advice on bankruptcy and debt issues. Their online intake system helps determine eligibility quickly.

Empire Justice Center

- **Website:** www.empirejustice.org
- **Coverage:** Statewide, with offices in Rochester, Albany, and other locations
- **Services:** Consumer law, housing, government benefits
- **Special focus:** Rural and upstate communities often underserved by other programs

Legal Aid Society of Northeastern New York

- **Website:** www.lasnny.org
- **Coverage:** Albany, Troy, Schenectady, and surrounding counties
- **Phone:** (518) 462-6765
- **Services:** Full-service civil legal aid including bankruptcy

Nassau Suffolk Law Services

- **Website:** www.nslawservices.org
- **Coverage:** Long Island
- **Phone:** (516) 292-8100
- **Services:** Comprehensive civil legal services including consumer law

Volunteer Lawyers Project of Onondaga County

- **Website:** www.onvlp.org
- **Coverage:** Syracuse and surrounding areas
- **Phone:** (315) 471-0212
- **Special feature:** Extensive volunteer attorney network

Finding Help Statewide in New York

LawHelpNY.org serves as the central portal for finding legal aid throughout New York. Enter your ZIP code and legal issue to find local providers. The site also includes:

- Self-help guides for common legal problems
- Court form libraries
- Information about legal rights
- Referrals to private attorneys for cases outside legal aid income limits

California Legal Aid Services

California's legal aid network is one of the most comprehensive in the nation, with specialized programs for different regions and communities.

Legal Aid Foundation of Los Angeles (LAFLA)

- **Website:** www.lafla.org
- **Phone:** (800) 399-4529
- **Coverage:** Los Angeles County
- **Services:** Bankruptcy representation, debt collection defense, foreclosure prevention
- **Special programs:** Immigrant rights, disability advocacy, consumer protection unit
- **Languages:** Services available in Spanish, Korean, Chinese, and other languages

LAFLA's bankruptcy program: They provide full representation in Chapter 7 cases and have specialized clinics for people considering bankruptcy alternatives.

Bay Area Legal Aid

- **Website:** www.baylegal.org
- **Phone:** (510) 250-5270
- **Coverage:** Alameda, Contra Costa, Marin, Napa, San Francisco, San Mateo, Santa Clara, Solano, and Sonoma counties

- **Services:** Consumer law, housing law, government benefits
- **Innovation:** They pioneered online legal aid delivery and offer extensive self-help resources

Legal Services of Northern California

- **Website:** www.lsnc.net
- **Phone:** (916) 551-2150
- **Coverage:** 23 northern California counties
- **Services:** Consumer law, housing, immigration, healthcare access
- **Rural focus:** Specialized programs for agricultural communities and remote areas

Central California Legal Services

- **Website:** www.centralcallegal.org
- **Coverage:** Central Valley, including Fresno, Kern, Kings, Madera, Merced, and Tulare counties
- **Phone:** (559) 570-1200
- **Special expertise:** Agricultural worker rights, consumer protection in rural communities

Legal Aid Society of San Diego

- **Website:** www.lassd.org
- **Phone:** (877) 534-2524
- **Coverage:** San Diego and Imperial counties
- **Services:** Full civil legal aid including bankruptcy and consumer law
- **Border expertise:** Specialized knowledge of cross-border financial issues

Public Law Center (Orange County)

- **Website:** www.publiclawcenter.org
- **Phone:** (714) 541-1010

- **Coverage:** Orange County
- **Services:** Consumer law, housing, immigration
- **Pro bono coordination:** Extensive network of volunteer attorneys

Finding Help Statewide in California

LawHelpCA.org is California's comprehensive legal aid locator. Features include:

- Detailed provider information by county and legal issue
- Eligibility prescreening tools
- Extensive self-help library
- Multilingual resources
- Mobile-friendly interface for accessing help on the go

Nonprofit Credit Counseling: Education and Debt Management

Nonprofit credit counseling agencies serve multiple roles in the debt relief process. They provide the mandatory credit counseling and debtor education courses required for bankruptcy, but they also offer comprehensive financial education and debt management programs.

What to Look for in a Credit Counseling Agency

HUD approval: For housing counseling services, look for HUD-approved agencies **DOJ approval:** For bankruptcy courses, agencies must be approved by the Department of Justice **NFCC membership:** The National Foundation for Credit Counseling maintains high standards for member agencies **Transparent pricing:** Legitimate agencies clearly disclose all fees upfront **No upfront fees:** Be wary of agencies requiring large payments before providing services

Recommended National Agencies with NY/CA Locations

National Foundation for Credit Counseling (NFCC)

- **Website:** www.nfcc.org
- **Phone:** (800) 388-2227
- **Services:** Credit counseling, debt management plans, bankruptcy education, housing counseling
- **New York locations:** Multiple offices throughout the state
- **California locations:** Extensive presence in major metropolitan areas
- **Fee structure:** Typically $25-50 for counseling sessions, sliding scale available

Money Management International (MMI)

- **Website:** www.moneymanagement.org
- **Phone:** (866) 889-9347
- **Services:** Credit counseling, debt management, bankruptcy courses, housing counseling
- **Delivery method:** Phone, online, and in-person counseling available
- **Special features:** Extensive Spanish-language services, military family expertise

GreenPath Financial Wellness

- **Website:** www.greenpath.org
- **Phone:** (877) 337-3399
- **Services:** Credit counseling, debt management, housing counseling, financial education
- **Unique approach:** Holistic financial wellness focus beyond just debt problems
- **Technology:** Advanced online tools and mobile app for ongoing support

InCharge Debt Solutions

- **Website:** www.incharge.org
- **Phone:** (877) 446-4722
- **Services:** Credit counseling, debt management, bankruptcy education, student loan counseling
- **Special expertise:** Strong focus on educational programs and financial literacy

What These Agencies Can Do for You

Pre-bankruptcy analysis: Help you understand whether bankruptcy is your best option or if alternatives might work better

Debt management plans: Negotiate with creditors for reduced interest rates and consolidated payments

Budget counseling: Develop realistic budgets and spending plans for your situation

Credit education: Understand how credit works and how to rebuild after financial difficulties

Housing counseling: Navigate foreclosure prevention options and understand your rights

Mandatory bankruptcy courses: Provide required credit counseling and debtor education certificates

Housing and Foreclosure Prevention: Keeping a Roof Over Your Head

Housing instability often triggers or accompanies financial crisis. Both New York and California have developed comprehensive programs to help residents avoid foreclosure and eviction.

New York Housing Resources

New York State Homeowner Protection Program (HOPP)

- **Website:** www.homeownerhelpny.org

- **Phone:** (855) 462-7395
- **Services:** Free foreclosure prevention counseling, legal assistance, mediation services
- **Eligibility:** Available to all New York homeowners facing foreclosure regardless of income
- **Key benefit:** Direct connection to HUD-approved housing counselors and legal aid attorneys

How HOPP works: When you call, they'll assess your situation and connect you with local resources. They can help negotiate with your lender, explore loan modification options, and provide legal representation if needed.

NYC Tenant Resource Portal

- **Website:** www.nyc.gov/tenantresourceportal
- **Phone:** 311 (within NYC)
- **Services:** Eviction prevention, rent stabilization information, tenant rights advocacy
- **Emergency help:** Same-day assistance for tenants facing immediate eviction
- **Legal clinic:** Free legal advice for housing issues

Right to Counsel NYC

- **Services:** Free legal representation for low-income tenants in eviction proceedings
- **Coverage:** Available in all five boroughs
- **Impact:** Dramatically reduces eviction rates for participating tenants
- **Access:** Automatic referral through housing court or direct application

New York State Rent Relief Program

- **Status:** Program has closed to new applications but existing cases are still being processed
- **Coverage:** Rental assistance and utility assistance for eligible households

- **Ongoing benefit:** Provides model for future emergency rental assistance programs

California Housing Resources

California COVID-19 Rent Relief Program

- **Website:** www.housing.ca.gov
- **Status:** Closed to new applications, but serving as model for future programs
- **Legacy resources:** Website maintains information about tenant rights and local assistance programs

Keep Your Home California

- **Status:** Original program ended, but resources remain available
- **Website:** www.calhfa.ca.gov
- **Ongoing services:** Information about current foreclosure prevention resources and homeowner assistance programs

California Mortgage Relief Program

- **Website:** www.camortgagerelief.org
- **Services:** Mortgage payment assistance for eligible homeowners
- **Eligibility:** Based on income and hardship criteria
- **Application process:** Online application with document upload capability

Housing Is Key

- **Website:** www.housing.ca.gov
- **Services:** Comprehensive housing assistance information portal
- **Resources:** Connects to local housing authorities, rental assistance programs, and homeless prevention services

California Department of Real Estate - Foreclosure Resources

- **Website:** www.dre.ca.gov

- **Services:** Consumer protection information, foreclosure consultant regulation, complaint filing
- **Education:** Detailed guides on foreclosure process and homeowner rights

Local Housing Authorities and Resources

Both states have extensive networks of local housing authorities that provide:

- **Section 8 housing vouchers**
- **Public housing**
- **Emergency rental assistance**
- **First-time homebuyer programs**
- **Housing counseling services**

To find your local housing authority:

- **New York:** Visit www.hcr.ny.gov for statewide directory
- **California:** Visit www.hcd.ca.gov for local agency listings

Utility Assistance: Keeping the Lights On

Financial crisis often means difficulty paying utility bills. Both states offer programs to prevent shutoffs and help with past-due amounts.

New York Utility Programs

Home Energy Assistance Program (HEAP)

- **Administration:** Local social services departments
- **Services:** Heating bill assistance, emergency utility shutoff prevention
- **Eligibility:** Income-based, generally up to 60% of state median income
- **Application:** Through local social services offices or online

Low Income Home Energy Assistance Program (LIHEAP)

- **Federal program administered locally**
- **Services:** Bill payment assistance, weatherization, emergency repairs
- **Seasonal availability:** Applications typically open in November

California Utility Programs

California Alternate Rates for Energy (CARE)

- **Services:** 20% discount on electric and gas bills for qualifying customers
- **Eligibility:** Income-based, up to 250% of federal poverty level for some programs
- **Application:** Through utility companies or community organizations

Low-Income Home Energy Assistance Program (LIHEAP)

- **Services:** Bill payment assistance, weatherization, crisis intervention
- **Administration:** Through local community action agencies
- **Emergency assistance:** Available for shutoff prevention

Government Benefits: Maximizing Your Safety Net

During financial crisis, it's crucial to access all available government benefits. Both states offer comprehensive benefit programs beyond federal offerings.

New York State Benefits

Supplemental Nutrition Assistance Program (SNAP)

- **Application:** Online at mybenefits.ny.gov or local social services
- **Emergency processing:** Available for households with urgent food needs
- **Asset limits:** Recently relaxed in many areas

Temporary Assistance for Needy Families (TANF)

- **Cash assistance:** For families with children
- **Work requirements:** May be waived during economic hardship
- **Connection to services:** Includes job training and support services

Emergency Assistance

- **Services:** One-time help with rent, utilities, or other crisis needs
- **Eligibility:** Varies by county but designed for crisis intervention
- **Application:** Through local social services departments

California State Benefits

CalFresh (SNAP)

- **Application:** Online at GetCalFresh.org or through county offices
- **Expedited service:** Available for households with immediate food needs
- **Student eligibility:** Expanded for college students in financial need

CalWORKs (TANF)

- **Cash aid and services:** For families with children
- **Homeless assistance:** Special provisions for families without housing
- **Education support:** Funding for job training and education programs

General Relief

- **County programs:** Cash assistance for individuals not eligible for federal programs
- **Varies by county:** Each county sets its own eligibility and benefit levels
- **Application:** Through county social services departments

Emergency Food and Basic Needs

New York Food Resources

Food Bank for New York City

- **Website:** www.foodbanknyc.org
- **Services:** Network of food pantries, mobile food trucks, prepared meal programs
- **Locate help:** Online pantry finder tool

Regional food banks serve different areas:

- **Foodlink** (Rochester region): www.foodlinkny.org
- **Food Bank of Central New York** (Syracuse): www.foodbankcny.org
- **Regional Food Bank of Northeastern New York** (Albany): www.regionalfoodbank.net

California Food Resources

California Association of Food Banks

- **Website:** www.cafoodbanks.org
- **Services:** Statewide network of food banks and pantries
- **Find help:** ZIP code search for local food assistance

Major regional food banks:

- **Los Angeles Regional Food Bank:** www.lafoodbank.org
- **San Francisco-Marin Food Bank:** www.sfmfoodbank.org
- **Second Harvest Food Bank** (Silicon Valley): www.shfb.org

Transportation and Other Essential Services

New York Transportation

Reduced-fare programs available through:

- **NYC:** Fair Fares program for low-income residents
- **Statewide:** Various county and regional transit authorities offer low-income discounts

California Transportation

Low-income discount programs offered by most transit agencies:

- **LA Metro:** LIFE program
- **San Francisco:** Muni Lifeline passes
- **Statewide:** Varies by local transit authority

Healthcare Access During Financial Crisis

New York Healthcare

New York State of Health (Health Insurance Marketplace)

- **Website:** www.nystateofhealth.ny.gov
- **Services:** Health insurance enrollment, Medicaid applications
- **Special enrollment:** Available during qualifying life events including financial hardship

Emergency Medicaid

- **Coverage:** Emergency medical services regardless of immigration status
- **Application:** Through hospitals or local social services

California Healthcare

Covered California

- **Website:** www.coveredca.com
- **Services:** Health insurance marketplace, Medi-Cal applications
- **Premium assistance:** Subsidies available based on income

Emergency Medi-Cal

- **Coverage:** Emergency and pregnancy-related services
- **Eligibility:** Based on income, not immigration status

Building Your Resource Network

Creating Your Personal Resource List

As you research these resources, create your own personalized list including:

Primary contacts for your most likely needs (legal aid, credit counseling, housing assistance) **Emergency numbers** for crisis situations (211, local homeless services, utility shutoff prevention) **Online resources** bookmarked for quick access during stressful times **Local offices** with addresses and hours for in-person services

Using 211 Services

Both New York and California participate in the 211 system:

- **Dial 2-1-1** from any phone for referrals to local services
- **Visit 211.org** for online resource directories
- **Text your ZIP code to 898-211** for local resource lists

Preparing for Appointments

When contacting any of these resources:

Gather your documents: Income statements, bills, court papers, identification **Prepare your questions:** Write down what you need help with specifically **Be honest about your situation:** Complete information helps providers serve you better **Follow up:** Keep notes about who you talked to and what they recommended

Common Mistakes to Avoid

Don't Wait Until Crisis

Apply early: Many programs have waiting lists or limited funding **Maintain relationships:** Stay in touch with case workers and service providers **Update information:** Keep your contact and income information current with all programs

Don't Overlook Local Resources

City and county programs often provide services not available at state or federal levels **Community organizations** may offer help that government programs don't provide **Religious and charitable organizations** often assist regardless of membership or belief

Document Everything

Keep records of all applications, correspondence, and services received **Save confirmation numbers** for online applications and phone calls **Take notes** during meetings and phone calls with service providers

Planning for the Future

Beyond Crisis Management

Once you've stabilized your immediate situation, these same resources can help with: **Financial education** to prevent future crises **Career development** through job training and education programs **Asset building** through matched savings programs and homeownership counseling **Credit rebuilding** through ongoing counseling and monitoring services

Giving Back

Many people who successfully navigate financial crisis later volunteer with the organizations that helped them. Consider: **Peer counseling** programs that train formerly distressed individuals to help others **Board service** with legal aid and nonprofit organizations **Community education** about financial literacy and consumer rights **Policy advocacy** to improve and expand services for others in crisis

Your Resource Quick Reference

Emergency Contacts

New York:

- **Legal Aid:** Call 211 or visit LawHelpNY.org
- **Housing Crisis:** (855) 462-7395 (HOPP)
- **Food Emergency:** Visit foodbanknyc.org or call 211
- **Benefits:** Visit mybenefits.ny.gov or call 211

California:

- **Legal Aid:** Call 211 or visit LawHelpCA.org
- **Housing Crisis:** Visit housing.ca.gov or call 211
- **Food Emergency:** Visit cafoodbanks.org or call 211
- **Benefits:** Call 211 or visit local county website

Court Information Quick Access

New York Bankruptcy Courts:

- **SDNY:** www.nysb.uscourts.gov
- **EDNY:** www.nyeb.uscourts.gov
- **NDNY:** www.nynb.uscourts.gov
- **WDNY:** www.nywb.uscourts.gov

California Bankruptcy Courts:

- **NDCA:** www.canb.uscourts.gov
- **CDCA:** www.cacb.uscourts.gov
- **EDCA:** www.caeb.uscourts.gov
- **SDCA:** www.casb.uscourts.gov

Remember: You don't have to navigate this alone. These resources exist specifically to help people in your situation. Don't hesitate to reach out - getting help is a sign of strength, not weakness.

In our final chapter, we'll help you put together everything you've learned into a concrete action plan for your fresh financial start.

24

Your Fresh Start Roadmap

Building the Life Bankruptcy Made Possible

You've done it. Whether you've just received your Chapter 7 discharge or completed your final Chapter 13 payment, you've successfully navigated one of life's most challenging financial processes. But here's what many people don't realize: the end of bankruptcy isn't really an ending at all - it's the beginning of the most empowering phase of your financial journey.

This chapter is your comprehensive guide to life after bankruptcy. We'll walk through exactly how to rebuild your credit, protect yourself from future financial pitfalls, and create the stable, secure life that bankruptcy was designed to make possible. Most importantly, we'll help you shift from survival mode to prosperity mode.

Understanding Your New Financial Reality

What Your Discharge Actually Means

When you receive your bankruptcy discharge, you're not just getting relief from debt - you're getting something much more valuable: a legal reset of your financial life. Here's what happens:

For Chapter 7 filers: Your discharge typically comes 3-4 months after filing. Most of your unsecured debts - credit cards, medical bills, personal loans - are legally eliminated forever. Creditors cannot call, write, sue, or take any collection action on these debts. Ever.

For Chapter 13 completers: After 3-5 years of making plan payments, you receive your discharge. Any remaining balance on eligible debts is wiped out, and you're current on all secured debts like your mortgage and car loans.

In both cases, you now have something precious: breathing room. No more sleepless nights worrying about collection calls. No more choosing between groceries and minimum payments. No more feeling trapped by insurmountable debt.

The Psychological Shift

Many people experience a complex mix of emotions after bankruptcy: relief, excitement, but sometimes also anxiety about the future. This is completely normal. You might wonder:

- "Will I ever be able to get credit again?"
- "How long until I can buy a house?"
- "What if I make the same mistakes again?"

These concerns are understandable, but here's the truth: millions of Americans have successfully rebuilt their financial lives after bankruptcy. You have all the tools you need to join them.

The Credit Rebuilding Blueprint

Phase 1: Assessment and Correction (Months 1-3)

Step 1: Obtain Your Credit Reports

Get your free annual credit reports from all three bureaus at www.annualcreditreport.com. This is the only official site for free reports - be wary of imposters charging fees or requiring credit card information.

What to look for:

- All discharged debts should show $0 balances
- Accounts should be marked "included in bankruptcy" or "discharged"
- No new collection accounts for discharged debts
- Accurate personal information (name, address, Social Security number)

Step 2: Dispute Errors Aggressively

Credit bureaus often make mistakes with bankruptcy information. Common errors include:

- Discharged debts still showing balances owed
- Accounts not marked as included in bankruptcy
- Duplicate entries for the same debt
- Wrong discharge dates

File disputes online with each credit bureau for any incorrect information. Under federal law, they must investigate and correct errors within 30 days.

Step 3: Document Everything

Create a file with:

- Your bankruptcy discharge papers
- Credit reports with disputed items highlighted
- Correspondence with credit bureaus
- Any settlement letters or payment confirmations

This documentation protects you if discharged debts resurface or if you face credit report errors.

Phase 2: Foundation Building (Months 3-12)

Step 4: Create Your Post-Bankruptcy Budget

Your bankruptcy gave you a fresh start, but budgeting keeps you on track. Use the 50/30/20 rule as a starting point:

- **50% for needs:** Housing, food, transportation, insurance, minimum debt payments
- **30% for wants:** Entertainment, dining out, hobbies, non-essential purchases
- **20% for savings and debt payoff:** Emergency fund, retirement, extra payments on remaining debts

Real example: Maria's post-bankruptcy budget

- **Monthly income:** $3,200
- **Needs (50%):** $1,600 (rent, groceries, car payment, insurance, utilities)
- **Wants (30%):** $960 (entertainment, dining out, clothing)
- **Savings (20%):** $640 (emergency fund, retirement contribution)

Step 5: Build Your Emergency Fund

Start small - even $25 per month adds up. Your goal is eventually having 3-6 months of expenses saved, but initially focus on reaching $1,000. This small cushion prevents minor emergencies from becoming major crises.

Emergency fund milestones:

- **Month 1-3:** $500 (covers most car repairs or minor medical bills)
- **Month 4-8:** $1,000 (handles most single emergencies)
- **Month 9-24:** $3,000-5,000 (provides real financial security)

Step 6: Begin Credit Rebuilding

Secured Credit Cards These are your best starting point. You deposit money (typically $200-500) which becomes your credit limit. The card reports to credit bureaus just like any other credit card.

Best secured cards for bankruptcy recovery:

- **Discover it Secured:** Offers cash back rewards and graduates to unsecured

- **Capital One Secured:** Low deposit options and automatic credit line reviews
- **Citi Secured:** Converts to unsecured with responsible use

Credit Builder Loans These unique loans help build credit while forcing you to save. You make monthly payments into a savings account, and the money is released to you when the loan is paid off.

How it works: You take a $1,000 credit builder loan with 12-month terms. You make $85 monthly payments for 12 months. At the end, you get your $1,000 back, plus you've built 12 months of positive payment history.

Authorized User Strategy If you have a trusted family member or friend with excellent credit, ask to be added as an authorized user on their account. Their positive payment history can boost your credit score quickly.

Important: Only do this with someone you trust completely, and make sure they have:

- Low balances relative to credit limits
- No late payments in the past two years
- A long credit history

Phase 3: Acceleration (Year 2 and Beyond)

Step 7: Diversify Your Credit Profile

As your credit improves, you can add different types of credit:

Retail Store Cards Often easier to qualify for than major credit cards. Use them for regular purchases you'd make anyway, then pay them off immediately.

Gas Station Cards Similar to retail cards but with broader utility. Perfect for building credit if you drive regularly.

Unsecured Credit Cards Once your credit score reaches 600-650, you may qualify for unsecured cards with better terms than secured cards.

Step 8: Optimize Your Credit Utilization

Keep your credit card balances below 30% of your limits, but ideally below 10%. This has a massive impact on your credit score.

Example: If you have a $1,000 credit limit:

- **Poor utilization:** $800 balance (80% utilization)
- **Good utilization:** $250 balance (25% utilization)
- **Excellent utilization:** $50 balance (5% utilization)

Step 9: Monitor Your Progress

Use free credit monitoring services like:

- **Credit Karma:** Free credit scores and monitoring
- **Credit Sesame:** Credit analysis and improvement tips
- **Annual Credit Report:** Official source for free annual reports

Track your credit score monthly and celebrate improvements. Most people see significant score increases within 12-18 months of consistent good habits.

Timeline: What to Expect When

Months 1-6: Foundation Phase

- **Credit score:** May initially drop 50-100 points due to bankruptcy
- **Available credit:** Secured cards and credit builder loans
- **Goals:** Clean up credit reports, establish budget, build emergency fund

Months 7-18: Building Phase

- **Credit score:** Should start increasing 10-30 points every few months
- **Available credit:** May qualify for store cards, better secured cards
- **Goals:** Maintain perfect payment history, increase emergency fund

Months 19-36: Growth Phase

- **Credit score:** Could improve 100+ points from post-bankruptcy low

- **Available credit:** Unsecured cards, better loan terms become available
- **Goals:** Consider major purchases like car or home if needed

Years 3-5: Establishment Phase

- **Credit score:** Should approach or exceed pre-bankruptcy levels
- **Available credit:** Access to prime credit products and competitive rates
- **Goals:** Long-term wealth building, homeownership if desired

Major Purchase Strategies

Buying a Car After Bankruptcy

Timing: You can typically get car financing 12-18 months after discharge **Rates:** Expect higher interest rates initially, but refinancing is possible later **Down payment:** Save for at least 10-20% down to get better terms **Loan terms:** Avoid loans longer than 5 years, regardless of lower payments

Michael's car buying strategy: Eighteen months after his Chapter 7 discharge, Michael needed a car. He saved $3,000 for a down payment and shopped at credit unions and smaller banks rather than dealer financing. He got a $15,000 car loan at 12% interest. Two years later, with improved credit, he refinanced at 6%, saving $2,400 over the remaining loan term.

Buying a Home After Bankruptcy

Chapter 7: Typically eligible for FHA loans 2 years after discharge **Chapter 13:** May be eligible for FHA loans 1 year after discharge with court permission **Conventional loans:** Usually require 4-7 years after bankruptcy

Preparation strategies:

- Save for larger down payment (3.5% minimum for FHA, but 10-20% gets better rates)
- Maintain perfect payment history on all accounts

- Keep housing debt-to-income ratio below 28%
- Work with lenders experienced in post-bankruptcy lending

Sarah's homeownership journey: Two years after her Chapter 7 discharge, Sarah qualified for an FHA loan. She had saved $15,000 for a down payment and closing costs, maintained a 720 credit score, and had stable employment. Her 3.5% down payment on a $200,000 home made homeownership possible much sooner than she expected.

Protecting Your Fresh Start

Red Flag Financial Products to Avoid

Payday Loans

- **Why they're dangerous:** Annual percentage rates often exceed 400%
- **The trap:** Designed to create dependency through rollover fees
- **Better alternatives:** Credit union payday alternative loans, cash advances from employers

Title Loans

- **Why they're dangerous:** You risk losing your car for short-term cash
- **The trap:** Most borrowers end up paying more in fees than they originally borrowed
- **Better alternatives:** Negotiate payment plans with creditors, seek assistance from nonprofits

Rent-to-Own Stores

- **Why they're dangerous:** You pay 2-4 times retail price for basic furniture and electronics
- **The trap:** Easy approval masks extremely high effective interest rates
- **Better alternatives:** Save for purchases, buy used, use layaway programs

Subprime Auto Loans

- **Why they're dangerous:** Interest rates above 20% keep you underwater on the loan

- **The trap:** Predatory dealers target bankruptcy filers with overpriced cars
- **Better alternatives:** Shop with credit unions, save for larger down payments, consider certified pre-owned

Building Financial Immunity

Diversify Your Income Don't rely solely on employment income. Consider:

- **Side hustles:** Freelancing, part-time work, gig economy
- **Passive income:** Rental property, dividend investing (when financially stable)
- **Skill development:** Increase your earning potential through education and training

Insurance as Protection Adequate insurance prevents financial catastrophes:

- **Health insurance:** Prevents medical bankruptcy
- **Disability insurance:** Protects income if you can't work
- **Life insurance:** Protects family from debt responsibility
- **Umbrella policy:** Protects assets from liability claims

Estate Planning Basics Even with modest assets, you need:

- **Will:** Directs asset distribution and names guardians for children
- **Power of attorney:** Allows someone to handle finances if you're incapacitated
- **Healthcare directive:** Specifies medical wishes

Advanced Strategies for Long-Term Wealth Building

Investment Principles for Bankruptcy Survivors

Start Simple Begin with target-date funds in retirement accounts. These automatically adjust risk as you age and require minimal knowledge or maintenance.

Prioritize Retirement Savings Take advantage of employer 401(k) matches - it's free money. Even $25 per month in a retirement account grows significantly over time due to compound interest.

Build Before You Invest Ensure you have:

- **Emergency fund:** 3-6 months of expenses
- **Stable housing:** Secure, affordable housing situation
- **Reliable transportation:** Dependable vehicle that's paid off or nearly paid off
- **Good insurance:** Adequate coverage for health, disability, and property

The Psychology of Money After Bankruptcy

Overcoming Financial PTSD Many bankruptcy survivors develop an unhealthy fear of credit or debt. While caution is good, excessive fear can prevent beneficial financial moves like:

- **Strategic use of credit:** Building credit history, earning rewards
- **Calculated risks:** Homeownership, education, business investments
- **Leverage opportunities:** Low-interest loans for appreciating assets

Finding Balance The goal isn't to never use credit again - it's to use credit wisely. This means:

- **Understanding terms:** Reading contracts and understanding interest rates
- **Having exit strategies:** Knowing how you'll pay off debt before taking it on
- **Maintaining perspective:** Debt is a tool, not an enemy, when used properly

When Filing Again Might Be Necessary

Understanding the Time Limits

If you find yourself in financial trouble again, you can't immediately file for bankruptcy. The waiting periods are:

Chapter 7 to Chapter 7: 8 years from the first filing date **Chapter 13 to Chapter 13:** 2 years from the first filing date**Chapter 7 to Chapter 13:** 4 years from the first filing date **Chapter 13 to Chapter 7:** 6 years from the first filing date (with exceptions for partial payment of unsecured debts)

Preventing the Need to File Again

Early Warning Signs Watch for these red flags:

- **Credit card balances increasing monthly**
- **Using credit for basic living expenses**
- **Making only minimum payments**
- **Borrowing money to pay other debts**
- **Avoiding opening bills or checking account balances**

Intervention Strategies If you notice warning signs:

- **Immediate budget review:** Cut all non-essential spending
- **Credit counseling:** Get professional help before crisis hits
- **Increase income:** Take on extra work or sell assets
- **Negotiate with creditors:** Many will work with you to prevent default

Success Stories: Real People, Real Results

David's Journey: From Foreclosure to Homeowner Again

Background: David filed Chapter 7 after losing his job and facing foreclosure. His credit score dropped to 480.

Strategy: David focused on rebuilding slowly and consistently:

- Used a secured credit card for small purchases, paying in full monthly
- Took a credit builder loan from his credit union
- Maintained perfect payment history on his car loan and rent
- Saved aggressively, living on 70% of his new job's income

Results: Three years later, David's credit score reached 720. He qualified for an FHA loan and bought a home with 3.5% down. His mortgage payment was lower than his previous rent.

Lisa's Transformation: From Medical Debt to Financial Security

Background: Lisa filed Chapter 7 due to medical bills from cancer treatment. She emerged debt-free but with damaged credit and medical anxiety about future costs.

Strategy: Lisa focused on both credit rebuilding and health protection:

- Obtained comprehensive health insurance through her employer
- Built an emergency fund specifically for medical expenses
- Used authorized user status on her mother's card to boost credit quickly
- Started a health savings account (HSA) for tax-advantaged medical savings

Results: Two years post-bankruptcy, Lisa had $10,000 in medical emergency savings, a 680 credit score, and peace of mind about future health costs.

Marcus's Evolution: From Impulsive Spender to Disciplined Investor

Background: Marcus filed Chapter 13 due to overspending and credit card debt. He completed his 5-year plan but needed to change his relationship with money.

Strategy: Marcus focused on behavioral change:

- Took a financial literacy course at his community college

- Used budgeting apps to track every expense
- Automated savings so he couldn't spend the money impulsively
- Found free and low-cost hobbies to replace expensive entertainment

Results: Five years after completing his Chapter 13 plan, Marcus had $25,000 in savings, was contributing 15% to retirement, and had developed healthy money habits that prevented future debt problems.

Your Personal Fresh Start Action Plan

Month 1: Assessment and Foundation

- [ ] Obtain credit reports from all three bureaus
- [ ] Dispute any errors related to bankruptcy discharge
- [ ] Create a realistic monthly budget
- [ ] Open a dedicated savings account for emergency fund
- [ ] Research secured credit card options

Month 2: Implementation

- [ ] Apply for one secured credit card with low fees
- [ ] Set up automatic transfers to emergency fund
- [ ] Establish utility accounts and other bills in your name (if needed)
- [ ] Consider credit builder loan from local credit union

Month 3: Habit Formation

- [ ] Make first secured card purchase and pay in full
- [ ] Review and adjust budget based on actual spending
- [ ] Set up calendar reminders for all bill due dates
- [ ] Research credit monitoring services

Months 4-6: Building Momentum

- [ ] Monitor credit score improvements monthly
- [ ] Increase emergency fund contributions if possible
- [ ] Consider authorized user opportunities with trusted family/friends
- [ ] Research auto insurance, health insurance, and other protection needs

Months 7-12: Expansion

- [ ] Apply for additional credit products if credit has improved
- [ ] Consider upgrading secured card to unsecured
- [ ] Set larger financial goals (car purchase, home down payment)
- [ ] Review and optimize all recurring expenses

Year 2+: Long-term Planning

- [ ] Explore homeownership if desired and feasible
- [ ] Increase retirement contributions
- [ ] Consider investment options for long-term wealth building
- [ ] Regularly review and update financial goals

Staying Motivated During the Journey

Celebrating Small Wins

Rebuilding after bankruptcy is a marathon, not a sprint. Celebrate these milestones:

- **First month of on-time payments**
- **Emergency fund reaching $500, then $1,000**
- **Credit score increasing by 50 points**

- **First credit limit increase**
- **Qualifying for better credit products**

Finding Support

Online communities can provide encouragement and advice from others in similar situations. Look for:

- Reddit communities focused on credit rebuilding
- Facebook groups for bankruptcy survivors
- Financial forums with sections on credit repair

Professional support remains available:

- Nonprofit credit counselors for ongoing guidance
- Financial planners for long-term wealth building
- Legal aid for any post-bankruptcy issues

Maintaining Perspective

Remember that bankruptcy doesn't define you - it's simply a tool you used to regain control of your financial life. Many successful people, including famous entrepreneurs and celebrities, have filed bankruptcy and gone on to achieve great financial success.

Your bankruptcy record will eventually fade from your credit report, but the financial skills and resilience you develop during rebuilding will serve you for life.

Looking Forward: Your Financial Future

The Compound Effect of Good Habits

The habits you develop post-bankruptcy - budgeting, saving, using credit responsibly - create compound benefits over time:

- **Good credit** leads to better interest rates, saving thousands on loans

- **Emergency savings** prevent future financial crises
- **Investment discipline** builds long-term wealth
- **Financial knowledge** helps you make better decisions throughout life

Giving Back

Many bankruptcy survivors eventually help others facing similar challenges. Consider:

- **Volunteering** with legal aid organizations
- **Mentoring** others going through bankruptcy
- **Sharing your story** to reduce stigma and provide hope
- **Supporting** nonprofit organizations that helped you

Final Thoughts on Your Journey

Bankruptcy gave you a second chance, but what you do with that chance is entirely up to you. You have the opportunity to build not just financial stability, but genuine financial freedom.

The path forward isn't always easy, but it's straightforward: spend less than you earn, save consistently, use credit wisely, and invest in your future. The compound effect of these simple actions, practiced consistently over time, will create the secure, prosperous life that bankruptcy made possible.

You've already proven you can handle financial adversity. Now you get to prove you can handle financial success.

Your bankruptcy is behind you. Your bright financial future lies ahead.

Congratulations on completing this journey, and best wishes for the prosperity that awaits you.

Glossary of Bankruptcy Terms

A

Adversary Proceeding - A lawsuit filed within a bankruptcy case to resolve disputes, such as challenging the dischargeability of specific debts or recovering fraudulent transfers.

Automatic Stay - A federal court order that immediately stops all collection activities by creditors when a bankruptcy case is filed, including foreclosures, repossessions, wage garnishments, and collection calls.

Asset Case - A Chapter 7 bankruptcy where the debtor has non-exempt property that the trustee can sell to pay creditors (occurs in less than 10% of cases).

B

BAPCPA - Bankruptcy Abuse Prevention and Consumer Protection Act of 2005, which reformed bankruptcy law and added the means test requirement.

Best Interests Test - A requirement in Chapter 13 that unsecured creditors receive at least as much as they would have received in a Chapter 7 liquidation.

Brunner Test - The three-part legal standard used by most courts to determine "undue hardship" for student loan discharge: (1) minimal standard of living test, (2) persistence test, and (3) good faith test.

C

Chapter 7 - "Liquidation bankruptcy" designed for low-income debtors to eliminate most unsecured debts in 3-4 months while keeping exempt property.

Chapter 11 - Business reorganization bankruptcy, rarely used by individual consumers except those with very high debt levels or complex financial situations.

Chapter 13 - "Reorganization bankruptcy" or "wage earner's plan" allowing debtors with regular income to repay debts over 3-5 years while keeping all property.

CMI (Current Monthly Income) - Average gross income over the six months before filing bankruptcy, used in means test calculations.

Co-Debtor Stay - Chapter 13 protection that prevents creditors from pursuing co-signers on consumer debts while the plan is active.

Cramdown - Chapter 13 power to reduce secured debt balances to the current value of collateral, treating the remainder as unsecured debt (available for vehicles owned 910+ days).

Credit Counseling - Mandatory course that must be completed within 180 days before filing bankruptcy, focusing on budget analysis and alternatives to bankruptcy.

D

Discharge - Court order that eliminates the debtor's legal obligation to pay certain debts, providing permanent protection from collection efforts.

Dischargeable Debt - Debts that can be eliminated in bankruptcy, typically including credit cards, medical bills, and personal loans.

Dismissal - Termination of a bankruptcy case without discharge, usually due to failure to meet requirements or complete plan payments.

Disposable Income - In Chapter 13, the amount available for debt payments after subtracting allowable living expenses from current monthly income.

E

Exemptions - Laws that protect certain property from being taken by creditors, allowing debtors to keep essential assets through bankruptcy.

Executory Contract - Ongoing contracts where both parties still have obligations to perform, which can be assumed or rejected in bankruptcy.

F

341 Meeting - "Meeting of Creditors" where the debtor testifies under oath about their financial affairs, typically lasting 10-15 minutes and rarely attended by creditors.

Feasibility - Chapter 13 requirement that the proposed repayment plan be realistic based on the debtor's income and expenses.

Filing Fee - Court costs for bankruptcy cases: $338 for Chapter 7, $313 for Chapter 13 (fee waivers available for very low-income filers).

G

Good Faith - Legal requirement that bankruptcy filing and Chapter 13 plans represent honest efforts to address debt problems, not attempts to abuse the system.

H

Hardship Discharge - Rare early discharge from Chapter 13 for debtors who cannot complete their plans due to circumstances beyond their control.

Homestead Exemption - Protection for equity in a debtor's primary residence, varying significantly by state ($27,900 federal vs. up to $678,000+ in California).

I

Insider - Family members, business partners, or other parties with close relationships to the debtor, subject to longer look-back periods for transfers.

Involuntary Dismissal - Court termination of a bankruptcy case due to debtor non-compliance, missed payments, or failure to meet requirements.

J

Joint Filing - Married couples filing bankruptcy together, sharing costs and procedures while both receiving discharge.

Judgment Proof - Status of debtors with no income or assets that creditors can legally seize, making collection impossible even with court judgments.

L

Lien - Legal claim against property securing payment of debt, which may survive bankruptcy even if personal liability is discharged.

Lien Stripping - Chapter 13 power to eliminate second mortgages and other junior liens when property value is less than senior debt.

Liquidation - Sale of assets to pay creditors, though most Chapter 7 cases are "no asset" and involve no actual liquidation.

M

Means Test - Income-based qualification test for Chapter 7, comparing debtor's income to state median and calculating disposable income for those above median.

Meeting of Creditors - See 341 Meeting.

Modification - Changes to confirmed Chapter 13 plans due to changed circumstances, requiring court approval.

N

No Asset Case - Chapter 7 bankruptcy where all debtor property is exempt, resulting in no asset sales (90%+ of Chapter 7 cases).

Non-Dischargeable Debt - Debts that survive bankruptcy, including student loans, recent taxes, child support, and criminal fines.

O

Objection - Formal challenge by creditors or trustees to discharge, exemptions, or plan confirmation.

Order for Relief - Court order officially commencing the bankruptcy case and triggering the automatic stay.

P

PACER - Public Access to Court Electronic Records system for accessing bankruptcy court documents and case information.

Plan - Chapter 13 repayment proposal outlining how debts will be addressed over 3-5 years.

Priority Debt - Debts that must be paid in full in Chapter 13, including recent taxes, child support, and certain government obligations.

Property of the Estate - All property owned by the debtor when bankruptcy is filed, subject to trustee administration unless exempt.

Pro Se - Self-representation in legal proceedings without an attorney.

R

Reaffirmation - Agreement to remain legally liable for specific debts despite bankruptcy discharge, requiring court approval.

Relief from Stay - Court permission for creditors to resume collection activities despite the automatic stay.

Ride-Through - Informal arrangement to keep property by continuing payments without reaffirming the debt.

S

Schedules - Detailed forms listing all debtor assets, debts, income, and expenses, filed with the bankruptcy petition.

Secured Debt - Debt backed by collateral that creditors can repossess or foreclose upon, such as mortgages and car loans.

Statement of Financial Affairs - Form detailing debtor's financial history, including recent transactions, payments, and business relationships.

Statute of Limitations - Time limit for creditors to file lawsuits, typically 3-6 years for consumer debts, varying by state.

Stay - See Automatic Stay.

T

341 Meeting - See Meeting of Creditors.

Trustee - Court-appointed official who administers bankruptcy cases, reviewing petitions, conducting 341 meetings, and distributing payments in Chapter 13.

U

Undersecured - Debt where collateral value is less than the amount owed, making the excess unsecured.

Undue Hardship - Difficult legal standard for discharging student loans in bankruptcy, typically requiring proof of persistent poverty and good faith repayment efforts.

Unliquidated Debt - Debt where the exact amount owed is disputed or uncertain.

Unsecured Debt - Debt not backed by collateral, such as credit cards, medical bills, and personal loans.

V

Voluntary Dismissal - Debtor's request to terminate their bankruptcy case, which may be granted by the court.

Voluntary Petition - The document filed to initiate a bankruptcy case.

W

Wage Earner's Plan - Another name for Chapter 13 bankruptcy, emphasizing its design for people with regular income.

Wildcard Exemption - Flexible exemption that can be applied to any property, providing maximum protection strategy options.

Legal Citations and References

11 U.S.C. - Title 11 of the United States Code, containing federal bankruptcy law.

FRBP - Federal Rules of Bankruptcy Procedure, governing bankruptcy court processes and requirements.

U.S. Trustee Program - Department of Justice division that oversees bankruptcy administration and approves credit counseling agencies.

This glossary provides definitions for key terms used throughout the bankruptcy process. For complete legal definitions and current law, consult the Bankruptcy Code, Federal Rules of Bankruptcy Procedure, and qualified legal professionals.

About the Author

Ngozi E. Bolin, Esq. brings over three decades of diverse legal experience including employment, personal injury, contracts, commercial litigation, real estate law and consumer bankruptcy law. Licensed to practice in both New York (1991) and California (2013), Ms. Bolin is one of the few attorneys with experience in the federal bankruptcy courts of America's two most populous states.

Ms. Bolin began her legal career as a Barrister & Solicitor of the Supreme Court of Nigeria (1989) before immigrating to the United States. Her diverse educational background includes studies under the British Commonwealth system and at Harvard Extension School.

Throughout her distinguished career, Ms. Bolin has specialized in helping individuals and families navigate financial crises through bankruptcy relief. Her practice encompasses the full spectrum of consumer bankruptcy matters, including Chapter 7 liquidation cases, Chapter 13 reorganization plans.

Ms. Bolin's legal expertise in different areas of law has been demonstrated through involvement in significant published cases including *Louis Capital Markets, LP v. Refco Group Ltd., LLC, et al.* (9 Misc.3d 283, 801 N.Y.S.2d 490, N.Y.Co. 2005), *Giordano v. Thomson, et al.* (438 F. Supp.2d 35, E.D.N.Y. 2005), and *Davis v. Commercial Bank of New York* (275 F.Supp.2d 418, S.D.N.Y. 2003).

Ms. Bolin's practice philosophy centers on making high-quality legal representation accessible through innovative service delivery models. She has pioneered unbundled legal services that allow clients to obtain expert guidance while managing costs effectively, reflecting her deep commitment to ensuring that financial crisis doesn't prevent people from accessing competent legal representation.

This book represents the culmination of Ms. Bolin's extensive experience in consumer bankruptcy practice, distilling decades of courtroom advocacy, client counseling, and case strategy into an accessible guide for both legal professionals and consumers navigating the bankruptcy process. Her unique perspective, combining international legal training with deep expertise in American bankruptcy law, provides readers with both comprehensive legal knowledge and practical wisdom gained through years of helping people achieve genuine financial fresh starts.

Made in the USA
Middletown, DE
05 November 2026

36562497R00309